# Communications in Computer and Information Science 2706

**Rationale**
The CCIS series is devoted to the publication of proceedings of computer science conferences. Its aim is to efficiently disseminate original research results in informatics in printed and electronic form. While the focus is on publication of peer-reviewed full papers presenting mature work, inclusion of reviewed short papers reporting on work in progress is welcome, too. Besides globally relevant meetings with internationally representative program committees guaranteeing a strict peer-reviewing and paper selection process, conferences run by societies or of high regional or national relevance are also considered for publication.

**Topics**
The topical scope of CCIS spans the entire spectrum of informatics ranging from foundational topics in the theory of computing to information and communications science and technology and a broad variety of interdisciplinary application fields.

**Information for Volume Editors and Authors**
Publication in CCIS is free of charge. No royalties are paid, however, we offer registered conference participants temporary free access to the online version of the conference proceedings on SpringerLink (http://link.springer.com) by means of an http referrer from the conference website and/or a number of complimentary printed copies, as specified in the official acceptance email of the event.

CCIS proceedings can be published in time for distribution at conferences or as post-proceedings, and delivered in the form of printed books and/or electronically as USBs and/or e-content licenses for accessing proceedings at SpringerLink. Furthermore, CCIS proceedings are included in the CCIS electronic book series hosted in the SpringerLink digital library at http://link.springer.com/bookseries/7899. Conferences publishing in CCIS are allowed to use Online Conference Service (OCS) for managing the whole proceedings lifecycle (from submission and reviewing to preparing for publication) free of charge.

**Publication process**
The language of publication is exclusively English. Authors publishing in CCIS have to sign the Springer CCIS copyright transfer form, however, they are free to use their material published in CCIS for substantially changed, more elaborate subsequent publications elsewhere. For the preparation of the camera-ready papers/files, authors have to strictly adhere to the Springer CCIS Authors' Instructions and are strongly encouraged to use the CCIS LaTeX style files or templates.

**Abstracting/Indexing**
CCIS is abstracted/indexed in DBLP, Google Scholar, EI-Compendex, Mathematical Reviews, SCImago, Scopus. CCIS volumes are also submitted for the inclusion in ISI Proceedings.

**How to start**
To start the evaluation of your proposal for inclusion in the CCIS series, please send an e-mail to ccis@springer.com.

Emma L. Tonkin · Gregory J. L. Tourte ·
Kristina Yordanova
Editors

# Annotation of Real-World Data for Artificial Intelligence Systems

## 9th International Workshop, ARDUOUS 2025
## Bologna, Italy, October 25–26, 2025
## Proceedings

Springer

*Editors*
Emma L. Tonkin
University of Bristol
Bristol, UK

Gregory J. L. Tourte
University of Oxford
Oxford, UK

Kristina Yordanova
University of Greifswald
Greifswald, Germany

ISSN 1865-0929 ISSN 1865-0937 (electronic)
Communications in Computer and Information Science
ISBN 978-3-032-09116-1 ISBN 978-3-032-09117-8 (eBook)
https://doi.org/10.1007/978-3-032-09117-8



This Springer imprint is published by the registered company Springer Nature Switzerland AG
The registered company address is: Gewerbestrasse 11, 6330 Cham, Switzerland

# Preface

This was the 9th instalment in a series of successful ARDUOUS (International Workshop on Annotation of Real World Data for Artificial Intelligence Systems; previously Annotation of useR Data for UbiquitOUs Systems) workshops and the first associated with ECAI (The European Conference on Artificial Intelligence), having in the past been part of PerCom, and, in 2024, the Informatik Festival.

The field of Artificial Intelligence (AI) has seen rapid development recent last years with a huge increase in the consumption of data and in the recognition of its influence on the developed AI systems. To address this shift from knowledge-based to data-driven AI systems development, the ARDUOUS workshop series explores various topics in data annotation for AI applications. Well-annotated data powers developments in many fields of AI such as training models in machine learning, computer vision, and natural language processing, learning representations in knowledge representation and reasoning or planning and search, and plays an important role in validating knowledge-based systems. Furthermore, ensuring the involvement of the relevant stakeholders increases the fairness, ethicality and trust in the annotations and ultimately in the resulting AI systems.

ARDUOUS aims to bring together researchers from the AI community who work on topics addressing the challenges involved in producing reliable and quality-assured annotation. The objective of the workshop is to offer a forum in which researchers can discuss 1) the role and impact of annotations in designing and validating AI applications, 2) the process of labelling, and the requirements to produce high-quality annotations for diverse settings and tasks, 3) innovative tools, interfaces and automated methods for annotating data, 4) methods for standardisation and normalisation in annotation practices, and 5) novel topics and approaches in this field.

The topics of the workshop include, but are not limited to:

- processes for and best practices in annotating data for AI systems
- AI methods towards automation of the annotation process
- experiences in the development, validation and sharing of data annotation protocols
- ensuring compliance with relevant legislation and best practice when building or applying ground truths
- human-centred and human-in-the-loop approaches to designing and deploying AI systems
- low-resource annotation workflows
- the role of annotation and its effects in ensuring fairness, ethicality and trust in AI
- annotation evaluation metrics: inter-indexer consistency, similarity, bias and subjectivity

This volume contains the papers presented at ARDUOUS 2025 - the 9th International Workshop on Annotation of Real World Data for Artificial Intelligent Systems, held on October 26th 2025 in Bologna, Italy, colocated with the 28th European Conference on Artificial Intelligence (ECAI). In this year's edition 16 submissions were registered.

All submissions underwent a peer review process to ensure that the papers accepted were of high quality. Each submission received three reviews by program committee members and external reviewers. The program committee chairs decided to accept 11 papers, resulting in an overall acceptance rate of 69%. Papers were received from India, Pakistan, Italy, Germany, the UK and the US, and from researchers in industry, academia and in other fields such as civil service.

This year, the program features a keynote talk by Stefan Lüdtke of the University of Rostock: Thriving on Less: Coping with Label Scarcity in Sensor-Based Human Activity Recognition. Accepted papers this year were in the broad areas of Activity Recognition, Annotation for Healthcare Applications, Ergonomics and Data Synthesis, and Annotation of Textual Data. The best paper prize was awarded to Hoan Tran, Veronika Potter, Umberto Mazzucchelli, Dinesh John and Stephen Intille, for their paper titled *"Towards Practical, Best Practice Video-Annotation to Support Human Activity Recognition"*.

We would like to acknowledge all reviewers who participated in the peer-review process, and thank all authors who submitted a contribution to ARDUOUS 2025. We believe that the accepted papers will stimulate good discussion in the area of data annotation.

October 2025

Emma L. Tonkin
Gregory J. L. Tourte
Kristina Yordanova

# Organization

## Workshop Chairs

| | |
|---|---|
| Emma L. Tonkin | University of Bristol, UK |
| Gregory J. L. Tourte | University of Oxford, UK |
| Kristina Yordanova | University of Greifswald, Germany |

## Organizing Committee

| | |
|---|---|
| Teodor Stoev | University of Greifswald, Germany |
| Dipendra Yadav | University of Greifswald, Germany |
| Fernando Moya Rueda | MotionMiners, Germany |

## Program Committee

| | |
|---|---|
| Abe Kazemzadeh | University of St. Thomas, USA |
| Aftab Khan | Toshiba Research Europe, UK |
| Frank Krüger | University of Applied Sciences Wismar, Germany |
| Jesse Hoey | University of Waterloo, Canada |
| Juan Ye | University of St. Andrews, UK |
| Stefan Lüdke | University of Rostock, Germany |
| Laura Scheinert | University of Exeter, UK |
| Daniele Riboni | University of Cagliari, Italy |
| Samaneh Zolfaghari | Mälardalens University, Sweden |
| Cèesar Ferri | Polytechnic University of Valencia, Spain |
| Ümit Şerifi | Tarsus University, Turkey |
| Josephine Thomas | University of Greifswald, Germany |
| Miquel Perello Nieto | University of Bristol, UK |
| Andrea Ferrario | University of Zürich, Switzerland |
| Jingjing Liu | University of Bristol, UK |
| Sumaiya Suravee | University of Greifswald, Germany |
| Mostafa Razavi Ghods | University of Greifswald, Germany |
| Tobias Pabst | University of Leipzig, Germany |

# Keynote

# Thriving on Less: Coping with Label Scarcity in Sensor-Based Human Activity Recognition

Stefan Lüdtke

Institute of Visual & Analytic Computing, University of Rostock, Germany
stefan.luedtke@uni-rostock.de

Human activity recognition (HAR) based on wearable sensor data plays a critical role in fields like healthcare, sports science or logistics [6], where it can help to uncover activity patterns of patients or workers, allowing optimization of treatment, training or work organization. Typically, HAR is based on supervised machine learning, e.g. using convolutional neural networks [5]. Deploying HAR in such diverse domains requires training of new models for each domain: Relevant activities, subject groups and movement patterns can be vastly different between domains, and models typically do not generalize across domains. Even in the same domain, novel activities or environments prevent the use of existing models, requiring retraining or fine tuning of models.

A major challenge in this context is the need for labeled training data. While obtaining raw sensor data is straightforward, obtaining ground truth labels is time-consuming and error-prone [11]. Thus, HAR developers often face the challenge of having only small amounts of labeled data available for model training.

In this keynote presentation, I will present an overview of methods that enable effective model training even with limited labeled data. The approaches discussed include: (a) Neuro-symbolic methods, which partially replace training data with prior knowledge; (b) Transfer learning, domain adaptation, and fine-tuning techniques, which leverage existing models; and (c) Making use of synthetic pre-training data as an indirect way to incorporate prior knowledge.

*Neuro-Symbolic Activity Recognition* Symbolic HAR methods leverage explicitly encoded prior knowledge about the domain to reduce or eliminate the need for labeled training data. For example, action preconditions and effects can be modeled using planning-based representations, leading to computational causal behavior models [2]. Hybrid approaches combine symbolic, knowledge-based representations of the domain structure with data-driven models like neural networks to model the mapping between sensor data and symbolic states [7]. Additional context features, such as process step information [4] or spatial location [6], can also enhance model robustness and reduce the need for labeled examples.

*Transfer Learning and Domain Adaptation* Another promising strategy involves reusing models trained on large datasets for new tasks or domains. In computer vision, this is commonly done using pre-trained models, e.g. pre-trained on ImageNet. While HAR lacks similarly large and standardized pre-training datasets, recent advances in unsupervised pre-training have begun to close this gap [12]. When no labeled data from the target domain are available, *domain adaptation* methods can be employed to align feature distributions between source and target domains, enabling zero-shot transfer [8, 1].

*Synthetic Data Generation* A promising idea to obtain pre-training data is to leverage pre-trained generative models. Recent developments in text-to-motion synthesis such as MotionCLIP [9], approaches based on diffusion models [10] and Text2Motion-GPT [13] enable the generation of realistic human motion from textual descriptions. These are typically represented as sequences of poses represented as a skeleton with joint positions and angles. These can be converted into IMU data streams, e.g., using biomechanical models. This opens up the possibility of generating large, diverse synthetic datasets for pre-training HAR models, reducing the dependence on real-world labeled data, as exemplified by IMU-GPT [3].

In summary, a large number of approaches have been proposed to cope with label scarcity in sensor-based HAR. While these methods demonstrate significant potential, there is still a considerable need for labeled data to achieve state-of-the-art performance in real-world deployments.

## References

1. Al Kfari, M.K., Lüdtke, S.: Domain adaptation in human activity recognition through self-training. In: Companion of the 2024 on ACM International Joint Conference on Pervasive and Ubiquitous Computing, pp. 897–903 (2024)
2. Krüger, F., Nyolt, M., Yordanova, K., Hein, A., Kirste, T: Computational state space models for activity and intention recognition. A feasibility study. PloS One, **9**(11), e109381 (2014)
3. Leng, Z., et al.: IMUGPT 2.0: language-based cross modality transfer for sensor-based human activity recognition. Proc. ACM Interact. Mob. Wear. Ubiquit. Technol. **8**(3):1–32 (2024)
4. Lüdtke, S., Rueda, F.M., Ahmed, W., Fink, G.A., Kirste, T.: Human activity recognition using attribute-based neural networks and context information. arXiv preprint arXiv:2111.04564 (2021)
5. Rueda, F.M., Grzeszick, R., Fink, G.A., Feldhorst, S., Hompel, M.T.: Convolutional neural networks for human activity recognition using body-worn sensors. In: Informatics, Vol. 5, pp. 26. MDPI (2018)
6. Niemann, F., Lüdtke, S., Bartelt, C., Hompel, M.T.: Context-aware human activity recognition in industrial processes. Sensors **22**(1), 134 (2021)
7. Rueda, F.M., Lüdtke, S., Schröder, M., Yordanova, K., Kirste, T., Fink, G.A.: Combining symbolic reasoning and deep learning for human activity recognition. In: 2019 IEEE International Conference on Pervasive Computing and Communications Workshops (PerCom Workshops), pp. 22–27. IEEE (2019)

8. Soleimani, E., Nazerfard, E.: Cross-subject transfer learning in human activity recognition systems using generative adversarial networks. Neurocomputing **426**, 26–34 (2021)
9. Tevet, G., Gordon, B., Hertz, A., Bermano, A.H., Cohen-Or, D. (2022). MotionCLIP: Exposing Human Motion Generation to CLIP Space. In: Avidan, S., Brostow, G., Cissé, M., Farinella, G.M., Hassner, T. (eds) Computer Vision – ECCV 2022. ECCV 2022. LNCS, vol. 13682, pp. 358–374. Springer, Cham (2022). https://doi.org/10.1007/978-3-031-20047-2_21
10. Tevet, G., Raab, S., Gordon, B., Shafir, Y., Cohen-Or, D., Bermano, A.H.: Human motion diffusion model. arXiv preprint arXiv:2209.14916 (2022)
11. Yordanova, K.: Challenges providing ground truth for pervasive healthcare systems. IEEE Pervas. Comput. **18**(2), 100–104 (2019)
12. Yuan, H., et al.: Self-supervised learning for human activity recognition using 700,000 person-days of wearable data. npj Digital Med. **7**(1), 91 (2024)
13. Zhang, J., et al.: Generating human motion from textual descriptions with discrete representations. In: Proceedings of the IEEE/CVF Conference on Computer Vision and Pattern Recognition, pp. 14730–14740 (2023)

# Contents

# Automating Ergonomics: Scalable AI for Technical Hand Grip Classification

# Automating Ergonomics: Scalable AI for Technical Hand Grip Classification

Simone Borghi[1(✉)], Fabio Grandi[2], Giuliano Iotti[3], and Margherita Peruzzini[2]

[1] Department of Engineering "Enzo Ferrari", University of Modena and Reggio Emilia (DIEF), Modena, Italy
simone.borghi@unimore.it

[2] Department of Industrial Engineering, University of Bologna (UNIBO), Bologna, Italy
{fabio.grandi11,margherita.peruzzini}@unibo.it

[3] Società Italiana di Ergonomia (SIE), Section Emilia Romagna, Bologna, Italy

**Abstract.** Recent studies show that most Work-Related Musculoskeletal Disorders (WMSDs) of the hand and wrist are the result of repeated stresses, caused by repetitive activities over a long time. Tools like ergonomics risk indexes, have been developed to assess upper limb overload in repetitive tasks: part of this evaluation is based on the observation of the number and frequency of Technical Hand Grips (THGs), differing by the number of fingers involved, the exerted forces and most affected regions. Ergonomists typically assess THGs manually via video review, which is time-consuming: a need arises for the automation of these procedures. The rapid and functional creation of AI models capable of classifying efficiently THGs presents some particular challenges: (1) labeling a huge amount of images at ergonomist-level, since, to the best of our knowledge, there are no useful datasets available; (2) considering object occlusions as an intrinsic requirement of realistic study of THGs; (3) moving towards the shared request of data anonymization. This work proposes an Active Learning system in which an initial model labels THGs from videos and consults an Oracle (ergonomist) only when uncertain. An implemented AI (GNN) model is trained on these carefully labeled data to replace the first rudimentary model. The process repeats until the desired model accuracy or data set size is reached. This has guaranteed: (1) a rapid labeling strategy and scaling of the THGs classification model that learns from selected "good" data; (2) implement an occlusion-robust model, by applying selective masking strategies; (3) anonymization through graph-structured data.

**Keywords:** Ergonomics · OCRA Index · Active Learning · Graph Neural Network · Technical Hand Grip Classification

## 1 Introduction

According to Govaerts et al. [1], the majority of WMSDs worldwide predominantly affect blue-collar workers; the most commonly affected anatomical regions are the back, shoulders/neck, and lower back, with 12-month prevalence rates


E. L. Tonkin et al. (Eds.): ARDUOUS 2025, CCIS 2706, pp. 3–15, 2026.
https://doi.org/10.1007/978-3-032-09117-8_1

ranging from 42% to 60%. Upper limb WMSDs incidence rates range from 4% to 26% and remain a major cause of absenteeism, with significant impacts on individual health and overall industrial productivity. In agreement with Global Burden of Disease 2019[1], in Italy, WMSDs are the most prevalent occupational disease, with an 88% increase reported between 2010 and 2017. They are estimated to account for 50% of work absences and 60% of permanent work-related disabilities. The incidence is higher among men than women, with certain occupational groups are particularly affected. More recent data show an increase in occupational diseases of 21.6%, from 72,754 in 2023 to 88,499 in 2024; the most frequent pathologies are those affecting the musculoskeletal system and connective tissue[2].

Furthermore, according to the review by da Costa et al. [2], between 2000 and 2012, the annual incidence rates of work-related upper extremity musculoskeletal disorders ranged from 0.08 to 6.3, while the prevalence rates ranged from 0.14 to 14.9. The highest incidence of work-related upper extremity musculoskeletal disorders is observed in rotator cuff syndrome, while cubital, radial, or ulnar nerve entrapment has the highest prevalence.
From these serious data emerges the importance of effective assessments for WMSDs prevention: ergonomics evaluation methods was born to meet these needs. Ergonomics[3], also referred to as human factors, is the scientific study of how people interact with their work environment. Its aim is to redesign tasks, tools, and spaces to fit the worker, rather than forcing the worker to adapt, thereby enhancing well-being, reducing the risk of injuries, and preventing work-related illnesses, such as WMSDs. Ergonomics is inherently a multidisciplinary field, and includes knowledge from medicine, physiology, biomechanics, psychology, and sociology [3], to name a few.

Over time, the need has emerged to develop ergonomics indexes, which are objective assessments based on standardized methods, recognized by law, to evaluate the physical risks workers face, to prevent WMSDs and other work-related diseases. Some of the most used ergonomics indexes are: **NIOSH Lifting Equation** [4], **REBA Index** [5], **RULA Index** [6] and **OCRA**(*OCcupational Repetitive Actions*) **Index** [7]. In this work, we focused on the latter, an ergonomic evaluation of the risks associated with the activity of the upper limbs and hands, according to Italian D.Lgs. 81/2008[4]. The elements under analysis for the OCRA Index are the frequency, number, and type of technical actions of the hands or Technical Hand Grips (THGs), the presence of complementary factors such as extreme temperatures and vibrations, and the applied forces. These evaluation

1 https://ergosante.fr/it/chiffre-accidentologie-tms-italie/.
2 https://www.inail.it/portale/it/inail-comunica/news.html.
3 https://iea.cc/about/what-is-ergonomics/.
4 https://www.ispettorato.gov.it/files/2025/01/TU-81-08-Ed.-Gennaio-2025-1.pdf.

methods are standardized and officially recognized by regulations[5]; assessments are typically conducted by trained ergonomists, who either analyze video recordings or perform real-time observations in loco. However, the process is time-consuming and still involves a degree of subjectivity, making it susceptible to human error. Furthermore, GDPR (EU Regulation 2016/679)[6], Italian Privacy Code law (D.Lgs. 196/2003)[7] and Non-Disclosure Agreement (Art. 1321 and 2598 of Civil Code[8]) impose restrictions on the collection and use of videos and images of humans, especially in industrial contexts where conflicts may arise between production needs and the rights of workers or third parties [8].
In light of what has been discussed, an automated ergonomic assessment system should be able to recognize movements and gestures of hands accurately over time, while ensuring data anonymization. This work aims to develop a semi-automated OCRA Index evaluation pipeline for identifying THGs, specifically: *Dirty Grip, Power Grip, Pinch Grip, Hook Grip*, and *Palmar Grip* (see Fig. 1 and the Source[9] for more information).

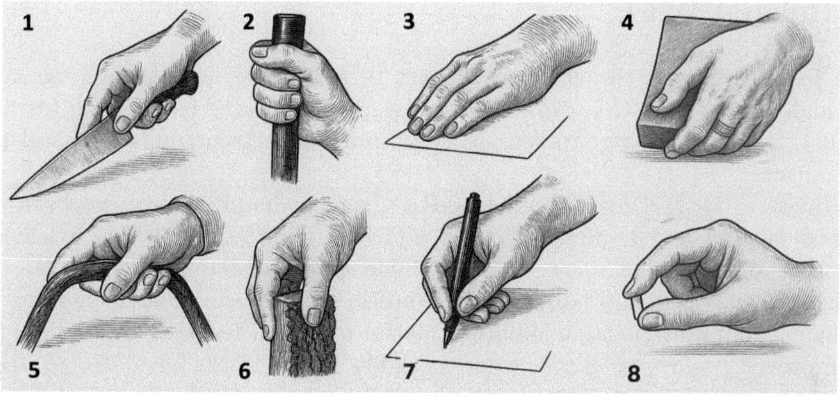


**Fig. 1.** The types of THGs according to the OCRA evaluation, investigated in this study. In details: *Dirty Grip* (**1**); *Power Grip* (**2**); *Pinch Grip* (**3**, **7** and **8**); *Hook Grip* (**4** and **5**); *Palmar Grip* (**6**).

To achieve this, we addressed key needs: (1) since no suitable THG-specific datasets exist, we had to create precisely (ergonomist level) labeled data; (2) real-world THG recognition occurs in presence of occluding objects: an efficient OCRA evaluation model must be accurate even in the presence of partial hands images; (3) this model will be used in industries with strict privacy rules, making

[5] https://osha.europa.eu/en/safety-and-health-legislation.
[6] https://www.garanteprivacy.it/regolamentoue.
[7] https://www.privacy.it/archivio/privacycode-en.html.
[8] https://www.normattiva.it/.
[9] https://www.univaq.it/include/utilities/blob.php?id=424&item=file&table=allegato&utm.

data anonymization crucial.
We chose an iterative approach using human-in-the-loop Active Learning and Graph Neural Networks (GNNs) architectures to meet these needs. Active Learning [9] is a machine learning approach in which the AI model is able to interactively query an Oracle, that could be a human or another information source, which, as a definition, provides correct information and is used as ground truth [10], to label new data with the goal of improving learning efficiency; this allows the model to scale quickly, as it learns from selected "good" data.
On the other hand, GNN models [11] are neural network architectures specialized for graph-structured data; it was adopted in this work for THGs classification based on 3D hand keypoints data. This paper is organized as follows: in Sect. 2, the state-of-the-art in hand pose recognition and automated labeling strategies will be addressed. The following Sect. 3 and Sect. 4 will provide an in-depth discussion of the solution implemented in this work, with technical details. Proposals for evaluation strategies will be discussed in Sect. 5.

## 2 Related Work

This section reviews the state of the art in semi-automatic hand pose labeling, highlighting how this work contributes and innovates (see Sect. 6 for more details). Several existing studies use computer vision techniques for hand pose recognition.
Kapitanov et al. [12] introduced HaGRID, a large hand gesture data set with 554,800 labeled and bounded images, addressing variability issues in existing data sets and covering more than 30 single and multihand gestures. Rastgoo et al. [13] developed sign language recognition models using depth cameras and advanced computer vision, combining spatial-temporal features and optical flow for improved performance over prior methods. Other works have also addressed the problem of semi-automatic hand poses labeling even in the presence of occlusions: in Hampali et al. [14], authors capture sequences with one or several RGB-D cameras and jointly optimize manually the 3D hand and object poses over all frames simultaneously. This approach allows for semi-automatic annotation of each frame with accurate pose estimates, despite significant occlusions. In Ienaga et al. [15], researchers proposed a semi-automatic system, based on human-in-the-loop Active Learning for bare hands poses recognition from images.

This work fits into this current research but responds to new and specific needs in professional ergonomic assessments summarized as:

1. Need to carry out numerous assessments in a short time; currently, an ergonomic assessment of THGs requires more than 1 h for a 1-minute of recorded activity (personal communication from a professional ergonomist).
2. Automation and support to the ergonomist for lengthy and complex assessments to limit human errors due to fatigue and inattention.

Furthermore, this assessment must be accurate for complex industrial assessments affected by occlusions, where video recording is subject to privacy issues.

## 3 Design of Proposed Solution

As previously described, the present work aimed to create a pipeline for semi-automatic labeling by means of an "human-in-the-loop" Active Learning approach for Technical Hand Grips (THGs) recognition. The challenges were to rapidly create an accurately labeled dataset of THGs images and 3D hand key-points graphs, suitable for training GNN classification models (but also more "classical' computer vision AI models) that support the ergonomists in their assessment and at the same time rapidly scale in power and accuracy, ideally becoming autonomous in a fully automated OCRA Index valuation. In this work, the model has been implemented to analyze not only collected videos, but also real-time recording, using ZED model depth cameras[10]. These particular stereoscopic cameras are excellent for accurate 3D recording of environments, objects, and people, and are already used for hand and full body tracking (see and [16]). Furthermore, the implementation of the THGs classification model must be robust and accurate even in the presence of occlusions. As shown in Fig. 2 the entire pipeline was organized as follows: (1) Videos of operators involved in manual work, recorded in advance or in real time using depth cameras, were

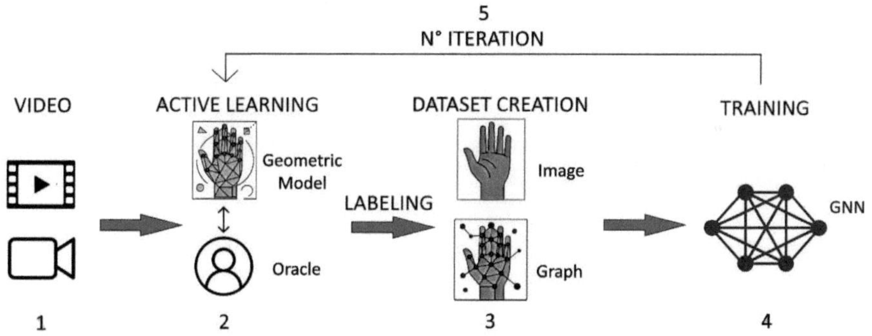


**Fig. 2.** THGs semi-automatic Active Learning labeling pipeline. Video inputs (**1**) were processed using an initial **Geometric Model** for semi-automated labeling; an **Oracle** assists when the model was uncertain or disagrees with the model's own evaluation (**2**). Labeled data of hands keypoints (**Graphs**) or **Images** (**3**) were used to train AI THGs classification models (for example **GNN**) (**4**) that will replace the **Geometric Model** to support the **Oracle** in labeling new video (**5**).

[10] https://www.stereolabs.com/en-it/products/zed-2.

used as input. (2) A Geometric Model based on a pre-existing Hand Tracking model performs a semi-automatic labeling, based on empirical constraints such as angles and average distances between particular hands' keypoints. An Oracle (ergonomist) intervenes with manual labeling in cases that were queried by the model or do not agree with the model itself. (3) The individual labeled frames were organized both as images, suitable for classical computer vision models, and as graphs of recorded hand keypoints. (4) The same data, through appropriate data augmentation and pre-processing strategies, was provided as a training dataset to a preliminary AI model (in the present analysis, to validate privacy maintenance strategies, a GNN). (5) This GNN model replaced the first rudimentary geometric model by actively helping the ergonomist in its evaluation; in parallel, the data will be saved in an even larger dataset and used to train an even more accurate model. This could be repeated until a model of desired accuracy is achieved or a satisfactory dataset is obtained.

## 4 Implementation

At the beginning of the pipeline, a rudimentary geometric model was implemented, which, based on distance and angle constraints between hand keypoints, partially supports Oracle in its evaluation. In this work, for all codes, we used the Python programming language[11], selected for its versatility, power, and wealth of libraries for data analysis, artificial intelligence, and computer vision (such as OpenCV [17] and PyTorch [18] Python Library). We use Mediapipe, an open-source, cross-platform framework developed by Google for building multimodal (video, audio, and sensor data) applied machine learning (ML) pipelines. It is designed to be efficient, flexible and easy to use, with a focus on real-time processing, such as hand tracking, object detection, pose estimation and more; the geometric model implemented was based on the pre-existing Mediapipe's hand tracking module (see Fig. 3 and [19]).

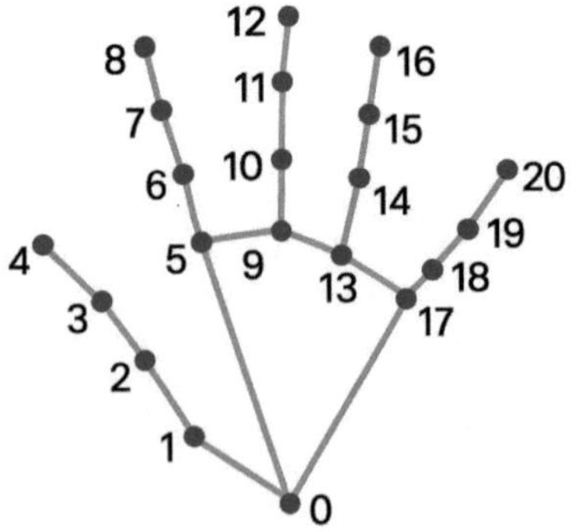


**Fig. 3.** Image of the 21 hand landmarks of the Mediapipe hand tracking model [19].

[11] https://www.python.org/.

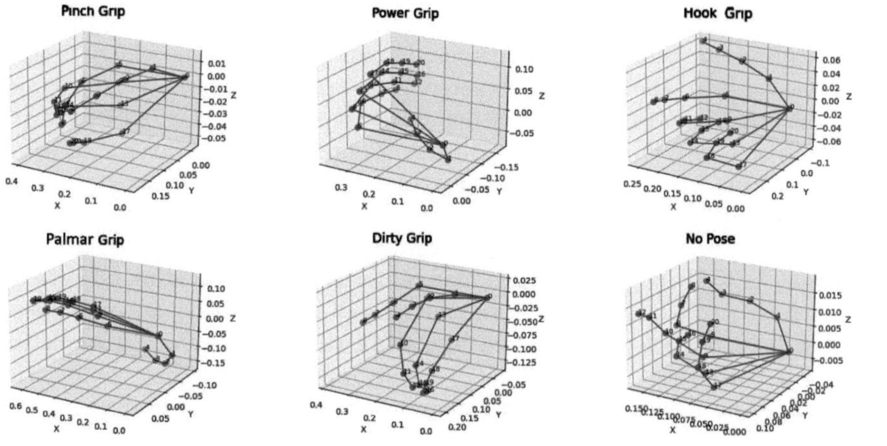


**Fig. 4.** Example of 3D keypoint graph structures for each of the THGs of interest, plus No Pose (**written in bold**).

This geometric model analyzes the geometric relationships from some of the 21 hand landmarks extracted from Mediapipe, to help the Oracle in THGs classification (focused on *Dirty Grip, Power Grip, Pinch Grip, Hook Grip*, and *Palmar Grip*). The classification criterion was set experimentally, based on a combination of Euclidean mean distances and angles between selected hand keypoints. After a careful analysis the keypoints thumb cmd (1), thumb tip (4), index tip (8), middle finger pip (10), ring finger pip (14), pinky tip (20) (see Fig. 3), from which the critical joints **8-4-20**, **10-4-14**, and **1-4-8** were selected, as they showed better ability to discriminate between THGs. For each joint, we calculated the angle (the tip of the thumb, i.e. point 4, was always used as the vertex of the angle) and average distance between keypoints, setting a specific threshold to identify the specific THG. If the distances and angles fell within this threshold, the THG was detected. These constraints were carefully tuned experimentally, ensuring fine-grained differentiation between similar THGs; however, overlapping thresholds were observed for different gestures. We set this as an initial query strategy: if a hand pose satisfies multiple THGs thresholds, the frame was marked as uncertain, and the system pauses to let the Oracle manually select the correct gesture from the complete list of THGs; at this stage, the Oracle can still intervene at will, when in disagreement with the model. This user-in-the-loop design ensures high labeling accuracy and facilitates the creation of clean, labeled datasets for further use. This script then saves data as images and 3D hand keypoints graph, labeled as: **Not Found**, that was, the model does not recognize the hand; **No Pose** where a hand is recognized, but with a pose that cannot be traced back to any of the THGs of interest or **THGs**, the correctly detected hand pose was attributable to one of the THGs of interest (*Dirty Grip, Power Grip, Pinch Grip, Hook Grip, Palmar Grip*). This simple geometric model will not be very accurate, but it will automate some of the labeling in the initial phase; remember that at this stage, it is always supervised by the Oracle. For an initial analysis, the geometric model/Active Learning strategy described above was used to label frames extracted from 7 freely available YouTube videos (total duration: 6,074 s; mean duration: 867.71 s; std duration: 789.78 s, variable frames/second or fps), featuring a diverse group of workers varying in sex and age, performing a range of manual tasks. In detail, the video depicted: (1) a little girl making a paper origami[12] (29.97 fps); (2) a girl making a paper airplane[13] (29.97 fps); (3) a woman manually kneading and flattening pasta dough to make tagliatelle[14] (25.00 fps); (4) various manual tasks such as building objects using various tools[15] (25.00 fps); (5) a butcher dividing a whole lamb into pieces[16] (23.98 fps); (6) a cook dividing and preparing various cuts from a whole leg of beef for a barbecue[17] (30.00 fps); (7) a lady making a crochet composition[18] (30.00 fps). The Active Learning strategy has been used for heterogeneous tasks and video, different by subject involved, registration duration, angle and magnification of the shot, use or non-use of tools and their type (to name a few there were used rolling pins, knives, bowls, stationery tools, hammers, drills, screws, crochet hooks, needles); this was an attempt to simulate what might be encountered during a real ergonomic assessment. This preliminary strategy allowed us to quickly obtain over 203 GB of data for a complex of 99584 labeled images and spatial 3D keypoints data. Further details are given in Table 1. As illustrated, the classes are highly unbalanced due to the variability of recorded THGs, which strongly depend on the type of task observed in the video. This imbalance is likely to occur in real-world scenarios as well, highlighting the need to incorporate suitable data compensation strategies into the processing pipeline. An initial GNN model for THG classification was trained on the 3D labeled spatial keypoints (see Fig. 4) from the first obtained data pool. This model is intended to replace the initial rudimentary geometric model in assisting the Oracle during its evaluations. As a first evaluation, the simple tree structure of the 21 keypoints was given as input to the model with a greater computational efficiency, reflecting the real anatomical structure of the hand, compared to a more connected graph structure. To train the GNN effectively, targeted data augmentation was applied to underrepresented classes to mitigate class imbalance, while a curriculum learning strategy was employed to expose the model to real-world occlusions gradually. For data augmentation, our GNN model employed geometric transformations including random scaling (0.8 to 1.2 factor), 3D rotations around the wrist joint (keypoint 0) for randomly selected angles between $-30$ and $+30°$, positional translations ($\pm 0.1$ units), and Gaussian noise (sigma $= 0.01$) to increase data variability and implemented selectively in less representative classes. To imple-

[12] https://www.youtube.com/watch?v=eEsx799dz8c.
[13] https://www.youtube.com/watch?v=x2vxFWFjR4M.
[14] https://www.youtube.com/watch?v=Bi5XGxw4oeY.
[15] https://www.youtube.com/watch?v=kzWjlhcc8Rw.
[16] https://www.youtube.com/watch?v=Uq_GB3ldQW8.
[17] https://www.youtube.com/watch?v=Xq00LNSAZzc.
[18] https://www.youtube.com/watch?v=F3WnFlIttCo.

ment the model in view of object occlusions that will be faced in the real evaluation, a curriculum learning approach was adopted. This strategy features progressive difficulty through anatomy-aware masking, where keypoints (see Fig. 3) were masked based on their probability of being occluded by an object (wrist: 20%, fingertips: 5%, intermediate joints: 30-55%), with masking intensity gradually increasing over 70% of the training period. The model architecture, trained on an NVIDIA GeForce RTX 3070 Laptop GPU, comprehends a series of graph convolutional layer 3→128→256→512→512 (input dimension 3 because of the three-dimensionality of the input data), batch normalization, ReLU activation, and increasing dropout rates (0.3-0.5), followed by global max pooling and a two-layer classifier with respective dimension 512 and 256 and output dimension equal to 6 (number of THGs plus No Pose classes). The training pipeline splits train and test at 80-20, respectively. The model training parameters were set with a learning rate of 0.001, an early stopping patience of 20, and a dropout rate of 0.5. We trained two separate but architecturally identical GNNs, one for the left and the other for the right hand.

**Table 1. THGs** of left (**SX Hand**) and right (**DX Hand**) hand obtained during the Oracle/Geometric Model active learning phase.

| THG | SX Hand | DX Hand |
|---|---|---|
| No Pose | 62507 | 22627 |
| *Dirty Grip* | 14 | 7 |
| *Power Grip* | 1513 | 814 |
| *Pinch Grip* | 19657 | 5986 |
| *Hook Grip* | 2015 | 739 |
| *Palmar Grip* | 75 | 21 |

## 5 Evaluation

The GNN model obtained according to the specifications described in Sect. 4 showed accuracies of 53.96% and 60.63% for right and left hand, respectively. For the evaluation phase described here, this model (named **"GNN Model"** for convention) will be placed alongside the initial geometric model (named **"Geo Model"**) used for the first labeling phase: the aim was to define whether the proposed strategy was able to accelerate the evaluation of THGs already at the first iteration. To this end, a YouTube video (called **"Validation Video"**), indicative of a real ergonomic evaluation, was selected. This video[19], set with a frame rate of 10 fps and selected in its most operational phase (between seconds 42 and 125), features the replacement and repair of pump parts, yielding a total

[19] https://www.youtube.com/watch?v=sqehpoNDxcc.

number of 238 frames useful for evaluation ("Not Found" hands excluded). The following protocol was hypothesized: the **GNN Model** and **Geo Model** were both used to support the **Oracle** in labeling the **Validation Video**; if, in a given frame and for a specific hand, the **GNN Model** and **Geo Model** provide contradictory evaluations of the THG, the **Oracle** was queried and proceeds with its labeling; the **Oracle**'s labeling was conducted blindly, meaning the models labeling was not shown; this to avoid biases. The evaluations performed by the **Oracle** are reported in Table 2. To evaluate the performance of the implemented pipeline, the agreement rate between the models and the Oracle was measured. This was defined as the number of THG comparisons in which both parties agreed, out of the total number of THG comparisons; this was expressed as a percentage. Results are reported on Fig. 5 and Table 3. The results of this preliminary evaluation demonstrated that both the **Geometric Model** and the **GNN Model** effectively assist the **Oracle** in its work, with agreement percentages improving as early as the first iteration, reaching, 73.01% for the left and 42.65% for the right hand with the **Geo Model** and 79.37% for the left and 39.71% for the right hand with the **GNN Model**. These findings suggest that a substantial portion of THG evaluations could be automated from the very first iteration.

**Table 2.** Number of **THGs** observed by the **Oracle** in the **Validation Video**, separated into left **(SX Hand)** and right hand **(DX Hand)**.

| THG | SX Hand | DX Hand |
|---|---|---|
| No Pose | 98 | 63 |
| *Dirty Grip* | 0 | 0 |
| *Power Grip* | 3 | 1 |
| *Pinch Grip* | 10 | 54 |
| *Hook Grip* | 0 | 1 |
| *Palmar Grip* | 14 | 15 |

## 6 Discussion

As seen in Sect. 2, most of the existing studies are based on the recognition of bare hands poses; in contrast, in real ergonomic evaluation of THGs, the model has to be accurate even in the presence of occlusions due to grasped objects. Furthermore, unlike gesture recognition, OCRA Index evaluations must be performed as objectively and accurately as possible, as any inaccuracies could result in a misjudgment of the operator's risk; the need for an Active Learning approach supported by specialized personnel to rapidly and efficiently improve the classification model is imperative. Finally, previous works relied on recordings and video footage, which, in modern industrial contexts, is not always allowed for privacy and security reasons. The proposed approach of GNN models trained

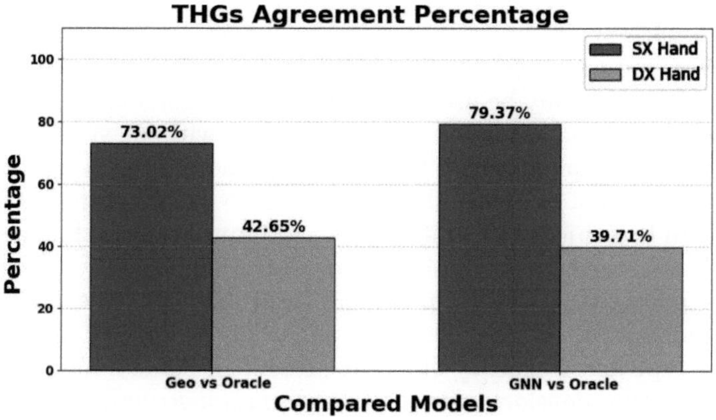


**Fig. 5.** Percentage of agreement in THGs classification between **Geometric Model** (**Geo**), **GNN Model** (**GNN**) and **Oracle** (**Oracle**) used as ground truth, for left (**SX**) and right (DX) **Hand**.

**Table 3.** Detailed count of the common **THGs** found between **Geometric Model** (**Geo**)/ **GNN Model** (**GNN**) and **Oracle** (**Oracle**) for left (**SX**) and right (**DX**) **Hand**. In orange the highest agreement values.

| | **SX Hand** | | **DX Hand** | |
|---|---|---|---|---|
| **THG** | **Geo vs Oracle** | **GNN vs Oracle** | **Geo vs Oracle** | **GNN vs Oracle** |
| No Pose | 92 | 97 | 56 | 53 |
| *Dirty Grip* | 0 | 0 | 0 | 0 |
| *Power Grip* | 0 | 3 | 0 | 0 |
| *Pinch Grip* | 0 | 0 | 2 | 0 |
| *Hook Grip* | 0 | 0 | 0 | 1 |
| *Palmar Grip* | 0 | 0 | 0 | 0 |

on 3D hand landmarks graphs, instead of more traditional convolutional neural networks (CNN), which require images to be trained, leading to privacy issues, tries to answer these needs. Furthermore, structured graph data are particularly suitable for the implementation of robust AI models in the presence of occlusions by implementing differential masking strategies at keypoints (curriculum learning), data augmentation, and other techniques. In light of these considerations, we believe that the main innovations of this work lie in: (1) the implementation of an Active Learning system for the semi-automatic labeling of THGs, encompassing both individual frames and 3D hand keypoints; (2) the rapid development of accurate and occlusion-robust GNN models and THG datasets; (3) the exploration of data anonymization strategies through the use of GNNs rather than

more traditional approaches such as CNNs (potentially implementable themselves). We also want to underline our strongly applicative approach: the protocol and scripts can potentially be used immediately by ergonomists, in their studies and in parallel creating new data and AI models, without slowing down their activity. What is presented in this work is not intended to be a rigid framework; oracle query strategies, as well as the details of GNN architecture and graph data processing, can be subject to modifications and improvements. Furthermore, the evaluations carried out on the **Validation Video** were purely indicative, highlighting the potential of the proposed protocol, but also the limitations due to the dependence on the specific video analyzed, its quality and characteristics, and the type and frequency of THGs presented. Some limitations emerged, which inspire future developments; first of all, graph-structured data offers the advantage of versatility as preprocessing and good data anonymization, but the limitation of being dependent on the pre-existing model (e.g., the Mediapipe model), with its technical limitations: this experience prompted us to compare other pre-existing AI models and to put forward the hypothesis of creating a new one, maybe combining GNN and CNN architecture, specific for ergonomics needs. Second, for an optimal evaluation of THGs, three-dimensionality is important: from videos obtained by stereoscopic cameras such as ZED this is not a problem; however from 2D videos, the three-dimensionality is created by guessing of the pre-existing AI model. Furthermore, we will strive to create an even larger and more varied dataset in terms of the type of operations performed, camera angles, resolution, and other details to improve the generalizability of the models.
We will endeavor to address these weaknesses in future research.

## 7 Conclusion

Our proposed strategy aimed to realize a semi-automated pipeline to help the ergonomist in classifying THGs, from videos or real-time footage; the system has the potential to scale rapidly in terms of model accuracy and data quality, to the point of becoming potentially autonomous in the OCRA Index evaluation, responding to the needs of a professional ergonomic assessment. Specifically, it was obtained that: (1) the implementation of an Active Learning strategy for THGs labeling using human-in-the-loop Active Learning approach, allows to obtain "good" data quickly, on which to iteratively train increasingly accurate AI models; (2) curriculum learning could enable to train models robust to occlusions, crucial for evaluating THGs in real-world settings; (3) the graph structure facilitates data anonymization, potentially removing the need to store images or videos, which are increasingly subject to privacy and security restrictions.

**Disclosure of Interests.** The authors declare that they have no competing interests.

## References

1. Govaerts, R., et al.: Prevalence and incidence of work-related musculoskeletal disorders in secondary industries of 21st century Europe: a systematic review and meta-analysis. BMC Musculoskelet. Disord. **22**, 1–30 (2021)
2. Costa, J.T., Baptista, J.S., Vaz, M.: Incidence and prevalence of upper-limb work related musculoskeletal disorders: a systematic review. Work **51**(4), 635–644 (2015)
3. Wilson, J.R.: Fundamentals of ergonomics in theory and practice. Appl. Ergon. **31**(6), 557–567 (2000)
4. Health. Division of Physical Sciences: NIOSH, Manual of Analytical Methods. US Department of Health and Human Services, Public Health Service, Centers (1994)
5. Hignett, S., McAtamney, L.: Rapid entire body assessment (REBA). Appl. Ergon. **31**(2), 201–205 (2000)
6. McAtamney, L., Corlett, E.N.: RULA: a survey method for the investigation of work-related upper limb disorders. Appl. Ergon. **24**(2), 91–99 (1993)
7. Stradioto, J.P., Michaloski, A.O., Paula Xavier, A.A., Colombini, D.: Comparison of RULA and checklist OCRA ergonomic risk methods for civil construction. Industr. Eng. Manage. Syst. **19**(4), 790–802 (2020)
8. Arputharaj, J.V., Prasad, D.D., Adu-Manu, K.S.: Navigating data privacy in industry 5.0: advanced strategies for sustainability. In: Soft Computing in Industry 5.0 for Sustainability, pp. 117–143. Springer (2024)
9. Brame, C.: Active learning. Vanderbilt University Center for Teaching, 1–6 (2016)
10. Settles, B.: Active learning literature survey. University of Wisconsin-Madison Department of Computer Sciences (2009)
11. Corso, G., Stark, H., Jegelka, S., Jaakkola, T., Barzilay, R.: Graph neural networks. Nat. Rev. Methods Primers **4**(1), 17 (2024)
12. Kapitanov, A., Kvanchiani, K., Nagaev, A., Kraynov, R., Makhliarchuk, A.: HaGRID–HAnd gesture recognition image dataset. In: Proceedings of the IEEE/CVF Winter Conference on Applications of Computer Vision, pp. 4572–4581 (2024)
13. Rastgoo, R., Kiani, K., Escalera, S.: Hand pose aware multimodal isolated sign language recognition. Multimedia Tools Appl. **80**(1), 127–163 (2021)
14. Hampali, S., Rad, M., Oberweger, M., Lepetit, V.: Honnotate: a method for 3D annotation of hand and object poses. In: Proceedings of the IEEE/CVF Conference on Computer Vision and Pattern Recognition, pp. 3196–3206 (2020)
15. Ienaga, N., Cravotta, A., Terayama, K., Scotney, B.W., Saito, H., Busa, M.G.: Semi-automation of gesture annotation by machine learning and human collaboration. Lang. Resour. Eval. **56**(3), 673–700 (2022)
16. Ashok, Y., Kumar Rohil, M., Tandon, K., Sethi, H.: VOEDHgesture: a multipurpose visual odometry/simultaneous localization and mapping and egocentric dynamic hand gesture data-set for virtual object manipulations in wearable mixed reality. In: Proceedings of the 16th International Conference on Agents and Artificial Intelligence (ICAART), pp. 1336–1344 (2024)
17. Bradski, G., Kaehler, A., et al.: OpenCV. Dr. Dobb's Journal of Software Tools, **3**(2) (2000)
18. Imambi, S., Prakash, K.B., Kanagachidambaresan, G.R.: PyTorch. Programming with TensorFlow: Solution for Edge Computing Applications, 87–104 (2021)
19. Marais, M., Brown, D., Connan, J., Boby, A.: An evaluation of hand-based algorithms for sign language recognition. In: 2022 International Conference on Artificial Intelligence, Big Data, Computing and Data Communication Systems (icABCD), pp. 1–6. IEEE (2022)

# Recommendations for Datasets Creation Process for Human Motion Generation in Industrial Simulations

Nilah Ravi Nair(✉), Jérôme Rutinowski, Moritz Roidl, and Alice Kirchheim

Chair of Material Handling and Warehousing, TU Dortmund University, Joseph-von-Fraunhofer Straße 2-4, Dortmund 44227, Germany
nilah.nair@tu-dortmund.de

**Abstract.** Humans are crucial for industrial layout planning and technological design, as seen in assembly lines and order-picking layouts. These fields aim to incorporate robots for human convenience and collaboration, striving towards Industry 5.0. As a result, simulation, virtual and digital twin environments are used to facilitate employee training, ergonomic evaluations, and task modelling. Human motion generation for robotics and industrial simulation environments can accelerate process analysis by simplifying the generation of human motions. Given the data-intensive nature of generative models, human motion datasets containing industrial scenarios, terminologies and appropriate textual annotation are necessary. Thus, the key contribution of this work is a novel dataset collection framework for futuristic, industrial, large-scale datasets that can be adapted to the dataset requirements of human motion generation models. In addition, we aim to bring together the human motion generation, dataset and industrial simulation community by providing a platform for discussion and exchange.

**Keywords:** Human Motion Generation · Industrial Simulation · Dataset Creation

## 1 Introduction

Even in highly digitised industries, humans play a vital role, such as in manufacturing, assembly, order picking, and packaging [48,49]. Recent years have seen an increased use of robots in industries to ease the strain on workers, tackle staff shortages and improve productivity [13,49]. Application of robots in industries may entail robot-only environments [14] or human-robot collaborative (HRC) environments [13]. Due to the challenge of achieving the dexterity and flexibility of human limbs, human-robot collaborative environments are highly desirable [10]. To ensure safety, collaborative robots follow safety standards such as safety stop, hand guiding, speed and separation monitoring, and power and force limiting [22], thus reducing overall productivity [40]. As a result, research focused


E. L. Tonkin et al. (Eds.): ARDUOUS 2025, CCIS 2706, pp. 16–35, 2026.
https://doi.org/10.1007/978-3-032-09117-8_2

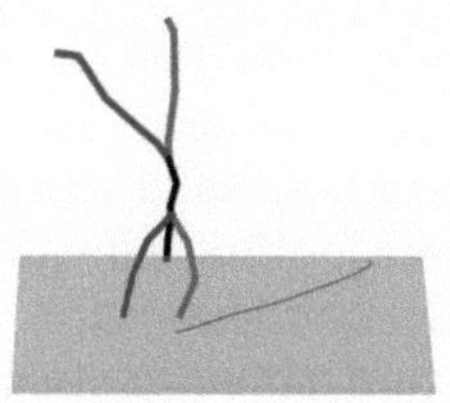

(a) MotionGPT [61] generated image.

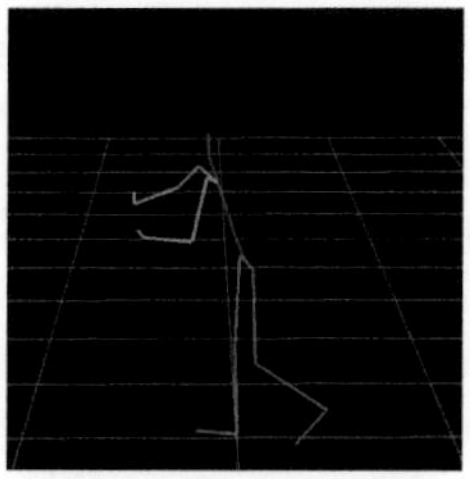

(b) Image obtained from LARa dataset [37].

**Fig. 1.** Figure 1 (a) is an example of motion generated for the prompt 'Person pushing a Cart' by MotionGPT [61] demo model. The snippet is of a person performing a cartwheel or handstand. The grey portion depicts the floor. The ideal generated snippet would be of a person pushing a shopping cart or logistics cart with one or both hands as shown in Fig. 1 (b) obtained from the logistics dataset LARa [37].

on bringing humans and robots closer by training the robots in simulation environments to interact with human models before implementing the solutions in real industries is in progress.

Industrial simulators facilitate training, maintenance, forecasting, planning and risk assessment [26,49]. Although human models are of interest in these simulators, the human models do not account for factors such as fatigue and human randomness, leading to inaccurate results [26,48]. Realistic human models could benefit robot training simulators [15]. Compared to algorithm-driven human models [15], developments in human motion generation (HMG) [59,61] and generative artificial intelligence (GenAI) present the possibility of obtaining human motion with ease, diversity, and control for simulation environments [62]. However, GenAI is data-driven, and the available datasets for HMG heavily focus on daily living activities, as seen in the AMASS dataset [32]. Figure 1 presents an image of motion generated from MotionGPT [61]. The generator related the term cart to cartwheeling. Consequently, appropriate human motion data depicting varied industrial scenarios with industrial terminologies is necessary.

Furthermore, there is a lack of publicly available datasets containing complex industrial activities rich in metadata. Metadata includes workers' physical characteristics, experience, dimension, and weight of the objects used, motion goals, and distance traversed [58]. The inclusion of such metadata benefits industrial simulation environments in process analysis. This dearth in the availability of datasets can be associated with the expenses in capturing the required processes and the subsequent data annotation tasks [26,36]. In addition, recording a single human is insufficient to capture the subtlety and diversity of human behaviour [34,40]. Thus, creating structured open-sourced datasets with high activity variability and subject characteristics is necessary [43].

Creating a well-structured industrial dataset with varied scenarios can be arduous. Although there are frameworks for motion annotation using large language models [30] and motion generation (MoGen) model evaluation [25], there are no frameworks for dataset creation. A human motion dataset creation framework is crucial when two distinct fields attempt to collaborate and communicate their requirements. For example, industrialists use specific motion terminologies, and the GenAI community requires human motion data in standard file formats. A framework of decentralised data collection and centralised presentation of human motion to generate industry-specific human motions is necessary to promote such exchanges. Thus, this work has two goals: to recommend a framework for creating a human motion dataset for data-driven HMG focused on industrial and robotics simulators and to bridge the gap between the dataset creators and the MoGen community by providing a platform for discussion and resource exchange. The framework is developed from recommendations from a dataset user perspective for dataset creators to help elucidate industrial simulation challenges and facilitate the GenAI community to use the industrial data with existing models.

This publication is structured as follows: Sect. 2 discusses the challenges in industrial simulations that HMG can tackle by surveying human motion datasets in industry, robotics and industrial simulation environments and the requirements of generative networks. Section 3 presents the key contribution of this work, a framework for human motion dataset creation. The proposed framework is developed based on seven recommendations, one provided for each stage of the dataset creation process. Finally, Sect. 4 discusses the future work required for incorporating HMG into industrial simulations.

## 2 Challenges in Industrial Simulation Environments

Understanding the challenges and requirements of industrial simulation, human-robot collaboration training, and datasets for training generative neural networks is vital to outlining an industrial human motion dataset creation framework.

### 2.1 Human-Robot Interaction

Recent years have seen research conducted to evaluate the impact of collaborative human-robot environments on productivity. For instance, [47] provides a study on robots assisting harvesters in strawberry fields and predicts that harvesting efficiency can improve from 81.8% to 92% with robots helping human harvesters. In the simulation, the robots assisted the harvesters by reducing the non-productive walking period by transporting harvesting trays. Robots can be employed for analogous tasks in warehouses. However, when robots approach humans or each other in these scenarios, the robots slow down to avoid accidental collisions. This safety precaution causes delays and reduces overall efficiency. In addition, high-speed robot models such as evoBOT [28] must be equipped with safety designs and fail-safes, including hand gesture recognition-based commands and monitoring of speed and distance between the robot and human. Furthermore, limitations on the operational power and force of the robots are necessary as described in [2], ISO 10218-2 and ISO/TS 15066 [12].

Various robotic algorithms are tested on ROS, Gazebo, PyBullet and Isaac Gym, which are state-of-the-art (SOTA) robotics simulation tools [13,21,45] used to train and test robot movements. However, these models do not simulate active human factors. Human factors refer to the ergonomics and interaction of humans with the elements of a system that it is part of [48]. [60] notes that concepts such as hybrid order picking with autonomous picking have rarely been studied and have significant research and implementation scope. Many researchers train robots in virtual environments and then transfer the trained models to real-world environments for further experimentation [21,29,45,54]. Consequently, one can conclude that simulators presenting humans and robots in collaborative settings specific to the industry are highly relevant for human-robot interaction and collaboration research.

HMG can contribute to these simulation environments by generating erratic human movements, grasping motions and close-quarter interactions for the safety training of the robots. Furthermore, text-conditioned and scene-conditioned HMG as a plug-in could help the roboticists focus on the robot training rather than the human model. Such safety training would facilitate leaving the human out of the initial training loop while improving the trust of the human volunteers at a later stage of testing the collaborative robot. Soft biometrics such as age, gender, height, weight, and handedness of the individual could further benefit robotics training environments.

### 2.2 Simulation Environments for Industry

As noted by [26], simulation models facilitate industry decision-makers to obtain practical insight into their specific scenario, such as logistics. Furthermore, simulations offer a dynamic, cost-effective experimental platform for seamlessly conducting various experiments and analyses. [38] simulated and evaluated the effect of worker stamina on worker hours. The authors used Simpy to simulate the worker environment to obtain algorithms for improving the performance of work-hours estimation on a small dataset. The authors note that since the simulator could not consider the constraints and noise of a real logistics environment, there is an evident gap between simulated and actual data, requiring further investigation. [27] presents a concept to create complex human motions for interaction with objects in production. The authors separate actions from object class semantics and couple them based on context and functional spaces in the geometric primitives defined simulation. The work presents a direction for HMG to simplify the action sequence generation and save time in animation.

Simulation environments to evaluate algorithms to estimate the intention of workers to ensure safe robotized warehouses are presented in [40]. The authors tested their algorithms on worker intention estimation in an interactive 3D simulation of a virtual reality warehouse environment developed in Unity3D. Furthermore, the algorithms were tested in a real-world laboratory warehouse. The algorithm could predict worker intention within reasonable expectations and offered the possibility of further development in the direction of system monitoring. In a similar research direction, [5] proposed using production system simulation in mixed reality to facilitate production planning by including human factors. Further, the technique realises human-centric production design. [49] presents a review on using digital human models for ergonomic assessment in industry. The authors suggest a potential gap between researchers' and industry's expectations, indicating the need for collaborative development of industrial applications of human models in simulations.

These works emphasise that the industry requires human simulation models where age, gender, height, and weight characteristics can be varied. Further, quantifying and manipulating the speed of the human, human-human interaction, distance covered, hand movement towards a set goal and a setting where interaction with objects can be modelled is required. In addition, industrial simulations could benefit from natural language-based terminologies for movement generation [33].

The authors [26] duly note that technical experts without domain knowledge often require comprehensive explanations of real-world systems to formulate models, including simulation environments, required by domain specialists. It is expected that GenAI can help bring together the two extremes – domain specialists and technical professionals – with the help of Natural Language Processing (NLP) based frameworks for building simulation models of logistics systems based on verbal descriptions. The possibility of domain experts creating logistics simulations using GenAI could exponentially increase productivity.

### 2.3 Industrial Human Motion Datasets

The authors of [7] review human motion analysis in an industrial context, such as human activity recognition, motion prediction, and gesture recognition. The authors presented 16 benchmark datasets for human analysis, their sensor technologies, type of interaction, availability of the human representation and public availability. Out of the 16 datasets, 11 datasets are publicly available. [58] notes that publicly available sensor datasets containing industrial domain activities, such as packaging, pushing a cart, scanning barcodes and picking orders, are rare due to the difficulty in collecting and annotating realistic datasets. However, [7] notes that industrial datasets have increased in the past years.

Various sensor technologies can be used in creating human motion datasets [39] noted that there is a preference for video data when creating datasets. However, motion capture (MoCap) sensors provide high-fidelity 3D data and can overcome the drawbacks of video data, such as occlusion and privacy concerns [39]. Full-body representations of the human body in a given dataset are valuable for HMG. However, with methods to convert sensors (for example, inertial measurement units (IMUs)) to full-body representation [31] and OpenPose [16] to obtain skeletal information from RGB data, there is flexibility to obtain full-body representations. Consequently, full-body representation of humans performing actions in industrial scenarios can be extracted from existing datasets created in the context of human action analysis [7]. As seen in [20], various

**Fig. 2.** Example of Digital Twin, where industrial scenarios can be visualised in Unity. Image from TU Dortmund University.

skeleton representations are feasible. One must ideally choose the representation when creating the dataset appropriately to ensure compatibility.

Datasets, such as InHARD dataset [9], UR10 [9], and HRI30 [23], consist of human-robot collaboration scenes in industrial settings that are manually annotated with their action classes. Accumulating these existing industrial datasets with human-robot and human-object interactions could facilitate the use of HMG for simulation environments such as AMASS [32] and HumanAct12 [18], supported in the creation of MotionGPT [61].

Understandably, each dataset provides features such as the availability of digital twin (example of digital twin in Fig. 2), skeletal information, semantic annotation and fine hand gestures based on the intended application. Given the arduous effort that the dataset creation process takes, ideally, one must account for features that would help in the reusability and extendability of the dataset for future research [44]. For example, the subject's characteristics in a given dataset affect the performance and generalisation of human motion analysis [34]. Datasets with metadata such as subject characteristics and work experience are valuable [37,58] to research on representation biases, person identification, anonymisation, and velocity profiling [19,34]. However, very few datasets provide this information. Similarly, though human skeletal information can help us use the dataset for varied scenarios, few datasets focus on simple hand movements or egocentric vision, as in the case of assembly. As a result, in an ideal case, the industrial dataset creators must be informed of the features to be included for further research using their datasets.

### 2.4 Human Motion Generation

GenAI has received exponential traction over the past few years, as has HMG. [62] notes that along with the generation of 'natural, realistic and diverse human motions', HMG should ideally be able to 'generate motion in alignment with the condition signal and account for nonverbal communication'. Human motion completion, editing, character control and locomotion in physical simulation environments do not fall under the scope of HMG [62]. Consequently, application fields, such as film production, video games, augmented reality/virtual reality (AR/VR), human-robot interaction, and digital humans are referred [62]. Three subtasks of HMG are text-conditioned, audio-conditioned, and scene-conditioned

HMG. To generate motion from natural language descriptions, one must learn the relation between the text and motion [62].

In a phenomenal effort, [32] collected and converted various human motion datasets into a consistent representation of the Skinned Multi-Person Linear (SMPL) model archive. However, the datasets within AMASS only had a single action class label for their sequences. This poses a challenge to text-conditioned motion generation. [42] created language labels for the action sequences in the AMASS dataset, referred to as BABEL. The authors note that BABEL [42] supports overlapping multiple action labels, providing dense annotations. Further utilising the AMASS dataset with BABEL language annotation, [56] provides synthetic 3D indoor scene descriptions for supporting text-conditioned HMG in 3D scenes. The authors leverage AMASS human motions and ScanNet 3D indoor scenes and provide 3D referential descriptions using Sr3D in addition to the BABEL action labels in [56]. These labelled data have paved the way for the works of [50] that facilitates highly semantic text-conditioned HMG, [11] HMG with goal-oriented movement and [55] text-conditioned motion generation within 3D environments. Unfortunately, the datasets discussed above focus on daily living activities such as walking, jogging, grabbing, and swimming. Thus, terms pertaining to industrial activities, such as pushing a cart, putting items into a plastic bag, and scanning items, may not have a text-to-motion relation. These datasets limit the usage of these networks specifically for HMG in industrial simulations. Though industrial datasets exist for human motion analysis, the use of these datasets for HMG was not identified during the literature survey for this work. Thus, this work's authors believe it is necessary to accumulate industrial datasets with textual and scene descriptions to train existing HMG networks for industrial simulations.

## 3 Recommendations for a Holistic Dataset for Human Motion Generation

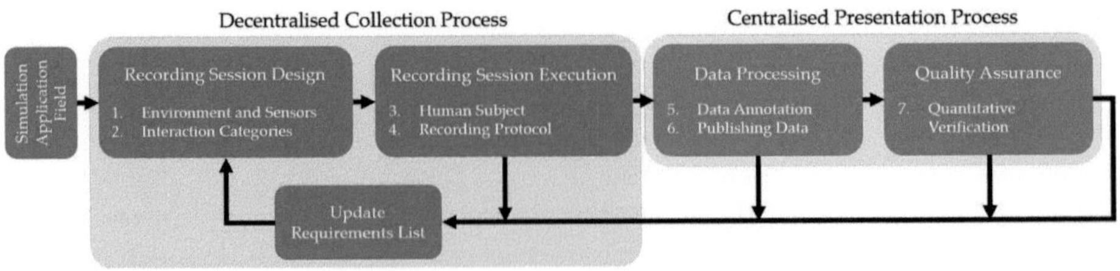


**Fig. 3.** Framework for human motion dataset generation for industrial simulations. The decentralised collection process is in blue, and the centralised presentation process is in green. Feedback from each stage updates the requirements list for future datasets. (Color figure online)

From Sect. 2, one can understand that the lack of data restricts the development of HMG neural networks and their scope of application areas. In addition, there exist various challenges in HMG for industrial simulations that need to be researched. There are ongoing efforts to create and enhance datasets for human motion analysis. Thus, a holistic industrial dataset with full-body representations can enhance HMG for simulation environments. Currently, dataset creators follow varied protocols for dataset creation, such as varied data formats, closed datasets, unavailability of metadata of the objects in the scenario, and the subjects' physical characteristics. In such a case, we face the problem of isolated datasets that may not be compatible. This scenario would essentially delay the development of a generalised HMG network that may be compatible with various industrial scenarios and support addressing the challenges that industrial simulations bring to HMG. As a result, concentrated efforts to bring together datasets to a similar format, like in the case of AMASS [32], may have to take place in frequent repetitions. However, this issue can be overcome by consistently providing relevant information at the dataset level by dataset creators. Motivated by [43], where the authors direct dataset creators towards considerations when creating human-analysis datasets, we provide the dataset creators a HMG developer data requirement perspective. The recommendations in [44] do not discuss features that must be considered for HMG. Thus, this work provides a framework to the reader and recommendations for creating a human motion dataset such that any datasets developed following the proposed framework would be compatible with the requirements of HMG datasets. The proposed framework of decentralised collection and centralised presentation is motivated by the work of AMASS [32].

Figure 3 presents the framework recommended for dataset collection, specifically for HMG. The following subsections will provide the reader with specific recommendations for each framework step. The framework is designed with the understanding that expecting one individual or group to create a large dataset encompassing varied industrial scenarios, objects, and robots is an impossible task. For example, dataset creators with in-depth information about assembly lines would be able to present their scenario more clearly than a logistician who is an expert in designing order-picking aisles. Further, there might be specific sub-processes of order picking, such as pick-by-light and pick-by-voice. Therefore, one must divide the processes and sub-processes of dataset creation for an industry based on expertise and re-group at a later stage. Each expert creates a dataset for their field of knowledge in a decentralised collection process and then later combines it with other fields through a centralised presentation process; then, one essentially creates a larger dataset compatible with each sub-dataset. A decentralised dataset collection process facilitates the creation of a multipurpose dataset, which could be used for human motion analysis, human motion generation, re-identification of subjects or reinforcement training of robots, depending on the modality of the data and metadata provided. Furthermore, this facilitates recording with new sensor technologies. To achieve a centralised presentation, a few criteria must be considered: standard file formats, recording protocol, metadata availability, and good annotations. The feedback from each stage of the dataset creation could be further used to update the requirements lists for a new dataset at a later stage. Modifying the dataset creation guidelines of [43] to suit motion generation, the following section elaborates Fig. 3.

### 3.1 Recording Session Design

Before creating a dataset, one must decide on the scope of the dataset. Next, the dataset features and recording sessions must be designed. Industrial scenarios to be recorded could be assembly, manufacturing, order-picking, or packaging. Depending on the expertise of the dataset creators, it is ideal to name the processes, sub-processes, objects interacted with, and human limbs used for the chosen scenario. The first stage in this process, after defining the scope of the dataset, is to identify the recording environment and the sensor system. The next stage is identifying the interaction categories. Multiple iterations of the environment's design and interaction of the recording scenario are necessary to ensure the robust design of the recording session.

**Environment and Sensors.** Video-based recordings of humans in industrial scenarios, especially in industrial settings, are not recommended as they may affect the employees' privacy [3], according to the European Union's General Data Protection Regulation (GDPR) [1]. Consequently, recreating the industrial environment within a laboratory with subjects of varied experience levels [58], and recording the scenario with a MoCap system or RGB-D camera would help collect appropriate motions [37]. Furthermore, a laboratory setting would help include human interactions with robots and drones in a safe and controlled environment, as presented in [51]. However, it is desired that dataset creators have a reference industrial scenario and attempt to recreate the same, if possible, to scale. Alternatively, given that the recording will take place in an industrial setting, appropriate sensor setups that provide ground truth information should be chosen. In addition, privacy-preserving practices such as blurring the faces of the individuals or extracting just the skeleton information while recording using tools such as OpenPose [35] are recommended.

Be it in an industrial or laboratory environment, once the recording scenario for the motion data has been defined, having an RGB-D video recording of the environment [8,56] can contribute to scene-conditioned HMG. In addition to facilitating work such as in [56], such RGB-D recordings would facilitate work in the direction of CAD model retrieval and object classification [8]. Alternatively, having a digital twin model with depth information, e.g., in Unity3D, would further enhance the available environment's metadata and provide information for scene interaction and goal-oriented movements. Although the existing MoCap datasets capture motion information, delicate finger movements are often not captured. It is highly recommended that dataset creators invest time and effort in recording these motions to ensure the dataset includes detailed finger movements. Converting the sensor data to SMPL models [6] and point-cloud data [8] would benefit further research. The authors of [32] use the C3D files obtained from the MoCap system to unify different datasets with the SMPL file format. An SMPL skin format of the recording can help identify issues with the skeleton rendered from the sensor pipeline. Further, this final format helps motion generation networks currently trained on AMASS to be fine-tuned to industrial scenarios.

**Recommendation 1:** The recording environment (e.g., industrial setting or laboratory) needs to be determined, framing the expectations for the dataset. Irrespective of the chosen environment, diverse natural movements and interactions of humans shall be recorded. Dimensional information about the objects in the scene, such as the height of shelves, the weight of cartons, and the distance between two points in a scene, shall be recorded. A point cloud model, digital twin model or multi-view video of the initial recording environment is an important asset. When considering sensors for human motion recording, a MoCap system is recommended to obtain ground truth information. Alternatively, RGB-D camera usage is recommended. In exceptional cases, pose extraction from videos or SMPL models from IMU sensors shall be considered. Multi-modal sensor systems are recommended as the best-case scenario for future research.

**Interaction Categories.** After defining the scope and designing the environment of the recording session, identify and name the processes, sub-processes, objects interacted with, and human limbs used in the scenario. Naming these various aspects helps the dataset creator identify processes for desired motion variability [37]. For example, when handling an item, the motion variability can be improved by including items of various sizes and weights at different shelf heights. In addition, this step helps identify activity class imbalances. For instance, if the dataset consists mainly of the 'walking' activity class and has fewer recordings of other activities, then the dataset creators could identify methods to increase recordings of less available activity classes.

Identifying the interaction categories can later help explain the recording to the annotators in the annotation process. In addition, this step facilitates the creation of a dictionary of the varied names by which a given object in the scene can be referred to. For instance, a carton can also be referred to as a box, bin or package. Having a terminology dictionary is beneficial in creating textual variability in the annotation stage. The terminology dictionary is not limited to the terms used for an object but should include the verbs that can be used for each interaction [58]. For example, 'he took the item from the robot' or 'the item was handed to him by the robot'. Given the inclusion of robots or drones in the industrial environment, human movements that would take place in these scenarios should be elaborated upon. For instance, if the human is expected to follow the robot, or if the robot is handing an item to the human, the hesitance or willingness of a human to interact with the robot [24] has to be expressed in words. Including such descriptions can later help explain the scenario in natural language during annotation and increase the variability of HMG. Depending on this step, one may need to modify the environment and sensor setup selected. Further, the dictionary created in this stage is subject to post-recording modification.

**Recommendation 2:** Identify and document the human interactions in the scene. Create a dictionary of possible verbs, objects, and behaviour based on the interactions. Verify inclusion and exclusion of terminologies by developing a process-sub-process pipeline of the chosen scenario. Finally, the interaction scenarios, the terminology dictionary, and the term definitions shall be documented.

### 3.2 Recording Session Execution

To obtain realistic human motion recordings, one should avoid biasing the individuals volunteering to perform motion in a pre-defined manner or performing action sequences with rigid body movement. Given the use of robots and drones, the recording environment should ensure the safety of the human volunteers. Humane conditions must be maintained while ensuring realistic motions. While recording sessions with a multi-modal sensor system, synchronisation of the start-stop time of the recording is essential. Alternatively, if timestamps are provided, ensure that the timestamps do not contain local time information such as daylight saving.

**Human Subjects.** Increase the variability in subject characteristics when selecting subjects to perform the activities of interest. In [34], the authors experimentally indicated that variability in subject traits increases the robustness of a neural network model. Furthermore, such variability of subjects' physical characteristics helps include ergonomics, process speed and handedness evaluations within the scene. Variability of the human subjects' physical characteristics has an additional advantage; the individuality or characteristics could further augment the dataset [19,53]. From an industrial perspective, variability in the subjects' work experience is desirable. For instance, an experienced subject packing an item would differ from a novice. Thus, selecting subjects with different work experiences and recording their metadata further enhances the dataset and creates distinct motion patterns.

Ethical and privacy concerns of the volunteers should be considered [3]. The dataset creators are responsible for ensuring that the information they collect from the volunteers complies with national or institutional regulations. Furthermore, they should ensure that the volunteers are aware of the data they provide and the potential uses of the data.

**Recommendation 3:** All work in which humans are recorded shall take ethical considerations into account. Although metadata such as gender, age, height, weight, handedness and work experience are desirable for human motion datasets, the volunteers must be well-informed about their subsequent data use. Sensitive data that is not required for industrial research shall be avoided.

**Recording Protocol.** [43] advocates creating a recording protocol for every dataset creation process. A recording protocol is expected to contain descriptions of the recording scenarios from the perspective of the volunteer performing the sequence of motion and a machine learning practitioner who would use the dataset. Furthermore, the recording protocol helps document the scenario's metadata, such as the weight and dimensions of the items in the scene. Additionally, given a mishap or faulty function of the drones and robots, describing the scenario in the recording protocol would help the researchers with data cleaning. For example, [37] entered the loss of MoCap reflector balls post-recording for a few subjects in their recording protocol. This indicated why a few recordings had to be removed due to faulty bone structure recording. The recording protocol can help annotate the scene's 3D scan or digital twin model. The goal of the recording protocol is that if the dataset creators must redo a recording, the information required to recreate the scene must be available. Thus, the recording protocol shall provide future dataset creators' perspectives on what was attempted and what can be further explored.

**Recommendation 4:** The recording protocol shall consist of the sensor placement on the body and recording environment, the process and sub-process pipeline, the dimensional information of the scene, and soft-biometric and work experience information of the volunteers. Further, sensor synchronisation, RGB-D image of the environment before recordings, and rendering pipeline or data acquisition pipelines used during the recording are essential information. Mishaps during recording (e.g., concerning sensors, volunteers, objects, or robots) must be accounted for. The creators shall include as much information as feasible.

### 3.3 Recorded Data Processing

A well-annotated, publicly available, and documented dataset can quicken the development of HMG research. Processing the recorded data is crucial to ensure the dataset's ease of use and visibility upon publishing the data. From this stage onwards, standard file formats are recommended as part of the centralised presentation requirement. This work considers annotation as part of processing the recorded data. However, an alternative scenario where the recorded data is published without annotation is feasible [52]. In such scenarios, visual data such as RGB data should be made public to facilitate annotation at a later stage or by a different group. Consequently, this stage is a transition between decentralised collection and centralised presentation.

**Data Annotation.** As discussed in [62], HMG has three sub-categories: text, speech and scene-conditioned HMG. From an industrial perspective, both text and scene-conditioned HMG are highly desirable. For text-conditioning, two forms of language annotations are desirable. The first is action annotation [42] and the second is descriptive texts [10]. Based on the exploration of the previous works [37,41,42,56], one could have three stages of annotation, namely, simple action annotation [37] or sequence labelling [42], description of the action with natural language [41] and finally, natural language description along with scene interaction [56].

Manual annotation is expensive in time and effort, as presented in [4]. However, the quality of manual annotation is unparalleled, as quality assurance methods can be implemented in this case. Crowdsourcing the descriptions is a method to increase variability in the natural language descriptions and reduce the annotation effort within a group. However, quality assurance can be complex without a manual revision process. Annotation tools [41,42] could help ease the annotation effort. Additionally, one could consider using existing motion descriptors [57] for initial annotation and then have the annotation revised by an expert. However, annotations provided by industrial experts are desirable to ensure the inclusion of industrial terminologies. Using the dictionary provided during the design stage supports this process. A mandatory revision by an annotation expert is recommended. Given the availability of action labels or action attributes, the use of large language models to generate textual data can be researched. Alternatively, video transcription tools can be used for annotation purposes [30]. A primary concern here could be the lack of textual diversity. Further research on using automated annotation for industrial scenarios is recommended.

Including subject information such as soft biometrics, perception of process speed, and indication of fatigue as annotation helps address the challenges and requirements of industrial simulations by HMG [46]. JSON or TEXT file formats should be used to save the annotations [56]. The start and end times of the annotated snippet should be mentioned. Timestamps with local information, such as daylight saving, should be avoided. Include language information of interest, such as *verb*, *noun*, and *object*. Separating the data into training, validation, and test sets is helpful for HMG researchers to compare different models.

**Recommendation 5:** The dataset creators shall provide quality annotations with diverse terms and verb usage. While the source of annotation can affect quality, the revision process helps increase annotation quality. Erroneous annotations must be avoided. Textual annotations similar to the ones found in HumanML3D [17] and KIT [41] are recommended. Use the terminology dictionary created in Sect. 3.1 to achieve annotation diversity.

**Publishing Data.** Following the FAIR principle is desirable, as mentioned in [43]. To achieve *Findability*, having machine-readable metadata is ideal. Furthermore, a well-maintained GitHub webpage specific to the dataset would increase visibility. To assure *Accessibility*, free-of-charge platforms that do not require registration are desirable. Thus, publishing the dataset on platforms such as Zenodo is recommended. Alternatively, a well-maintained website with login credentials can be considered to protect volunteer information and account for downloads. However, these pose the risk of gradual degradation in cases where maintenance is lacking. File formats are a critical criterion to ensure *Interoperability*. Therefore, ensure the availability of C3D, BVH, and SMPL models with NPY or PKL file formats for human motion [32,41]. Account for the skeletal structure followed. Point cloud and 3D models of the environment and RGB videos with blurred faces of volunteers are assets [37]. Ensure not to use non-standardised file formats. Finally, for *Reusability*, publishing the recording protocol along with a detailed dataset description is recommended. Ensure that the description of the terms used is available.

**Recommendation 6:** The recording files shall be clearly and appropriately named based on subject information, scenario, and repetition of recording. Ideally, raw file formats, such as C3D obtained from MoCap systems, shall be made available along with specific file formats, such as .npy, .pkl or .bvh. These file formats are used for neural network training and animation. Documentation shall include recording protocol, annotation label explanation, subject information, and the annotation procedure. Faulty data shall be documented, and erroneous labels shall be avoided through label revision. The incorrect data shall ideally be placed in separate folders to avoid confusion. The recording scenario's digital twin or point cloud model shall be provided. The datasets shall be hosted on platforms with version tracking and open access.

### 3.4 Quality Assurance

(a) LARa data with erroneous hand [37]. (b) LARa data with erroneous hand in a different angle[37]. (c) LARa SMPL data with erroneous hand [37].

**Fig. 4.** Error in recording must be corrected or marked during checking [37].

Quality assurance plays a significant role before and after the dataset is published. Before publishing the dataset, quality assurance of the recorded data could be in the form of visual inspection to ensure that the body structure obtained and the SMPL data created do not have significant inconsistencies and visual disfigurations as shown in Fig. 4. As discussed previously, if these frames cannot be corrected, the dataset creators must either mark them as unusable or remove them from the published data. Long duration of such instances can introduce erroneous motion generation in the MoGen neural network.

Training a generative model on the created dataset would be beneficial after publishing the data. Fine-tuning an SOTA HMG model on the created dataset has two benefits. The first benefit is that it acts as a quality assurance of the formatting of the created data, for example, the ease of use of the new data, along with benchmark HMG datasets. The second benefit is that standard HMG metrics can be analysed for possible deviations. For example, how the new dataset affects the fidelity, diversity, and condition consistency [62] of an existing model can help determine the quality of the new dataset. This testing process, by fine-tuning, extracts glaring inconsistencies in the data. One must note that the model characteristics and domain drift would affect the resulting generation. However, identifying a neural network for MoGen that may provide the best fidelity and visual quality is not considered a part of the quality assurance stage. A visual verification stage of the generated data is recommended, where an industrial simulation expert visually verifies the generated motions. Alternatively, this step can further the research in HMG to tackle the challenges brought forward by industrial simulations and provide a platform for the HMG community to request motion or metadata.

**Recommendation 7:** Appropriate state-of-the-art models [62] and evaluation metrics [25] shall be used to test the quality of the acquired data. A platform to facilitate discussion on the dataset shall be provided.

### 3.5 Discussion

The growth in AI-based technologies is rooted in the availability of datasets. Each new dataset created is to account for challenges that were unaccounted for in an older version of the dataset. As a result, dataset creation is a recursive process. The expectation of one dataset creator to generate large enough data that would be beneficial to the masses is unrealistic. Consequently, a cumulative dataset creation process is the ideal and feasible option. To help new dataset creators contribute to the process, it is necessary to account for challenges considered and simplifications made during the recording and annotation process. When creating a new dataset, the requirements list must be updated based on these criteria.

As seen in Sect. 2 in [7], a few industrial datasets with full-body representations are compatible or convertible to the skeletal formats used for HMG. However, textual annotations are lacking, as provided by [17]. Following [30], one could attempt re-annotating the data or using the existing terminology to create an annotation using large language models. A concentrated effort to accumulate existing industrial datasets and convert them to formats usable for HMG, similar to the effort taken by the creators of AMASS, is necessary for industrial simulations. Finally, to start and facilitate a conversation between the industrial simulation community, dataset creators and the HMG community, we provide a GitHub[1] repository. The repository will contain information on existing industrial datasets, links to modules on dataset formatting for HMG and annotation tools and a discussion forum for the community.

## 4 Conclusion and Future Works

Dataset creation is an arduous task. However, the availability of rich datasets is necessary to facilitate the GenAI community in developing promising tools

[1] The relevant code snippets and references are available on https://github.com/nilahnair/Industrial-Human-Motion-Dataset-for-HMG.

and methods that increase the efficiency of various applications. This work outlines a dataset creation framework for industrial dataset creators to follow that would allow the use of their dataset for human motion generation. The work provides an industrial practitioner who aims to create industrial data for Human Motion Generation for Industrial simulation, preliminary information on the data requirements of HMG. The features proposed in this work are detailed based on experience and surveys of the current datasets used for HMG. Furthermore, the work presented further challenges that HMG needs to tackle in industrial simulation environments.

As future work, the existing industrial datasets should be converted to HMG usable formats following a centralised presentation process. This process will provide more perspective on features that need to be considered in this framework. Next, industrial dataset creators should be made aware of the framework. Feedback from dataset creators and the HMG community can help further refine the framework. Finally, the communication platform to bring industrial simulation creators, dataset creators, and the human motion generation community together should be publicised and curated to help in the fluid exchange of data and challenges.

**Acknowledgments.** This research has been funded by the Federal Ministry of Research, Technology and Space of Germany and the state of North Rhine-Westphalia as part of the Lamarr Institute for Machine Learning and Artificial Intelligence.

## References

1. Regulation (EU) 2016/679 of the European Parliament and of the Council of 27 April 2016 on the protection of natural persons with regard to the processing of personal data and on the free movement of such data, and repealing Directive 95/46/EC (General Data Protection Regulation) (Text with EEA relevance) (2016)
2. Arents, J., Abolins, V., Judvaitis, J., Vismanis, O., Oraby, A., Ozols, K.: Human-robot collaboration trends and safety aspects: a systematic review. J. Sens. Actuator Netw. **10**(3), 48 (2021)
3. Asghar, M.N., Kanwal, N., Lee, B., Fleury, M., Herbst, M., Qiao, Y.: Visual surveillance within the EU general data protection regulation: a technology perspective. IEEE Access **7**, 111709–111726 (2019)
4. Avsar, H., Altermann, E., Reining, C., Rueda, F.M., Fink, G.A., ten Hompel, M.: Benchmarking annotation procedures for multi-channel time series HAR dataset. In: 2021 IEEE International Conference on Pervasive Computing and Communications Workshops and other Affiliated Events (PerCom Workshops), pp. 453–458. IEEE (2021)
5. Baroroh, D.K., Chu, C.H.: Human-centric production system simulation in mixed reality: an exemplary case of logistic facility design. J. Manuf. Syst. **65**, 146–157 (2022)
6. Bashirov, R., et al.: Real-time RGBD-based extended body pose estimation. In: Proceedings of the IEEE/CVF Winter Conference on Applications of Computer Vision, pp. 2807–2816 (2021)

7. Benmessabih, T., Slama, R., Havard, V., Baudry, D.: Online human motion analysis in industrial context: a review. Eng. Appl. Artif. Intell. **131**, 107850 (2024)
8. Dai, A., Chang, A.X., Savva, M., Halber, M., Funkhouser, T., Nießner, M.: Scannet: richly-annotated 3d reconstructions of indoor scenes. In: Proceedings of the IEEE Conference on Computer Vision and Pattern Recognition, pp. 5828–5839 (2017)
9. Dallel, M., Havard, V., Baudry, D., Savatier, X.: Inhard-industrial human action recognition dataset in the context of industrial collaborative robotics. In: 2020 IEEE International Conference on Human-Machine Systems (ICHMS), pp. 1–6. IEEE (2020)
10. Simone, V., Pasquale, V., Giubileo, V., Miranda, S.: Human-robot collaboration: an analysis of worker's performance. Procedia Comput. Sci. **200**, 1540–1549 (2022)
11. Diomataris, M., Athanasiou, N., Taheri, O., Wang, X., Hilliges, O., Black, M.J.: WANDR: intention-guided human Motion Generation. In: Proceedings of the IEEE/CVF Conference on Computer Vision and Pattern Recognition, pp. 927–936 (2024)
12. Faria, C., et al.: Safety requirements for the design of collaborative robotic workstations in Europe–a review. In: Advances in Safety Management and Human Performance: Proceedings of the AHFE 2020 Virtual Conferences on Safety Management and Human Factors, and Human Error, Reliability, Resilience, and Performance, July 16-20, 2020, USA, pp. 225–232. Springer (2020)
13. Farinelli, A., Zanotto, E., Pagello, E., et al.: Advanced approaches for multi-robot coordination in logistic scenarios. Robot. Auton. Syst. **90**, 34–44 (2017)
14. Fragapane, G., Koster, R., Sgarbossa, F., Strandhagen, J.O.: Planning and control of autonomous mobile robots for intralogistics: literature review and research agenda. Eur. J. Oper. Res. **294**(2), 405–426 (2021)
15. Fritzsche, L., Ullmann, S., Bauer, S., Sylaja, V.J.: Task-based digital human simulation with editor for manual work activities–industrial applications in product design and production planning. In: DHM and Posturography, pp. 569–575. Elsevier (2019)
16. Giulietti, N., Todesca, D., Carnevale, M., Giberti, H.: A real-time human pose measurement system for human-in-the-loop dynamic simulators. IEEE Access (2025)
17. Guo, C., et al.: Generating diverse and natural 3d human motions from text. In: Proceedings of the IEEE/CVF Conference on Computer Vision and Pattern Recognition (CVPR), pp. 5152–5161 (2022)
18. Guo, C., et al.: Action2motion: conditioned generation of 3d human motions. In: Proceedings of the 28th ACM International Conference on Multimedia, pp. 2021–2029 (2020)
19. Hallyburton, T., Nair, N.R., Moya Rueda, F., Grzeszick, R., Fink, G.A.: Anonymisation for Time-Series Human Activity Data. In: International Conference on Pattern Recognition, pp. 17–32. Springer (2025)
20. Han, F., Reily, B., Hoff, W., Zhang, H.: Space-time representation of people based on 3d skeletal data: a review. Comput. Vis. Image Underst. **158**, 85–105 (2017)
21. de Heuvel, J., Zeng, X., Shi, W., Sethuraman, T., Bennewitz, M.: Spatiotemporal attention enhances lidar-based robot navigation in dynamic environments. IEEE Robot. Autom. Lett. (2024)
22. Inam, R., Raizer, K., Hata, A., Souza, R., Forsman, E., Cao, E., Wang, S.: Risk assessment for human-robot collaboration in an automated warehouse scenario. In: 2018 IEEE 23rd International Conference on Emerging Technologies and Factory Automation (ETFA). vol. 1, pp. 743–751. IEEE (2018)

23. Iodice, F., De Momi, E., Ajoudani, A.: Hri30: an action recognition dataset for industrial human-robot interaction. In: 2022 26th International Conference on Pattern Recognition (ICPR), pp. 4941–4947. IEEE (2022)
24. Ishihara, T., Nitta, K., Nagasawa, F., Okada, S.: Estimating interviewee's willingness in multimodal human robot interview interaction. In: Proceedings of the 20th International Conference on Multimodal Interaction: Adjunct, pp. 1–6 (2018)
25. Ismail-Fawaz, A., Devanne, M., Berretti, S., Weber, J., Forestier, G.: Establishing a unified evaluation framework for human motion generation: a comparative analysis of metrics. arXiv preprint arXiv:2405.07680 (2024)
26. Jackson, I., Jesus Saenz, M., Ivanov, D.: From natural language to simulations: applying AI to automate simulation modelling of logistics systems. Int. J. Prod. Res. **62**(4), 1434–1457 (2024)
27. Jonek, M., Tuli, T.B., Manns, M.: Constraints for motion generation in work planning with digital human simulations. In: Proceedings of the Changeable, Agile, Reconfigurable and Virtual Production Conference and the World Mass Customization & Personalization Conference, pp. 567–574. Springer (2021)
28. Klokowski, P., et al.: evoBOT–design and learning-based control of a two-wheeled compound inverted pendulum robot. In: 2023 IEEE/RSJ International Conference on Intelligent Robots and Systems (IROS), pp. 10425–10432. IEEE (2023)
29. Liebers, C., et al.: Keep the human in the loop: arguments for human assistance in the synthesis of simulation data for robot training. Multimodal Technol. Interaction **8**(3), 18 (2024)
30. Lin, J., et al.: Motion-x: a large-scale 3d expressive whole-body human motion dataset. Adv. Neural. Inf. Process. Syst. **36**, 25268–25280 (2023)
31. Liu, L., Yang, J., Lin, Y., Zhang, P., Zhang, L.: 3d human pose estimation with single image and inertial measurement unit (IMU) sequence. Patt. Recogn. **149**, 110175 (2024)
32. Mahmood, N., Ghorbani, N., Troje, N.F., Pons-Moll, G., Black, M.J.: AMASS: archive of motion capture as surface shapes. In: Proceedings of the IEEE/CVF International Conference on Computer Vision, pp. 5442–5451 (2019)
33. Manns, M., Mengel, S., Mauer, M.: Experimental effort of data driven human motion simulation in automotive assembly. Procedia CIRP **44**, 114–119 (2016)
34. Nair, N.R., Schmid, L., Reining, C., Moya Rueda, F., Pauly, M., Fink, G.A.: Representation biases in time-series human activity recognition with small sample sizes. In: International Conference on Pattern Recognition, pp. 33–48. Springer (2025)
35. Nakano, N., et al.: Evaluation of 3d markerless motion capture accuracy using openpose with multiple video cameras. Front. Sports Active Living **2**, 50 (2020)
36. Naumann, A., Hertlein, F., Zhou, B., Dorr, L., Furmans, K.: Scrape, cut, paste and learn: automated dataset generation applied to parcel logistics. In: 2022 21st IEEE International Conference on Machine Learning and Applications (ICMLA), pp. 1026–1031. IEEE (2022)
37. Niemann, F., et al.: Lara: creating a dataset for human activity recognition in logistics using semantic attributes. Sensors **20**(15), 4083 (2020)
38. Okadome, Y., Aizono, T.: Adversarial data-selection based work-hours estimation method on a small dataset in a logistics center. Comput. Industr. Eng. **164**, 107872 (2022)
39. Olugbade, T., et al.: Human movement datasets: an interdisciplinary scoping review. ACM Comput. Surv. **55**(6), 1–29 (2022)
40. Petković, T., Puljiz, D., Marković, I., Hein, B.: Human intention estimation based on hidden Markov model motion validation for safe flexible robotized warehouses. Robot. Comput. Integrated Manufact. **57**, 182–196 (2019)

41. Plappert, M., Mandery, C., Asfour, T.: The KIT motion-language dataset. Big Data **4**(4), 236–252 (2016)
42. Punnakkal, A.R., Chandrasekaran, A., Athanasiou, N., Quiros-Ramirez, A., Black, M.J.: BABEL: bodies, action and behavior with english labels. In: Proceedings of the IEEE/CVF Conference on Computer Vision and Pattern Recognition, pp. 722–731 (2021)
43. Reining, C., Nair, N.R., Niemann, F., Rueda, F.M., Fink, G.A.: A tutorial on dataset creation for sensor-based human activity recognition. In: 2023 IEEE International Conference on Pervasive Computing and Communications Workshops and other Affiliated Events (PerCom Workshops), pp. 453–459. IEEE (2023)
44. Reining, C., Niemann, F., Moya Rueda, F., Fink, G.A., ten Hompel, M.: Human activity recognition for production and logistics-a systematic literature review. Information **10**(8), 245 (2019)
45. Ren, P., et al.: InfiniteWorld: a unified scalable simulation framework for general visual-language robot interaction. arXiv preprint arXiv:2412.05789 (2024)
46. Schaub, K.G., et al.: Ergonomic assessment of automotive assembly tasks with digital human modelling and the 'ergonomics assessment worksheet'(eaws). Int. J. Hum. Factors Model. Simulation **3**(3–4), 398–426 (2012)
47. Seyyedhasani, H., Peng, C., Jang, W.j., Vougioukas, S.G.: Collaboration of human pickers and crop-transporting robots during harvesting–Part II: simulator evaluation and robot-scheduling case-study. Comput. Electron. Agriculture **172**, 105323 (2020)
48. Sgarbossa, F., Grosse, E.H., Neumann, W.P., Battini, D., Glock, C.H.: Human factors in production and logistics systems of the future. Annu. Rev. Control. **49**, 295–305 (2020)
49. da Silva, A.G., Mendes Gomes, M.V., Winkler, I.: Virtual reality and digital human modeling for ergonomic assessment in industrial product development: a patent and literature review. Appl. Sci. **12**(3), 1084 (2022)
50. Tevet, G., Gordon, B., Hertz, A., Bermano, A.H., Cohen-Or, D.: Motionclip: exposing human motion generation to clip space. In: European Conference on Computer Vision, pp. 358–374. Springer (2022)
51. Thumm, J., Trost, F., Althoff, M.: Human-robot gym: Benchmarking reinforcement learning in human-robot collaboration. In: 2024 IEEE International Conference on Robotics and Automation (ICRA), pp. 7405–7411. IEEE (2024)
52. De la Torre, F., Hodgins, J.K., Montano, J., Valcarcel, S.: Detailed human data acquisition of kitchen activities: the CMU-multimodal activity database (cmu-mmac). In: Workshop on Developing Shared Home Behavior Datasets to Advance HCI and Ubiquitous Computing Research, in Conjuction with CHI. vol. 2009 (2009)
53. Upchurch, P., et al.: Deep feature interpolation for image content changes. In: Proceedings of the IEEE Conference on Computer Vision and Pattern Recognition, pp. 7064–7073 (2017)
54. Wang, C., Du, B., Xu, J., Li, P., Guo, D., Liu, H.: Demonstrating HumanTHOR: a simulation platform and benchmark for human-robot collaboration in a shared workspace. arXiv preprint arXiv:2406.06498 (2024)
55. Wang, Z., et al.: Move as you say interact as you can: language-guided human motion generation with scene affordance. In: Proceedings of the IEEE/CVF Conference on Computer Vision and Pattern Recognition, pp. 433–444 (2024)
56. Wang, Z., Chen, Y., Liu, T., Zhu, Y., Liang, W., Huang, S.: Humanise: language-conditioned human motion generation in 3d scenes. Adv. Neural. Inf. Process. Syst. **35**, 14959–14971 (2022)

57. Yazdian, P.J., Liu, E., Lagasse, R., Mohammadi, H., Cheng, L., Lim, A.: Motion-script: natural language descriptions for expressive 3d human motions. arXiv preprint arXiv:2312.12634 (2023)
58. Yoshimura, N., Morales, J., Maekawa, T., Hara, T.: Openpack: a large-scale dataset for recognizing packaging works in iot-enabled logistic environments. In: 2024 IEEE International Conference on Pervasive Computing and Communications (PerCom), pp. 90–97. IEEE (2024)
59. Zhang, M., et al.: Motiondiffuse: text-driven human motion generation with diffusion model. IEEE Trans. Patt. Anal. Mach. Intell. (2024)
60. Zhang, M., Grosse, E.H.: How to model human-robot collaborative logistics systems: systematic literature review and future perspectives. IFAC-PapersOnLine **58**(19), 379–384 (2024)
61. Zhang, Y., et al.: Motiongpt: finetuned LLMS are general-purpose motion generators. In: Proceedings of the AAAI Conference on Artificial Intelligence. vol. 38, pp. 7368–7376 (2024)
62. Zhu, W., et al.: Human motion generation: a survey. IEEE Trans. Patt. Anal. Mach. Intell. (2023)

# Toppled Realities: Challenges in Generation and Validation of Synthetic Data

Percy Lam[1(✉)], Weiwei Chen[1,2], Lavindra de Silva[1], and Ioannis Brilakis[1]

[1] Department of Engineering, University of Cambridge, Civil Engineering Building, 7a JJ Thomson Avenue, Cambridge CB3 0FA, UK
phl25@cam.ac.uk

[2] Bartlett School of Sustainable Construction, University College London, 1-19 Torrington Place, London WC1E 7HB, UK

**Abstract.** In advancing automation in infrastructure maintenance, collecting comprehensive datasets is arduous. While synthetic data provides a promising avenue to address real data shortages, problems remain in creating and validating the generations. This position paper aims to push the boundary in generating synthetic data without prior training samples and validating the synthetic generation by vision language models (VLM), as learned from our exploratory trials.

Our exploratory trials attempted to generate new toppled road lights in road scene images with several inpainting and image editing tools, and ultimately resorted to a more deterministic approach of "create, prepare, stylise and inpaint". When validating the synthetic toppled road lights, we explored the possibility of automating prompt engineering and made four main observations. Whilst exploration and exploitation can be seen, responses were sensitive to the text prompts. The model struggled with the dilemma of adhering to the instruction without good results and self-hallucinating for good results by goal misspecification. From the exploratory trials, we posit that finding the right starting point is important for generating synthetic data that appears real. VLMs can be more widely adopted for detection and validation with more meticulous auto-prompt engineering.

**Keywords:** Synthetic data · Defect detection · Vision Language Models · Prompt engineering

## 1 Introductions

Infrastructure supports our daily lives and is essential to economic activities. Artificial intelligence may bring revolutionary advancements to our infrastructure and public services [30]. A significant advancement in society would be to automate infrastructure maintenance to provide better service at a lower economic and environmental cost [24]. Taking roads as an example, despite bespoke multi-modal cameras [31] and advanced analytical programmes for maintenance planning [2], the state of practice in building a comprehensive defect classifier remains reliant on extensive field data collection and preparation. The ability


E. L. Tonkin et al. (Eds.): ARDUOUS 2025, CCIS 2706, pp. 36–50, 2026.
https://doi.org/10.1007/978-3-032-09117-8_3

to cover comprehensive types of defects is notably constrained by the types of instances that can be collected with limited data collection. Whereas being comprehensive is vital to automating road maintenance, the lack thereof creates a bottleneck for enhancing inspection and repair.

Synthetic data may alleviate the shortage of real-world samples. This study focuses on synthetic imagery, which provides extra patterns to enrich supervised learning for detectors, few-shot learning or evaluation of vision language models (VLM) and visualisation. Problems remain when some objects are hard to synthesise and need better validation methods. This position paper explores the two problems and proposes conceptual recommendations in synthetic data generation and validation. Supported by an exploratory trial on toppled road lights, the authors make the following recommendations:

- The choice of the starting point for generating synthetic data impacts the quality and realism of the output. Much work can be done to control the generation of non-human objects.
- Objects that are more physically sophisticated may need to be produced with more deterministic approaches.
- VLM may provide better interpretability, explainability and robustness in validating synthesised data than the past approach of measuring image disturbance metrics in a deep learning object detector.
- Automated prompting may be a promising direction in adopting VLM as a validation tool. Implements such as seeking explanations in addition to a binary Yes/No answer may alleviate hallucinations.

## 2 Related Works

The kinds of synthetic data and visual patterns generated depend on the research direction. Some research focused on the success of **creating extra instances**, where researchers tended to replicate annotated instances they already had with generative models such as generative adversarial networks (GAN) and diffusion models. Past research replicated road objects [6] and medical entities such as brains [26] and tumours [34]. Architectures such as CycleGAN [40] or StyleGAN [15] could also change the image styles during replication, such as from more accessible to more expensive types of medical imaging [28].

Aside from changing the styles of the entire synthesised image, several prior works brought objects from another dataset/data source and stylised them to **align with and paste onto the destination images**. Past successes involved direct copying and pasting [14] and using CycleGAN [3]. It may also be possible by first collecting real instances or creating instances from generative AI, then inpainted them onto destination images with style transfer [17].

Others attempted to create more visual patterns by **capturing the same object from different views**. Visualisation engines such as Nvidia replicator, Blender or Unreal Engine could be helpful. These engines also built in the ability to generate different photorealistic conditions such as lighting, time of day and weather. Researchers in engineering created multiview synthetic data for construction equipment [20], barrels [5] and industrial defects [22], while beyond engineering groceries [35] and wild animals [23] were synthesised. If 3D scene models were available, more complex capturing conditions like following waypoints and logics would be possible [1].

Noteworthy were the **methods to validate synthetic data**. Researchers traditionally produced synthetic data as part of their research to improve the detection of their desired targets. They would train and evaluate detectors with multiple architectures [6,14], different real data proportions [22] or parameters [26] and potentially different computer vision tasks [35] to substantiate the data synthesis. Some visual metrics such as Frechet Inception Distance [26] and the Structural Similarity Index Measure (SSIM) [6,26] could also be employed to assess the abruptness (the lack of similarity) caused by the data generation methods. More recently, prompt-image alignment was assessed in the technical reports of the generative models [11] and further advancements such as numerical reasoning (counting the numbers of targeted objects) were proposed [13].

Past research underscored several gaps in knowledge yet to be addressed. Some objects may not be as easy to synthesise as "copy (with whatever manipulations) and paste". Especially in inpainting scenarios, keeping the background unchanged while maintaining the realism of the inserted synthetic object remained an obstacle. VLM presented itself with an opportunity to interpret the alignment of the synthesised objects to the requirements, as it was pre-trained with a vast dataset. Apart from the technical reports of the image generators, however, other synthetic data research rarely considered using VLM as a validation tool. If VLM were valuable tools to investigate, the way users prompt them to evaluate synthesised content would become an important concern. This challenge would grow as VLM advances so that they not only detect synthetic inserts but also differentiate synthetic inserts from real objects.

## 3 The Exploratory Trials

The authors performed exploratory trials to create synthetic toppled road lights and made recommendations for this position paper. The task of the trial was to create a realistic fallen metallic lamp post in the driving lane of the supplied road scene images to imitate scenes of road obstructions. While road lights are abundant on motorways, they are rarely toppled, and this makes real data collection difficult. Toppled road lights nonetheless posed a road hazard that should be captured by a comprehensive road defect classifier [18] to support automated road maintenance. The authors attempted to synthesise toppled road lights and validate the generated images with VLM with different approaches.

### 3.1 Synthetic Data Creation

**Inpainting** is a method to insert an object into an existing image. Inpainting edits specific parts of an image through a mask that highlights the areas to be edited [12]. The first experimented creation method involves using a mask in the driving lane and inpainting an object by a purpose-built text-to-image generative model. Stable Diffusion 3.5 medium (SD 3.5) [7] by Stability AI [29] is chosen as it is a leading text-to-image generative model that operates within 12GB GPU VRAM of the Nvidia RTX 3080 Ti used for experiments.

Beyond the purpose-built text-to-image generative models, **foundation models** have very recently been equipped with image editing capabilities. The authors tried to prompt in gemini-2.0-flash-preview-image-generation (via Google Vertex AI prompt gallery) [9] to amend 10 road scene images. The authors used the first prompt[1] to edit road lights in the 10 images. For images that failed to augment road lights realistically, a more instructive second prompt[2] will be adopted.

The third attempt involves the "create, prepare, stylise and inpaint" approach in [17] summarised in Fig. 1. Real road lights are first detected by a VLM Florence-2 [36] and segmented from the background by Segment Anything [16]. The detected bounding box undergoes style transfer to get a derelict aesthetic style with SD 3.5. The segmentation mask enables us to prepare a binary mask from the segmented instance for later infilling. The stylised road light crop is then rotated and pasted onto the pavement.

**Fig. 1.** The "create, prepare, stylise and inpaint" approach synthesised more realistic toppled road lights.

### 3.2 Prompting and VLM Validations

Aside from visually inspecting images generated by methods in Sect. 3.1, VLM shows potential in interpreting and evaluating synthetic data. The fundamental problem with using VLMs for validation is that they may miss objects clearly visible to humans. The authors first queried the state-of-the-art VLM Gemini-2.5-Pro [10] and Gemini-2.5-Flash [8] benchmarked in LMArena [4] for the fallen metal poles with the synthesised images on the webapp. The first queries were

[1] "Add me a toppled road light behind the truck ahead of the car.".

[2] "Detect a road light from the image, then make an impression like it's toppled.".

unsuccessful, revealing **perceptual, semantic and contextual problems** of the models. The models may have omitted features obvious to human eyes, such as slender posts appearing similar to debris. Synthetic features created subtly in preserving realism make the features harder to detect. Semantics in the input prompts may not capture or describe the desired object well enough. The context that the VLM observed the targeted object may be different from a human, such as concluding features as "digital artefacts" rather than genuine objects.

The authors attempted to find suitable query prompts by **automating prompt engineering**. Past work on LLM embraced self-consistency, that the question that yields correct responses is more likely to follow a correct rationale [32]. When engineering the prompts, the tool shall manage engagements in exploration to find a diversity of prompts that yield good scores in the validation set, and exploitation to grind for higher scores when ascertaining a good prompt [37]. Meta prompting [39] enabled abstract frameworks to be provided to VLM/LLM, such as instructions about the optimisation goal, instead of the actual target objects to be found.

We implemented a pipeline similar to ORPO [37] but with images to VLM. Figure 2 illustrates the mechanism composed of two VLM chatbots, the question master and the evaluator. The interactions can be broken down as follows:

1. The question master asks the evaluator a question[3]
2. The evaluator evaluates the question and returns it a binary Yes/No answer and a justification. The accuracy score is also calculated and fed to the question master.
3. The question master interprets evaluator's responses against a given detection target[4], which was more stringent than a generic task in ORPO.
4. The question master follows its interpretation and refines the query prompt with explanations why it refines in such a manner. During the refinement, the question master looked at not only the past prompt and the score, but also the justifications that led to the answers.

The experimental setup looks for toppled road lights in a validation set of 10 synthetic images, and runs on Gemini-2.0-Flash-001 [8] for 10 iterations in each run at 0 temperature. The human oracle then chooses the best query prompt identified by the ORPO (allowing some leeway for more reasonable prompts) and tests it against the full synthetic dataset of 100 images, of which 62 images are classified "Yes" and 38 "No".

Three setups are tested to illustrate the (lack of) strength of the query prompts. In each of the setups, the chatbot was first given a warmup question, "What defect can you see from the road?" to provide context to subsequent detections. The validation setups are as follows:

1. The best prompt from auto-prompt engineering

[3] Start with "Can you see any obstructions on the road?".

[4] "Obstructions that count are those that are abnormal to the road, not mist, fog or water splashes, not road vehicles or not components normally on the road surface".

2. A casual prompt[5] with a verifying module
3. A refined prompt by human-in-the-loop[6] with a verifying module

Some answers were found to be vulnerable to hallucinations, especially those coming from casual query prompts. The authors employed a verifying module to eliminate contextual hallucinations of out-of-scope answers. The module receives the binary Yes/No answer and the justifications from the detector and reviews whether the detected obstruction aligns with the defined scope[7]. For identifying toppled road lights, the scope encapsulates the general expected appearance of a long and thin metallic object in the middle of the road. The system is instructed not to re-detect defects to avoid overriding previous detection, and only use the image as a context for the textual justification given by the detector. Metrics such as precision, recall, accuracy and F1 scores are calculated from each setup across 5 trials. They are evaluated with the final answer at the end of the verifying module.

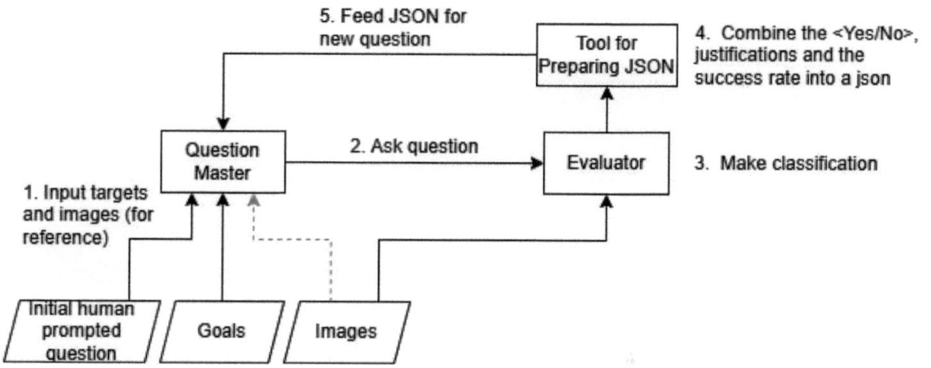


**Fig. 2.** A schematic of the implemented auto-prompt engineering pipeline.

[5] "Does the image contain any obstruction on the road? Please answer with a justification.".

[6] "Carefully examine the road surface and immediate surroundings in the middle distance directly ahead. Identify and describe any objects or features that are not part of the normal road infrastructure (e.g., markings, pavement), not traffic and not the smoke or water splash that disturbs the images. Consider size, shape, and orientation in your description. Are there such objects? Please justify.".

[7] Prompted with "I was looking for obstruction in front of the vehicle from the drivers' perspective. The obstruction appears to be a long and thin object, could be cylindrical or rectangular. The obstruction may be metallic in colour or sometimes a white patch remains. The object is not part of the road infrastructure. Based on the old justification, is there an obstruction of what I described in the image? Explain your reasoning here?".

# 4 Results and Discussions

Using the methods detailed in Sect. 3, this section shows and discusses the results of the exploratory trials. Drawing lessons from the results, this position paper makes several recommendations on creating and validating synthetic data.

## 4.1 Results on Synthetic Data Generation

The first attempt to inpaint with a text prompt and a mask of a road light rotated from the roadside failed because the mask was too slender to generate anything in it. Even when we enlarged the mask to a blob and retrieved an object, the object looked unreal (Fig. 3). In the hopes of inserting a more realistic object, we attempted to insert an image of a real rotated road light into the mask as a visual prompt via the IP-adapter [38], but were unsuccessful as the diffusion step could not reconstruct the input image. We suspected inpainting with off-the-shelf text-to-image generation models failed because the models were not pre-trained to create "toppled road lights".

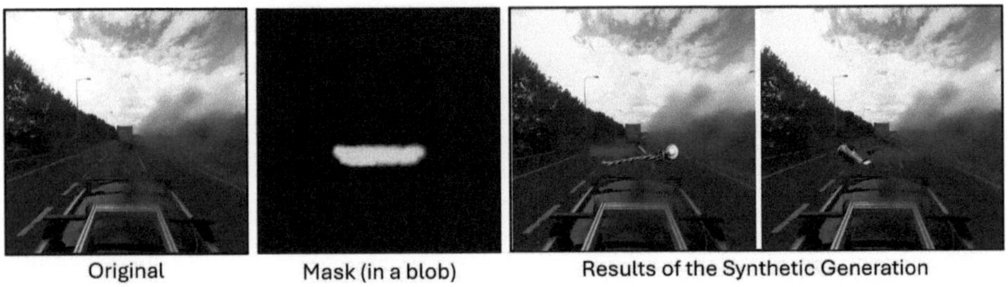


**Fig. 3.** Inpainting with off-the-shelf generation models did not return real toppled lights.

In the second attempt to use foundation models to generate images, Gemini-2.0 demonstrated processes that resembled a chain of thought [33]. The model first edited the image to include at least one road light, typically along the road median. It then modified the light or added a new one to topple ahead of the image-capturing vehicle, and concluded with an image caption[8].

Results in Fig. 4 showed 6 out of 10 edited images contained a bent or distorted road light lying on the ground. The lights were however all in wrong perspectives and felt fake. Parts of the original image, for instance the truck ahead, were unnecessarily modified. The remaining 4 images returned linear objects that did not resemble a road light. The model tended to generate over-saturated images, similar to what happened with excessively high guidance scale in text-to-image generative models. The authors tried to improve realism in the second

[8] such as "A tall, grey road light pole, bent and lying horizontally across the right lane of a highway, behind a blue and red truck driving in the distance, as seen from the perspective of a car travelling behind it. The sky is overcast with patches of blue, and the road is wet, with rain droplets visible on the camera lens.".

**Fig. 4.** Some distorted road lights may have been generated but all generations appeared not sufficiently realistic.

run but the model could not detect any existing road lights and produced similar images. The two runs demonstrated that while foundation models aligned the input text with the output visualisation, the synthesised images were not realistic enough for forthcoming tasks.

The third attempt resulted in more realistic synthetic data. Owing to the more deterministic approaches in extracting real road lights and pasting their augmented version, this method retains the difficult shape of the road lights (long and slender). The result showed in Fig. 1 was visually more satisfactory than previous attempts.

### 4.2 Results on Auto Prompt Engineering

Experiments on auto-prompting first showed exploration and exploitation behaviour, and secondly reflected the sensitivity to the initial input semantics. Table 1 showed the log of one of the trial runs. From the original query prompt, the prompt was modified to find features on the road surface and returned positive answers like pavement cracks and patches (the asterisk in Run 3). Regardless of the correctness, the model did not pick up the features we desired[9] and moved on to find "objects or pieces of material" in the next iteration. Receiving no positive responses, the question explored an alternative approach in the next iteration and seek distinctions on the material composition and yielded 9/10 correct. This question was taken to the validation test to represent auto-prompting.

The other two observations mirrored each other: the model could perform the right task but yielded poor results, or it could self-hallucinate to achieve false good results with a misspecified goal. In one of the runs, the model dismissed questions that yielded positive responses inconsistent with the detec-

[9] as we demanded objects "foreign in the road ahead" instead of "abrupt on the road surface or above" in other runs.

**Table 1.** Query prompts and justifications made by the question master in one of the runs. Whilst the model was shown exploring different questions, the accuracy score highly depends on the input semantics.

| Run | Question | Justifications | Score |
|---|---|---|---|
| 0 | Are there any ['obstruction'] in this image? State your justification also. Obstructions that count are those that are abnormal to the road, not mist, fog or water splashes, not road vehicles or not components normally on the road surface | | 0 |
| 3 | Excluding vehicles, road markings/reflectors/cones/signs, and weather effects (fog, spray, puddles), is there any visually distinct feature, texture, or item ON the flat, drivable road surface that looks like it doesn't belong there? Consider variations in shape, color, or texture compared to the surrounding pavement, even if small or low contrast. | Previous questions focusing on object types (debris, foreign object) failed. This question shifts focus to visual anomaly detection on the road surface itself, asking about features/textures that break the pattern, while still applying the necessary exclusions and considering subtlety. | 100* |
| 4 | Excluding vehicles, standard road features (markings, signs, etc.), and weather effects (fog, puddles, etc.), is there a distinct OBJECT or piece of material lying ON the drivable pavement? Focus on items that are separate from the road surface itself, even if they are flat, small, or visually similar to the pavement texture. Ignore variations like cracks, patches, or wear that are part of the road surface structure. | Attempt 4 identified road surface defects (cracks, patches), not foreign objects. This question refines the visual anomaly approach by re-emphasizing distinct 'objects' or 'material' lying *on* the pavement and explicitly *excluding* variations *of* the road surface itself (cracks, patches, wear) to better align with the target definition of foreign items. | 0 |
| 5 | On the drivable road surface ahead, is there any item present whose material appears different from the surrounding asphalt or concrete pavement? Exclude vehicles, standard road infrastructure (markings, signs, cones, reflectors, barriers), and weather effects (fog, spray, puddles). Importantly, disregard imperfections *within* the pavement like cracks, patches, or wear. Focus only on identifying discrete items lying *on top* of the road surface that seem to be made of a different substance (e.g., metal, plastic, wood, fabric, debris, etc.), even if small or low contrast. | Previous attempts struggled to differentiate subtle foreign objects from road defects. This question focuses explicitly on the *material composition* difference between an item lying *on* the road and the pavement itself, providing examples of foreign materials while maintaining exclusions for infrastructure, vehicles, weather, and road surface imperfections (cracks, patches). | 90 |

tion target, even though subsequent iterations failed to find positive responses, pointing sprays/mist as the primary issue and therefore all returned negative. Conversely in another run, the model self-hallucinated and claimed to have a positive response by acknowledging a mist as a road hazard. Subsequent iterations exploited this hallucinated finding to permit mist and obtain all "Yes" responses, bypassing the restrictions in the detection target. The misspecification behaviour exposed a weakness of using a score, in that the model may circumvent restrictions in order to achieve better scores.

### 4.3 Results on VLM Validation

Despite the exploration and exploitation by the auto-prompting mechanism, the detection results were unsatisfactory when validated on all 100 synthetic images. As shown in Table 2, the auto prompt returned about 47% accuracy, which was slightly above using a casual prompt (45%) but considerably worse than using a human-in-the-loop refined prompt (65%). A more remarkable shortfall happened with the F1 score, which was hampered substantially by the vast false negatives and the subsequent lack of recall. We suspected that VLM fell short of generating good prompts because there were more than 1 goal to be optimised. This led to further enquiries about the perceptual, semantic and contextual problems of VLM and the eventual approach to adopt a human-refined prompt.

An obvious solution to address the perceptual, semantic and contextual problems is to refine the prompt until the VLM can pick up the synthesised objects. There is however a significant risk of prompt over-refinement because models are found to have a tendency to align responses to the query and create confirmation bias [25] to potentially false positive answers. Confirmation bias happens in scenarios such as self-deceiving to have made a mistake when instructed to check if an answer was "wrong" [21]. Models are also very sensitive to the exact construction of the text prompt [19,27]. When a prompt is constructed so exactly that it encompasses an almost "overfitting" description, it may lose robustness beyond the tested image.

**Table 2.** Human-in-the-loop refined prompt showed superior detection performance to the automated prompt and a casual prompt, mainly contributed by having significantly better recall.

| | Precision | Recall | Accuracy | F1 |
|---|---|---|---|---|
| Autoprompt | $0.748 \pm 0.07$ | $0.210 \pm 0.06$ | $0.468 \pm 0.04$ | $0.325 \pm 0.08$ |
| Casual prompt + verified | $0.594 \pm 0.08$ | $0.374 \pm 0.04$ | $0.452 \pm 0.06$ | $0.459 \pm 0.05$ |
| Refined prompt + verified | $0.662 \pm 0.02$ | $0.891 \pm 0.03$ | $0.647 \pm 0.03$ | $0.759 \pm 0.02$ |

### 4.4 Recommendations on Synthetic Data Generation

The exploratory trial elucidates two problems with synthetic data that some objects are hard to synthesise realistically and are hard to detect with VLM. The following two subsections summarise the lessons learned from the exploratory trials and make recommendations to users and developers.

When creating new objects, understanding the problem and finding the right starting point may bring better results and save processing effort. **Text-to-image generation** on Gemini or ChatGPT is a convenient starting point to see if the "pre-trained world" already understands the desired object. If the users **require an initial training set**, the solution may be to generate a similar enough object by generative AI (foundation models or more purpose-built generative models such as SD3.5) and build on from there. Failing that, it may be wise to collect some data where the desired data may exist or look for datasets online that can be adapted or stylised for your tasks. Moreover, if the synthetic data generation is hindered by their **difficult shapes**, such as the thin masks in the pilot study, users are recommended to rely on more deterministic methods in style transfer and geometric transformations, instead of the more unconstrained ways like denoising diffusion models.

Apart from finding the right tools to start the data generation, more discussions are required on how to make synthetic data more realistic. This not only confines realism to the RGB pixel space, but also other attributes such as depths, shadows and luminance. Apart from bringing algorithmic advancements in generating images, it may benefit users to discuss how to generate different categories or forms of instances. There had been a lot of discussions online about controlling the generation of human appearance, but more can be done academically for different kinds of objects.

### 4.5 Recommendations on Validating Synthetic Data

Past literature shows how to evaluate synthetic data with image creation metrics and human visual inspection. They are useful in indicating how much an image has been disturbed from the baseline and whether people like the generated images. They however do not help describe the objects that are being created.

Much past research has generated instances and trained them in an object detector. Even if the generated instances are visually inspected and approved (which is not a prerequisite), it runs a risk that models beyond that bespoke object detector will not be able to interpret what the instances are. This hurts the result explainability–why the model makes a certain prediction, and reproducibility - only the researcher has access to the detector. Robustness is also a concern that a few differences in the "real-world" datasets will render the detector useless, as it may have learned something implausible. Issues surrounding the explainability, reproducibility and robustness of using synthetic data in conventional object detectors call for better validation methods.

Seeking interpretations from VLMs may be an effective and convenient way to validate the synthesised data. Validating with VLM roughly forms a closed loop from text (plus image) to synthetic images through the generative AI, and from synthetic images to text by vision question and answering. The loop ends by verifying from the text that the synthetic images are within what the model understands and what the user desires to generate. Completing the loop however requires the right prompts (and/or context) given to the VLM.

This leads to the question of how to prompt VLM. Users cannot explicitly prompt for the desired objects, otherwise models tend to provide positive answers aligning with the prompt. Besides the confirmation bias, we also noted potential contextual differences in the way VLM understands text prompts from humans. They may classify which features are digital artefacts outright, but humans may be more tolerant about the generation quality. Even being digital artefacts does not mean the synthetic generation fails. In fact, synthetic instances are by nature digital artefacts and being flagged meant they exist, regardless of how real they are. The prevalent method is still to find a suitable prompt manually, but reliable automation shall not be precluded.

If researchers would like to pursue the avenue of auto-prompting, such as the exploratory trial, the models would need to take into account the aforementioned handicaps. The VLM needs to explore query prompts better across various detection problems, such as those on the perception, semantics and contexts. Recent research also showed LLM had a tendency to approve what it generated for itself. A key insight from the auto-prompting tests in Sect. 3.2 is that validation requires a second source of information to confirm or refute a model output, such as outputting a score or binary Yes/No with an explanation. This can be done more systematically for more meticulous auto-prompting.

## 5 Conclusions

This research examines problems in creating and validating synthetic data through synthesising toppled road lights in road scene images in exploratory experiments. As opposed to approaches in prior work, experiments began without any suitable instances. Attempts were made to produce toppled road lights unsuccessfully by inpainting with text-to-image generation models and image editing by foundation models. The authors eventually resorted to a deterministic approach of "create, prepare, stylise and inpaint" and received visually satisfactory results. Reflecting on the experiments, the authors recommend users to find a suitable starting point for their synthetic generation tasks, and call for further research in generating different forms of defects with more realism.

The issue then propagates to validating the synthesised toppled road lights. While traditional evaluation methods of image creation metrics and human visual inspection are not sufficient, adopting VLM poses another set of problems. VLM is prone to perceptual, semantic and contextual handicaps, and exhibits confirmation bias and sensitivity towards the input prompt. The authors attempted to find a suitable prompt by automating prompt engineering. We observe that although models exhibited exploration and exploitation behaviour, mixed detection scores dragged the models into a dilemma of finding prompts as strictly instructed without positive responses, or misspecifying goals to self-hallucinate false positive responses. Despite the promises of soliciting explanations alongside a binary Yes/No answer, the overall lack of robustness in the auto-refined prompt necessitated the authors to manually refine a question prompt by human-in-the-loop. Acknowledging potential improvements to the result explainability, reproducibility and robustness, more research has to be done in validating synthetic data with VLM.

**Acknowledgments.** The author (P Lam) is funded by the UK Engineering and Physical Sciences Research Council (EPSRC) Centre for Doctoral Training in Future Infrastructure and Built Environment: Resilience in a Changing World (FIBE2) [grant number EP/S02302X/1] and sponsored by the National Highways, Costain and Trimble Solutions. This work is supported by the Digital Roads, UK EPSRC [grant number EP/V056441/1].

## References

1. Acharya, P., et al.: Using synthetic data generation to probe multi-view stereo networks. In: Proceedings of the IEEE International Conference on Computer Vision. vol. 2021-October, pp. 1583–1591. Institute of Electrical and Electronics Engineers Inc. (2021). https://doi.org/10.1109/ICCVW54120.2021.00183
2. AgileAssets: How AgileAssets PMS Predicts Pavement Preservation and Deterioration (2020). https://www.youtube.com/watch?v=cEZJyxLFAlk
3. Branikas, E., Murray, P., West, G.: A novel data augmentation method for improved visual crack detection using generative adversarial networks. IEEE Access **11**, 22051–22059 (2023). https://doi.org/10.1109/ACCESS.2023.3251988
4. Chiang, W.L., et al.: Chatbot arena: an open platform for evaluating LLMs by human preference. In: Proceedings of the 41st International Conference on Machine Learning. ICML'24, JMLR.org (2024)
5. Damian, A., Filip, C., Nistor, A., Petrariu, I., Mariuc, C., Stratan, V.: Experimental results on synthetic data generation in unreal engine 5 for real-world object detection. In: 2023 17th International Conference on Engineering of Modern Electric Systems, EMES 2023. Institute of Electrical and Electronics Engineers Inc. (2023). https://doi.org/10.1109/EMES58375.2023.10171761
6. Dewi, C., Chen, R.C., Liu, Y.T., Jiang, X., Hartomo, K.D.: Yolo V4 for advanced traffic sign recognition with synthetic training data generated by various GAN. IEEE Access **9**, 97228–97242 (2021). https://doi.org/10.1109/ACCESS.2021.3094201
7. Esser, P., et al.: Scaling rectified flow transformers for high-resolution image synthesis (2024). http://arxiv.org/abs/2403.03206
8. Google: Gemini 2.0 Flash (2025). https://console.cloud.google.com/vertex-ai/publishers/google/model-garden/gemini-2.0-flash-001?inv=1&invt=Abwxcg
9. Google: Gemini 2.0 Flash Image Generation (2025). https://cloud.google.com/vertex-ai/generative-ai/docs/models/gemini/2-0-flash?hl=en&authuser=1#image-generation
10. Google: Gemini 2.5 Pro Preview (2025). https://console.cloud.google.com/vertex-ai/publishers/google/model-garden/gemini-2.5-pro-preview-03-25
11. Google Imagen 3 Team: Imagen 3. Tech. rep., Google DeepMind (2024)

12. Hugging Face: Inpainting. https://huggingface.co/docs/diffusers/en/using-diffusers/inpaint
13. Kajić, I., et al.: Evaluating numerical reasoning in text-to-image models. In: Proceedings of the 38th Conference on Neural Information Processing Systems (NeurIPS 2024) (2024). http://arxiv.org/abs/2406.14774
14. Kanaeva, I.A., Ivanova, J.A.: Road pavement crack detection using deep learning with synthetic data. In: IOP Conference Series: Materials Science and Engineering. vol. 1019. IOP Publishing Ltd (2021). https://doi.org/10.1088/1757-899X/1019/1/012036
15. Karras, T., et al.: Alias-free generative adversarial networks. In: Proceedings of the 35th International Conference on Neural Information Processing Systems, pp. 852–863. Curran Associates Inc., Red Hook, NY, USA (2021). https://doi.org/10.48550/arXiv.2106.12423, https://nvlabs.github.io/stylegan3
16. Kirillov, A., et al.: Segment anything (2023). https://segment-anything.com
17. Lam, P., Chen, W., De Silva, L., Brilakis, I.: Integrating multi-source visual synthetic data for multi road defect detection (2025). https://doi.org/10.17863/CAM.118150
18. Lam, P.H., Chen, W., Brilakis, I.: Analysing the conditions of road assets with a network thinking. In: Kassim, M., Tagliabue, L.C., Amor, R., Sreckovic, M., Chassiakos, A. (eds.) Proceedings of the 2023 European Conference on Computing in Construction and the 40th International CIB W78 Conference. Heraklion, Greece (2023). https://doi.org/10.35490/EC3.2023.169
19. Lee, J.H., Shin, J.: How to optimize prompting for large language models in clinical research (2024). https://doi.org/10.3348/kjr.2024.0695
20. Lee, J.G., Hwang, J., Chi, S., Seo, J.: Synthetic image dataset development for vision-based construction equipment detection. J. Comput. Civil Eng. **36**(5) (2022). https://doi.org/10.1061/(asce)cp.1943-5487.0001035
21. Liu, F., AlDahoul, N., Eady, G., Zaki, Y., Rahwan, T.: Self-reflection makes large language models safer, less biased, and ideologically neutral (2024). http://arxiv.org/abs/2406.10400
22. Mohanty, S., Su, E., Ho, C.C.: Reinforcement learning optimized digital twin based synthetic data generation for defect detection of titanium spacer, p. 6. SPIE-Intl. Soc. Optical Eng. (2023). https://doi.org/10.1117/12.2673529
23. Mu, J., Qiu, W., Hager, G., Yuille, A.: Learning from synthetic animals. In: 2020 IEEE/CVF Conference on Computer Vision and Pattern Recognition (CVPR), pp. 12383–12392. Seattle, WA, USA (2020). https://doi.org/10.1109/CVPR42600.2020.01240, https://github.com/JitengMu/
24. National Highways: Connecting the Country: Our Long Term Strategic Plan to 2050. Tech. rep., National Highways, Guildford, UK (2023)
25. O'Leary, D.E.: Confirmation and specificity biases in large language models: an explorative study. IEEE Intell. Syst. **40**(1), 63–68 (2025). https://doi.org/10.1109/MIS.2024.3513992
26. Pinaya, W., et al.: Brain imaging generation with latent diffusion models. In: Mukhopadhyay, A., Oksuz, I., Engelhardt, S., Zhu, D., Yuan, Y. (eds.) DGM4MICCAI 2022. Lecture Notes in Computer Science, vol. 13609. Springer Nature Switzerland, Cham (2022). https://doi.org/10.1007/978-3-031-18576-2, https://link.springer.com/10.1007/978-3-031-18576-2
27. Razavi, A., Soltangheis, M., Arabzadeh, N., Salamat, S., Zihayat, M., Bagheri, E.: Benchmarking prompt sensitivity in large language models (2025). http://arxiv.org/abs/2502.06065

28. Song, Y., Chong, N.Y.: S-CycleGAN: semantic segmentation enhanced CT-ultrasound image-to-image translation for robotic ultrasonography (2024). http://arxiv.org/abs/2406.01191
29. Stability AI: Stable Diffusion 3.5 Medium (2024). https://huggingface.co/stabilityai/stable-diffusion-3.5-medium
30. The Secretary of State Science, I., by Command of His Majesty, T.: AI Opportunities Action Plan (2025). https://www.gov.uk/government/publications/ai-opportunities-action-plan/ai-opportunities-action-plan
31. Trimble Inc.: Trimble MX9 Mobile Mapping Solution. Tech. rep., USA (2022). www.trimble.com
32. Wang, X., et al.: Self-consistency improves chain of thought reasoning in language models. In: ICLR 2023. arXiv preprint (2022). http://arxiv.org/abs/2203.11171
33. Wei, J., et al.: Chain-of-thought prompting elicits reasoning in large language models. In: Proceedings of the 36th International Conference on Neural Information Processing Systems, pp. 24824–24837. Curran Associates Inc., New Orleans, LA, USA (2022). http://arxiv.org/abs/2201.11903
34. Wolleb, J., Bieder, F., Sandkühler, R., Cattin, P.C.: Diffusion models for medical anomaly detection (2022). http://arxiv.org/abs/2203.04306
35. Wong, M.Z., Kunii, K., Baylis, M., Ong, W.H., Kroupa, P., Koller, S.: Synthetic dataset generation for object-to-model deep learning in industrial applications. PeerJ Comput. Sci. **2019**(10) (2019). https://doi.org/10.7717/peerj-cs.222
36. Xiao, B., et al.: Florence-2: advancing a unified representation for a variety of vision tasks (2023). http://arxiv.org/abs/2311.06242
37. Yang, C., et al.: Large language models as optimizers. In: ICLR 2024. arXiv preprint (2023). http://arxiv.org/abs/2309.03409
38. Ye, H., Zhang, J., Liu, S., Han, X., Yang, W.: IP-Adapter: text compatible image prompt adapter for text-to-image diffusion models (2023). http://arxiv.org/abs/2308.06721
39. Zhang, Y., Yuan, Y., Yao, A.C.C.: Meta Prompting for AI Systems (2023). http://arxiv.org/abs/2311.11482
40. Zhu, J.Y., Park, T., Isola, P., Efros, A.A.: Unpaired image-to-image translation using cycle-consistent adversarial networks. In: Proceedings of the IEEE International Conference on Computer Vision. vol. 2017-October, pp. 2242–2251. Institute of Electrical and Electronics Engineers Inc. (2017). https://doi.org/10.1109/ICCV.2017.244

# Activity Recognition

# Retrieval-Based Annotation for Multi-Channel Time Series Data of Human Activities

Fernando Moya Rueda[1(✉)], Nilah Ravi Nair[2], Raphael Spiekermann[3], Erik Altermann[3], Philipp Oberdiek[4], Christopher Reining[2], and Gernot. A. Fink[3]

[1] Motion Miners, Dortmund, Germany
fernando.moya@motionminers.com
[2] Materials Handling and Warehousing, TU Dortmund University, Joseph-von-Fraunhofer-Str. 2-4, Dortmund 44227, Germany
[3] Pattern Recognition in Embedded Systems Group, TU Dortmund University, Otto-Hahn-Str. 16, Dortmund 44227, Germany
[4] ControlExpert GmbH, Marie-Curie-Straße 3, Langenfeld 40764, Germany

**Abstract.** Recent years have seen a rise in the number of labelled human activity datasets to support supervised learning of activity recognition. However, synchronisation and manual annotation of various multi-channel time-series data are cumbersome. Prior research focused on creating datasets that are convenient to annotate, leading to a scarcity of natural activity data that includes various subjects and activities. Therefore, an offline manual annotation tool for efficient labelling activities is desired. This work presents a semi-automatic annotation technique for multi-channel time-series human activity data, utilising a retrieval-based approach to reduce annotation effort. We present an annotation tool that accepts a variety of input data types and supports both manual and semi-automatic annotation. We benchmark the different approaches.

**Keywords:** Annotation · Retrieval · Multi-channel time series data · Annotation tool · Semi-automatic annotation

## 1 Introduction

With the advent of Industry 4.0 and 6G networks, the integration of intelligent technologies into human daily life has accelerated [7]. Advancements in sensor technology integrated into hand-held devices such as smartphones and smartwatches have generated a large amount of unused human activity data. The available multi-channel time-series data can facilitate several applications, e.g., human activity or soft-biometric classification, medical analysis for diseases such as Parkinson's, or human-robot interaction. Supervised machine learning methods require cleaned, formatted, and annotated data to learn meaningful connections and extrapolate to unseen data. Creating datasets abiding by these requirements is time-consuming and expensive, especially if experts are required for the annotation process [33].


E. L. Tonkin et al. (Eds.): ARDUOUS 2025, CCIS 2706, pp. 53–73, 2026.
https://doi.org/10.1007/978-3-032-09117-8_4

*Annotation.* Annotation is application-specific. According to [37], in Natural Language Processing (NLP), annotation refers to the addition of metadata to text, aiding machine learning tasks such as classification or segmentation. Similarly, [21] defines annotation in computer vision as assigning keywords or categories to images for recognition tasks. Extending this, we define annotation of multi-channel time-series data for Human Activity Recognition (HAR) as assigning labels to data samples, recorded under a defined protocol, for purposes such as activity classification or identification.

Annotations can be performed online during the activity or offline after recording. Online annotation may be performed by the subject [44], a dedicated annotator [25], or through automated methods followed by human validation. Offline and real-time annotations are often handled by trained annotators [33], with no involvement from the subject. Offline annotation can be done individually, in groups, or via crowdsourcing. Annotation revision is crucial for consistency and error reduction [33]. For multi-channel time-series data, such as from Inertial Measurement Unit (IMU), pairing with visual data (e.g., RGB video or Optical marker-based Motion Capture (MoCap)) is recommended to support label validation, error detection, and synchronisation during offline annotation [41].

*Label Ontology.* Activity label ontology is a critical research area [50]. Models trained on lab-based datasets often underperform in real-world HAR scenarios [50]. Broad labels like walking or lying down, common in many HAR datasets, are insufficient for capturing complex real-life activities. Recent work focuses on fine-grained labels and attributes [31], such as picking up a bowl or pushing a cart, which require greater annotation specificity and potentially prior annotator training. Given the complexity of multi-channel time-series data and detailed label structures, annotation tools are recommended to support the process [2]. Tools featuring semi-automatic, retrieval-based techniques can reduce cognitive load and improve annotation efficiency.

*Annotation Tool.* Manual annotation of time-series data for HAR is costly, time-intensive, and mentally demanding. [3] highlighted the annotation effort for the Logistic Activity Recognition Challenge (LARa) dataset [33], emphasizing the need for semi-automatic methods. In response, [43] proposed interactive, semi-automated annotation tools. Building on this, our prior work [2] introduced a retrieval-based feature to ease annotation by simplifying sequence validation tasks. Such tools support efficient dataset generation and promote targeted HAR research by reducing the annotation burden.

### 1.1 Objectives and Structure

This contribution extends the retrieval-based semi-automatic annotation based on the work of [2] published in the iWOAR2022. [2] proposes human activity retrieval for annotating multichannel time-series data for HAR. This retrieval ranks segments of data. It uses predictions of attributes from a deep architecture and ranks them based on their similarity to a query. A simple manual annotation then consists of accepting or rejecting the ranked segments. In [2], we compared the performance of the retrieval against manual annotations and explored two similarity measurements.

This contribution:

- expands the retrieval method to video data and performs the annotation task given by the Arduous Challenge 2022 on the CMU-MMAC kitchen dataset.
- presents Sequence Attribute Retrieval Annotator (SARA), an offline annotation tool developed based on the feedback of annotators and dataset creators of the e LARa dataset [33], created explicitly for time-series HAR.
- revisits a few annotation tools for multi-channel time series annotation of HAR datasets and examples of metrics one can use for annotation evaluation.

## 2 Related Works

HAR has been a longstanding research focus due to its relevance in areas such as daily living, elderly care, ergonomics, logistics, and behavioural analysis [14]. Numerous datasets have been developed to support machine learning and AI-based approaches in HAR [43]. Research has predominantly emphasised algorithm development, sensor selection, motion analysis, dataset complexity, and domain-specific applications [14].

More recently, attention has shifted toward the importance of semantic label annotation. Semantic attributes support transfer learning [31] and enable context-aware behaviour modelling in knowledge-based approaches [54]. Early work by [9] introduced binary semantic attributes for activities, building on attribute-based representations from computer vision [15]. Such representations are valuable in zero-shot learning and class generalisation. Methods leveraging uncertainty sampling and evolutionary algorithms have shown comparable or improved performance over conventional class prediction [9,31].

Efforts to semantically enrich activity annotations have also focused on rule-based approaches [54], later extended for automated model generation [53]. Despite their utility, annotation remains costly in terms of time and manpower, leading to frequent outsourcing [39]. As a result, few works directly examine annotation effort [3] and provide annotation guidelines and quality evaluation strategies [3,39].

### 2.1 Manual Annotation

[42] highlighted the lack of studies addressing annotation effort and consistency in multi-channel time-series HAR. While dataset creation is sometimes discussed, annotation details—particularly time and manpower—are often vague. For instance, annotating one minute of order-picking activity required 26 min using synchronised video and IMU data [16], though consistency-check methods were not disclosed. In a lab-based setting, [43] reported 2.5 min of annotation per recorded minute, aided by simplified sequences like walking, though classification performance varied. The OPPORTUNITY dataset required 7-10 h of annotation per 30 min of video [45], achieving only 56% accuracy in a follow-up study [10]. Annotation remains labour-intensive across domains: 27 h of car-tracking video

demanded eight person-months [51], while SUN RGB-D took over 2,000 h for 10,335 images [48]. For the LARa dataset, [33] reported a total of 19.75 days, averaging 37.5 min per one-minute recording.

To justify the development of annotation tools, researchers have piloted evaluations to quantify effort and user experience. For example, [36] compared manual and semi-automated annotations of accelerometer data, showing reduced annotation time with algorithmic support. Similarly, [35] emphasized setup and processing time for their MaD GUI tool. Fully-crossed annotation tasks–where multiple annotators label the same data–have recently been adopted to assess consistency and inform discussions on defining ground truth in HAR [3].

## 2.2 Semi-automatic Annotation

Semi-automatic annotation is especially desirable for time-series data, as it reduces manual effort and the reliance on support videos or online procedures. For instance, [29] leveraged gait cyclicity and pressure sensors to detect foot-ground contact phases, reducing annotation and revision time by 17% compared to fully manual approaches. Similarly, [13] applied dynamic time warping (DTW) for semi-supervised labelling of logistics activities, proposing clustering based on similar body movements to improve annotation quality. [43] and [3] proposed a semi-automatic annotation framework using three neural networks trained on the LARa dataset [33]. Retraining on a small subset of annotated data enabled significant reductions in annotation effort–up to 62.83% [3]. However, the use of fixed-size windows led to fragmented annotations. To address this, [23] introduced SLIC, a clustering algorithm based on k-means, which improved post-processing efficiency by 56%.

While online annotation offers potential to reduce offline effort, it suffers from reliability issues due to user forgetfulness or task interference [52]. Active learning approaches offer a targeted alternative, where a classifier predicts activity labels and uncertainty estimates are used to prompt users for confirmation only when necessary [11]. Such strategies may also be adapted for offline use, for instance, through retrieval-based annotation methods.

*Retrieval.* Unlike recognition-based methods for semi-automatic annotation, retrieval approaches return ranked candidates based on similarity to a user-defined query. A typical scenario is Query by Example (QbE), widely used in content-based image retrieval [8], where a sample input guides the search. However, QbE has limitations, particularly for rare samples, as users must first locate a suitable example–often a tedious or infeasible task [49]. To address this, semantic-based retrieval offers an alternative by using binary attributes–also known as visual attributes–to represent class semantics [15]. Both query and data are projected into this attribute space, enabling retrieval via nearest-neighbour search. This method has shown success in keyword spotting [49] and cuneiform spotting [46], where it is known as Query-by-String (QbS) and Query-by-eXpression (QbX), respectively. Further discussion of retrieval-based annotation is presented in Sect. 3.

### 2.3 Annotation Metrics

Annotation metrics are essential for evaluating annotation quality. Tools like ANVIL [22] offer metrics such as histograms, Cohen's $\kappa$ for inter/intra-annotator agreement [30], and confusion matrices. Cohen's $\kappa$ has been used in several studies to assess annotation consistency [2,54], while annotation time is another commonly reported metric [3]. Krippendorff's *alpha* is also employed to measure agreement among multiple annotators [24]. Cohen's $\kappa$ ranges from $-1$ to 1, with higher values indicating stronger agreement [30]. Krippendorff's *alpha* serves a similar purpose, particularly for multi-rater settings. Beyond agreement metrics, uncertainty estimation is increasingly considered. Uncertainty may arise from temporal misalignment or annotator confidence in segment labels [26]. Although not a direct quality metric, uncertainty can enhance model training. For instance, label transition uncertainty (label jitter) can be incorporated through adaptive label smoothing [26], and soft labels allow multiple labels per segment with associated confidence scores [19].

### 2.4 Annotation Tools

Annotation tools for HAR assist in labelling multi-channel time-series data, typically recorded from sensors like IMUs. Due to the lack of visual context, it is often necessary to visualise such data alongside motion capture or synchronised multi-angle video streams. Alternatively, self-annotation–where the subject annotates in real time–has been explored, though it suffers from reliability and privacy concerns [52].

Despite growing interest in annotation strategies [12], the design and evaluation of annotation tools themselves remain underexplored. Most dataset creators develop bespoke tools tailored to their specific needs [33]. However, building user-friendly, reusable tools poses challenges due to the trade-off between flexibility and usability [22]. Flexible tools require complex features and powerful analysis capabilities, while usability emphasises simplicity and ease of use. Instead of viewing the diversity of tools as a limitation, [22] advocates for interoperability to leverage the diverse capabilities of tools. In this context, we review selected annotation tools for multi-channel time-series data, outlining their features, input formats, and interface design, aiming to guide future tool development and dataset creation efforts. This overview focuses on time-series annotation tools and excludes video-based systems requiring subject tracking or segmentation.

**Summary of Annotation Tool Features.** The following information is presented based on the available documentation and/or access to different annotation tools. This work does not survey pure video-based annotation tools, which predominantly require features such as subject selection, segmentation, tracking, and multiple subject annotations. Key features relevant to HAR include support video integration, synchronisation with time-series sensor data, semi-automatic or automatic labelling, visualisation and relabelling capabilities, and annotation analysis. From a usability perspective, necessary tool capabilities include clear documentation, an intuitive interface, support for various file formats, executable installers, and accessible source code for customisation.

Table 1 summarises these features across the reviewed tools, aiming to assist dataset creators, researchers, and annotators in selecting suitable tools and potentially reducing development effort. The SPHERE self-annotation tool is excluded, as it primarily supports annotation by the subject post-activity, which does not align with conventional offline annotation workflows. The tool characteristics analysed are Annotated Media (primary data annotated), Supported Media (auxiliary inputs like video), and Application (web-based, open-source, last update). Additional Features include semi-automatic annotation, media synchronisation, and annotation/data analysis. While the type of analysis is not detailed, this table refers broadly to methods supporting inter-annotator agreement and data exploration. Platform compatibility (OS/web) is also noted, relevant for privacy and data sharing in HAR contexts.

**Table 1.** Feature summary for the previously available annotation tools.

| Tool | Annotated Media | | | Supported Media | | | Application | | | Additional Features | | |
|---|---|---|---|---|---|---|---|---|---|---|---|---|
| | Video | MoCap | Other | Video | MoCap | Other | Platform | Open Source | Last Update | Semi-auto. Ann. | Synch. | Analysis |
| **ELAN** | X | - | Audio | X | - | Audio | OS[a] | X | 12.05.2023: Rel. 6.5 | No | Yes | No |
| **ANVIL** | X | X | Audio | X | X | Audio | OS | - | 29.08.2017: Rel. 6.0 | No | Yes | Yes |
| **Signalinger Pro** | - | - | IMU | X | - | - | Both[b] | X | 2021 | Yes | No | No |
| **NOVA** | X | X | - | - | - | Audio | OS | X | 31.08.2023 Ver 1.2.6.2 | Yes | No | Yes |
| **SAT-GDAD** | - | - | IMU & Pressure | X | - | IMU & Pressure | OS | - | - | Yes | Yes | Yes |
| **SDAT-mSAR** | X | - | - | X | - | IMU | Web | - | - | Yes | Yes | Yes |
| **Advene** | X | - | - | - | - | - | OS | X | 29.6.2023 Rel: 3.13.1 | Yes | Yes | No |
| **WDK** | - | - | OBD | X | - | - | OS | X | 20.01.2020 | Yes | Yes | Yes |
| **MaD GUI** | - | - | OBD | X | - | - | OS | X | 3.06.2023: Rel. 1.0.2 | Yes | Yes | Yes |
| **LARa** | X | X | - | X | - | - | OS | X | 17.05.2022 | Yes | No | No |

[a] Refers to Operating System

[b] Both refers to the availability of both web-based and native application

Common issues encountered included a lack of tool accessibility, missing documentation, or inactive development. Tools developed for specific datasets tended to be less accessible, while general-purpose tools like ELAN and ANVIL proved more widely available. Recent annotation tools emphasise user-friendly interfaces, semi-automatic support, and open-source availability. Usability studies and neural-assisted annotation features further underline the growing relevance of annotation tooling, as demonstrated in the LARa annotation tool. Local annotation tools are often preferred to ensure data privacy, particularly when handling recordings of identifiable human subjects. This applies both to manual annotations and tools incorporating semi- or fully automated methods. Automated annotation suggestion mechanisms—based on previous labels, attribute dependencies, or neural predictions–have proven effective in reducing annotation time [3]. Retrieval-based approaches integrate these strategies, requiring annotators primarily to validate suggestions, which is elaborated in the next section.

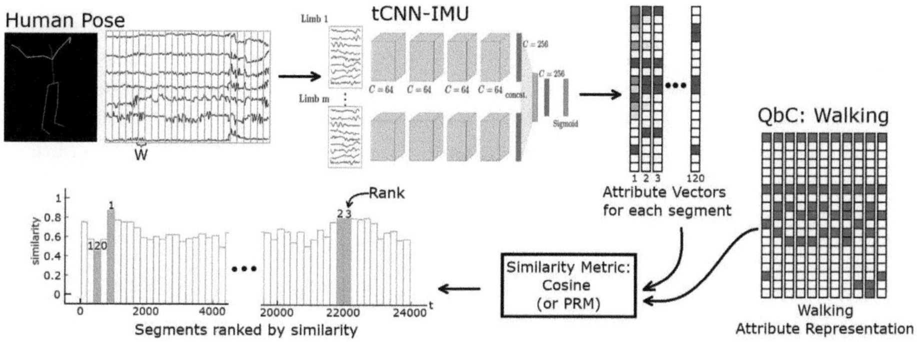


**Fig. 1.** This figure shows the Retrieval Pipeline. First, a recording of a human is segmented and forwarded through a network. The resulting attribute vectors are processed by the GDAP, comparing against the attribute representation of a class using a similarity metric (Cosine similarity in this example). The similarity of a segment is the similarity to the nearest neighbour of the query's attribute representation. The retrieval list is then sorted in descending order by the score value. The numbers on the highlighted bars show the order in which they would be presented to the Annotator.

## 3 Retrieval-Based Annotation Tool of Multi-Channel Time Series Human Activity Data

This contribution extends upon our previous work in [2], which evaluates the viability of retrieval for annotating multi-channel time-series data for HAR tasks. As discussed, the retrieval is based on works in word spotting [49] and will be considered as an alternative method of obtaining automated annotations for the semi-automated annotation pipeline, discussed in [3]. In their semi-automated approach, MoCap recordings are segmented and forwarded through a tCNN-IMU [32] to annotate them automatically. Following this, a human revises the annotations and corrects any errors. We propose to use retrieval instead of automatic annotation. With retrieval, this process might be more straightforward as the reviser can focus on one class at a time and accept or reject examples of that class instead of having to switch mentally between classes with a complete recording. The retrieval pipeline uses GDAP [2] for processing predicted attribute representations of sequences. Figure 1 presents the retrieval-based annotation method.

### 3.1 Attribute-Based Human Activity Retrieval

As discussed in Sect. 2, two types of queries are usually helpful to search for a word: Query by String (QbS) and Query by Example (QbE). Here, the focus will be on three equivalents of QbS in HAR. There are three possible retrieval methods: Query by Class (QbC), Query by Attribute (QbA), and Query by Attribute Representation (QbAR). Retrieval provides a list of results that is sorted by relevance to a query. Queries are evaluated by segmenting recordings and forwarding each segment through a tCNN-IMU network, which returns pseudo-probabilities for the presence of each attribute. For QbA, the only relevant network output is the one corresponding to the queried attribute, which can be used to sort all segments. All other attributes can be ignored. In the case of QbAR, the query is a vector compared to the network's output vector, focusing on a specific combination of attributes. QbC sorts segments based on Nearest Neighbor (NN), measuring the similarity between the predicted attributes and an attribute representation $A$. For QbC, there are multiple attribute representations to choose from for each class, $p(c|a) = 1(c = g(a))$. Then, we used the GDAP [28] for computing the predicted attribute vectors with activity classes—we use two similarity metrics, the cosine similarity and the Probabilistic Retrieval (PRM) [46].

### 3.2 Introducing SARA

SARA stands for Sequence Attribute Retrieval Annotator. SARA, developed and modified based on the LARa annotation tool [33], includes desirable features and attempts to overcome limitations as found in the LARa annotation tool. In alignment with the LARa annotation tool, SARA focuses on MoCap and video annotations. However, it is noted that SARA was not intended to be a video annotation tool with features such as subject tracking and multiple subject annotations. We recommend other tools, such as [38], for video-based multiple-human activity annotation, including subject tracking, segmentation, and pose estimation.

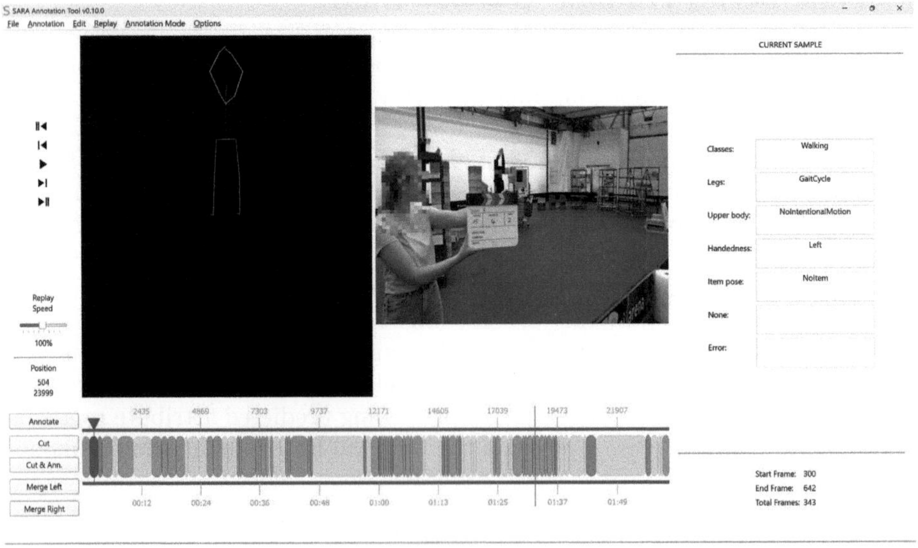


**Fig. 2.** SARA annotation tool interface.

Fig. 2 shows the user interface of SARA. A few features of SARA are the possibility of presenting both MoCap and video simultaneously, simultaneous viewing of multiple videos, within-tool synchronisation of MoCap or video recordings, and a method of semi-automatic annotation. Additionally, based on the experience with the LARa annotation tool, the developers of SARA ensured intuitive keyboard shortcuts to facilitate fast navigation. The visual interface was chosen after discussions with logisticians and students, who have previously been the primary user base for the LARa annotation tool. Furthermore, the interface is complemented with configurable text size and pop-up window size from the settings. These features were included and assessed based on the concepts of *usability* and *human-computer interaction* as discussed in [20].

To begin a new annotation process, a structure or blueprint for the annotations of the dataset must be formally defined. For SARA, the formalisation of the classes and/or attributes following an annotation hierarchy is achieved with the help of a JSON file. This hierarchy, referred to as *annotation scheme*, must be loaded when setting a new dataset in SARA. Additionally, SARA facilitates the inclusion of a dependency file, along with the scheme, under a dataset. Dependencies are an exhaustive enumeration of all possible annotations. Dependencies can be loaded from a CSV file. If dependencies are loaded, manual annotation can be sped up drastically by filtering out options incompatible with the current selection of classes and/or attributes. However, it is essential to mention that dependencies function efficiently, given that the class-to-attributes combinations are known beforehand and/or can be listed by the dataset designer. Consequently, the dependency file can be uploaded later onto the SARA annotation tool. An interesting feature that may be included in the future is a neural network that can learn the dependencies or the relations between attributes/classes while the user is annotating and can help suggest the most likely combinations.

SARA is a work-in-progress. As a result, we invite developers and researchers to modify SARA to suit their requirements and provide recommendations for constant improvement. In Sect. 6, a few ideas from the SARA developer on the possible modifications and extensions that could be built into the tool have been elaborated. To ensure longevity and ease of use of the tool, SARA was developed on Python, open-sourced, and well-documented to facilitate modification from both researchers and developers alike. The key value of SARA is to maintain ease of use for researchers from fields other than computer science. Thus, along with installations through PyPI package and Github, a detailed description of the tool, its instructions, Windows executables, and the SARA manual can be found in Zenodo[1]. The annotations of LARa and Kitchen dataset created on SARA can be found in the same link.

Section 4 presents the interface study results of the SARA in comparison to the LARa as well as the results of the video-based retrieval annotation method of the SARA annotation tool designed for the Kitchen Dataset.

## 4 Results

This contribution performs fully-crossed annotation tasks to evaluate the retrieval-based annotation method. This evaluation considers a fair approach for measuring the quality of the annotation, as also presented in the original manuscript [2], and proposed by [3,43]. Despite being cumbersome and impractical, fully crossed annotation tasks must be quantified, as the community strongly assumes manual annotation as the ground truth. However, this is hardly the case

[1] DOI: https://doi.org/10.5281/zenodo.8189341.

in reality. Annotations depend enormously on human interpretation; thus, manual annotation has to be carefully revised, as discussed in different versions of the Arduous Workshops.

This section discusses the experiments, developments, and results considered as part of the tool's augmentation and the implementation of the retrieval method. First, we present the datasets used for annotation purposes to illustrate the complexity of the annotation labels and the annotation process. Next, we present the manual and retrieval annotation evaluation on the MoCap dataset, namely, the LARa dataset. Next, the annotation effort of the Kitchen dataset, as part of the Arduous Challenge, is presented. Finally, the experiments focused on the annotation tool are elaborated. Specifically, we evaluate the performance and preference measure of the annotation tool based on the concepts of usability and human-computer interaction [20].

### 4.1 Datasets

SARA annotation tool was developed focused on the LARa dataset [33] and Kitchen dataset as part of the Arduous Challenge 2022, which is a subset from the CMU MMAC dataset. Here, we elaborate on the details of these datasets.

**LARa Dataset.** LARa, or the Logistics Activity Recognition Challenge, is a dataset that consists of completely annotated optical motion capture systems and inertial measurement unit recordings of humans performing order picking and packaging activities in a logistic environment [33]. The annotation labels consist of classes and attributes explicitly designed to accommodate logistics scenarios and to facilitate transfer learning. The LARa dataset was created in a controlled laboratory environment where logistics scenarios were set up. Three scenarios were considered. The first is a simplified order-picking scenario, the second is a real-world order-picking and consolidation system, and the third is a real-world packaging process. The point of interest in these scenarios is that the subjects who perform the activities are only briefed on the logistics process and are not informed on how to perform the activities themselves. Consequently, the activities consist of natural human movements. Each recording of LARa has a duration of two minutes.

The LARa annotation tool was developed to facilitate the detailed annotation process to create the dataset. Two experienced annotators trained ten annotators. LARa v1 consisted of the recordings and their corresponding annotations of 14 subjects. Further expanding the dataset, LARa v2 included the recordings and corresponding annotations of subjects 15 and 16, corrections to previous annotations, and an extended README file. [3] used the recordings from subjects 15 and 16 as the test set for a tCNN-IMU network [32] trained on the subjects of LARa v1 to perform their experiments.

LARa v3[2] now includes the SARA annotation tool executable, the MoCap data modified to suit SARA import, annotations from the work of [3], and a few erroneous MoCap files to facilitate uncertainty evaluations. This version would also include the manual to SARA.

[2] DOI: https://doi.org/10.5281/zenodo.8189341.

**Kitchen Dataset.** As discussed, the Kitchen dataset is an annotated subset of the CMU MMAC dataset, published as part of the Arduous Challenge 2022. The dataset consists of subjects cooking different items, such as brownies, eggs, and sandwiches, in a kitchen environment. Though the actual dataset consisted of MoCap, On-body device (OBD) data, video, and audio data, the challenge organizers had specifically mentioned avoiding the use of MoCap and audio data for the annotation process of the challenge. As part of the Arduous Challenge, the annotation schema and the annotations of a few recordings to facilitate semi-automatic annotations were also provided.

There were two parts to the challenge. The first part was to conduct manual annotation of the given recordings. This would include the annotation tool that was used to annotate and settings towards the annotation labels proposed by the Arduous Challenge 2022. The quality of the annotations was evaluated using Cohen's kappa, annotation time, and learning curve. The second was to perform semi-supervised or automated annotation. The evaluations of the annotation from the network would be based on precision, recall, accuracy, and F1 score.

### 4.2 Metrics

Two experiments are conducted to evaluate the retrieval-based annotations for HAR. First, retrieval is assessed on the LARa dataset for HAR, measuring its global performance. A global retrieval metric on the LARa testing set allows for quantifying the performance of retrieval on annotation tasks without carrying out a specific annotation experiment. Second, the annotation tool with a retrieval mode is used for an annotation task. Then, the effort of annotating recordings of a dataset is evaluated in terms of annotation time and consistency, following the same procedure from [3,43] for comparison. The retrieval metric and consistency are introduced as follows,

**Retrieval Metrics.** We choose the well-known and broadly used interpolated *Average Precision (AP)* [4] as the performance metric for our retrieval tasks. The AP is computed for every single query as follows:

$$AP = \frac{1}{T} \sum_{n=1}^{N} P(n) \cdot rel(n),$$

where, $P(n)$ denotes the *precision* for a cut off at position $n$ in the retrieval list. The indicator function $rel(n)$ evaluates to 1 if the $n$-th position in the list is relevant with respect to the query and 0 otherwise. The total amount of relevant elements is represented by $T$, and the length of the retrieval list is represented by $N$. In our scenario, the length of the retrieval list, $N$, is defined by the number of windows within one single recording, $r$. The performance for each recording $r \in R$ is obtained by computing the mean overall average precisions from a single recording, $r$, see Eq. 1, where, $Q$ denotes the total amount of queries and $AP_r(q)$ the average precision for query $q$ in record $r$.

$$mAP_r = \frac{1}{Q} \sum_{q=1}^{Q} AP_r(q), \quad (1) \qquad = \frac{1}{R} \sum_{r=1}^{R} mAP_r \quad (2)$$

Afterward, the overall performance is evaluated by computing the mean overall $mAP$s from a set or $R$ recordings, see Eq. 2 .

The result of this metric shows the viability of the method for the entire dataset and gives insights into how well it works on larger datasets.

**Consistency Metric.** We use Cohen's $\kappa$ as a consistency metric. Cohen's $\kappa$ emphasizes agreement, and it does not consider one annotation as the ground truth or LARa-labels, contrary to performance metrics such as accuracy or the F1-measure. What is called the ground truth in HAR is here regarded as an annotation perspective. This perspective strongly depends on the HAR application, context, annotator experiences, protocols, activity definitions, and semantics. Researchers in HAR still debate the meaning of the ground truth.

### 4.3 Retrieval Evaluation on LARa

We evaluated the retrieval-based annotation for HAR through two experiments: assessing retrieval performance on the LARa dataset via $mAP$, and integrating retrieval into a semi-automated annotation process, measuring time and consistency as in [3]

Using the LARa annotation tool with four annotators, we observed faster annotation times with retrieval-based methods (cosine and PRM) compared to manual annotation, with reduced mental load and improved efficiency through ranked suggestions and editable attributes. Retrieval-based annotations showed substantial agreement among annotators ($0.61 < \kappa \leq 0.8$), matching or exceeding consistency in prior work [3,40], even for low-performing attributes, except for *Handy Unit*[3].

### 4.4 Retrieval Evaluation on Kitchen Dataset

For the Arduous Challenge 2022, the LARa tool was adapted to support RGB video from the CMU-MMAC dataset. Annotation labels were restructured into a class-attribute format to ease selection. One experienced annotator manually annotated three recipes—Brownie, Eggs, and Sandwich —using simplified labels and a dependency-based selection interface to speed up the process. Annotation times and revision efforts are summarised in the Supplementary Material.

To extend this, the SARA tool incorporated retrieval-based annotation using a shared ResNet-18 and recipe-specific MLPs. Manual annotations were compared to retrieval-based ones in terms of time and consistency; See the Y Material for tables. While retrieval supported faster annotations in some cases, overall time was similar or slightly longer due to network loading and prediction quality. Cohen's $\kappa$ showed substantial to high agreement across most recordings, indicating promising potential with further improvements to the retrieval network.

### 4.5 Concepts of Usability and Human-Computer Interaction of Annotation Tools

User-centered design was central to developing the SARA annotation tool, with experienced annotators involved throughout. Inspired by [20], SARA incorporated key HCI principles, addressing user motivation, experience, and interface

[3] See Supplementary Material for a detailed results description.

comfort. Usability was evaluated through both performance (e.g., annotation time, errors) and preference (user opinions), following the framework in [20]. Given limited resources, a comparative evaluation was conducted with two new annotators from different backgrounds. Both tested LARa and SARA tools using recordings from the LARa and Kitchen datasets, applying both manual and retrieval-based annotations. Annotation duration, interruptions, and comments were recorded, and consistency was measured via Cohen's $\kappa$. Post-annotation surveys were used to assess preference. The following sections summarize these results.

**Performance Measure.** To evaluate the annotation tools, total annotation time and Cohen's $\kappa$ were used as performance measures. Annotators first completed test runs on both tools to familiarise themselves with the interface and annotation process; these were excluded from evaluation. Each annotator then annotated one recording from the LARa and one from the Kitchen dataset using both LARa and SARA tools, in any order of their choosing. It was assumed that the impact of the tool interface would outweigh any memory effects due to the annotation duration. The annotators were requested to send the files via Sciebo and note the annotation time on a Google Excel sheet after the annotation process. In case of queries, the annotators contacted an annotation expert.

**Table 2.** Performance Evaluation: Annotation time of each annotator on the respective tool, inclusive of revision time.

| Annotator | Record | LARa | SARA |
|---|---|---|---|
| | | hh:mm | hh:mm |
| *A5* | **LARa** | 1:40 | 1:33 |
| | **Kitchen** | 1:16 | 1:12 |
| *A6* | **LARa** | 0:51 | 0:39 |
| | **Kitchen** | 1:12 | 0:22 |

From Table 2, it can be noted that annotator *A6* took considerably more time to annotate with the LARa annotation tool in comparison to the SARA annotation tool. An average difference of 18 min 25 sec can be observed between the annotation durations on both tools for the four recordings in total.

It is to be noted that these values do not account for the time taken to install the annotation tools on the systems of the annotators. Both annotators had a MACOS, where installation of the LARa annotation tool was difficult due to library issues. Consequently, both annotators used a Windows OS NUC where the annotation tool was pre-installed for annotation purposes. Installing the SARA annotation tool on MACOS version *macOS Big Sur Version 11.0* has some issues with the packages. This was overcome by creating a compatible version on PyPi, which can be directly installed on the mentioned MACOS.

Three Cohen's $\kappa$ comparisons were made (Table 3): (1) between manual and retrieval annotations per annotator, (2) inter-annotator consistency, and (3) alignment with expert-reviewed LARa labels. Annotator $A_6$'s manual annotations using the LARa tool were lost due to file corruption, highlighting the need for reliable backup mechanisms like those in SARA. Annotator $A_5$ showed high

**Table 3.** Between-annotator consistency $\kappa$ of activity class annotation of a test recording from one subject by 2 annotators for the LARa dataset recording.

| | | | SARA | | | |
|---|---|---|---|---|---|---|
| Procedure | | | Manual | | Retrieval | |
| | | | A5 | A6 | A5 | A6 |
| LARa | Manual | A5 | **0.8115** | 0.3519 | **0.7328** | **0.6875** |
| | Retrieval | A5 | **0.6783** | 0.2915 | **0.8632** | 0.5756 |
| | | A6 | **0.6242** | 0.2939 | **0.7301** | **0.6809** |
| LARa Labels | | | **0.7234** | 0.3235 | **0.7678** | **0.6567** |

agreement between manual and retrieval annotations across tools. Retrieval-based inter-annotator consistency was substantial, with SARA outperforming LARa. Despite limited training, both annotators showed encouraging agreement with the LARa labels, especially in retrieval mode. For the Kitchen dataset, inter-annotator agreement using SARA manual mode reached $\kappa = 0.8160$, indicating high consistency.

**Preference Measure.** The questionnaire designed for this experiment was essentially comparative between the LARa and SARA annotation tools. However, the questions were designed such that the annotator would have the freedom to discuss or elaborate on certain discomforts or preferences they came across during the annotation procedure.

The questions were:

- Which tool did you find visually appealing?
- Which tool enabled you to annotate easily?
- Which tool was easier to learn during the test phase?
- Which tool had easily accessible icons?
- Are there any modifications you would like to see?
- Which tool did you find overall easier and satisfactory to use?
- Did you have issues while using the tools, for example, bugs, non-responsive interface, etc.?
- Is there some feature you would have liked in the new tool?

Both annotators favored SARA for its visual design and usability. While one found both tools comparable in learnability and icon accessibility, they slightly preferred SARA for its shortcut functionality and clear visual layout, which supported efficient annotation review. Dependency structures and multiple video views in SARA were noted to ease adaptation to annotation guidelines and resolve ambiguities.

One annotator suggested improvements to video navigation via separate toggles or frame controls; the other expressed satisfaction with current features. Both unanimously preferred SARA overall, citing stability and design. In contrast, LARa faced issues like installation difficulties and system crashes. Suggestions for future SARA features included on-demand button descriptions, though one annotator offered no further input due to limited exposure to annotation tool capabilities.

**Table 4.** Semantic Attributes in LARa Dataset, Cohen's $\kappa$.

| Attributes | LARa Label | LARa vs. SARA | |
|---|---|---|---|
| | | Manual | Retrieval |
| I-A Gait Cycle | 0.91 | 0.78 | 0.66 |
| I-B Step | 0.85 | 0.42 | 0.34 |
| I-C Standing Still | 0.87 | 0.40 | 0.66 |
| II-A Upwards | 0.98 | 0.31 | 0.49 |
| II-B Centred | 0.91 | 0.23 | 0.73 |
| II-C Downwards | 0.99 | 0.83 | 0.84 |
| II-D No Int. Motion | 0.92 | 0.30 | 0.58 |
| II-E Torso Rotation | - | - | - |
| III-A Right Hand | 0.92 | 0.32 | 0.63 |
| III-B Left Hand | 0.93 | 0.32 | 0.70 |
| III-C No Hands | 0.98 | 0.68 | 0.80 |
| IV-A Bulky Unit | 0.95 | 0.00 | 0.37 |
| IV-B Handy Unit | 0.87 | 0.37 | 0.43 |
| IV-C Utility/Auxiliary | 0.92 | 0.72 | 0.58 |
| IV-D Cart | 1.00 | - | - |
| IV-E Computer | 1.00 | - | - |
| IV-F No Item | 0.98 | 0.58 | 0.81 |
| V-A None | - | - | - |
| VI-A Error | - | - | - |

**Preference Measure - Industrial Partners.** SARA annotation tool was used by the LARa project's industrial partner – Motion Miners GmbH – to facilitate annotations of their industrial recordings. The annotators were requested to complete a survey specifically designed for them. In this case, there is no comparison with the LARa annotation tool. Furthermore, the annotators didn't provide any specific annotations that would be used for performance evaluation. They discuss their opinion about SARA after the annotation process. The two annotators had no prior experience in annotation beyond that with SARA. The industrial partners were asked the following questions:

- Is SARA visually appealing?
- Have you used any other HAR annotation tools before?
- Are there any modifications you would like to see in the tool?
- Did you have issues using the tool, e.g., bugs, not responsive interface, etc.?

As discussed, the annotators had no prior experience with any other annotation tool. They mentioned that they found SARA both well-structured and easy to use. With respect to modifications to the tool, the annotators pointed toward a few bug fixes, such as no clear separation between the main window and the annotation window in the light mode, an empty *About* under the Options tab, and changing positions of the annotation labels within the annotation pop-up window.

# 5 Discussion

Building on [2], this work explores retrieval-based semi-automatic annotation on video data from the Kitchen dataset, as introduced in the Arduous Challenge 2022. A comprehensive overview of annotation tools for multi-channel time-series data is presented—distinct from traditional video annotation tools—as the focus lies on media synchronization, time-series analysis, and usability.

The SARA annotation tool, featuring integrated retrieval-based annotation, was introduced and evaluated on both the LARa and Kitchen datasets. While promising results were seen with LARa, the Kitchen dataset required further refinement of the retrieval network. Performance and preference comparisons between SARA and LARa highlight the advantages of incorporating human-computer interaction principles into tool design. Retrieval annotations showed strong alignment with expert labels, supporting the value of semi-automatic and semi-supervised annotation strategies for future dataset development.

## 5.1 ARDUOUS Workshop Comments

The SARA annotation tool was presented at the Arduous Workshop 2023 during the PERCOM conference in Atlanta, USA. Feedback gathered from the session highlighted several enhancement opportunities.

**Annotation Scheme:** Concerns were raised about the degree of freedom annotators have in modifying the annotation scheme, especially when label developers and annotators are different groups. Unrestricted modifications could introduce inconsistencies. A suggested solution was a web-based annotation scheme management system, allowing annotators to propose changes for reviewer approval and system-wide updates.

**Visualisation of Time-Series Data:** Currently supporting only MoCap and video, participants recommended expanding SARA to visualise and synchronise other time-series data, such as IMU, alongside existing modalities.

**Integrated Annotation Evaluation Metrics:** To promote annotation quality, integrating evaluation metrics like Cohen's Kappa and annotation duration directly into the tool was suggested. Such features would encourage users to assess and improve dataset consistency and quality seamlessly.

**Uncertainty-based Retrieval Enhancements:** While SARA's retrieval module provides frame frequency visualisations, it lacks uncertainty-based selection. Workshop participants recommended incorporating uncertainty-driven retrieval strategies to refine the annotation suggestions.

**Web-Based Application:** Although the executable version improved usability over LARa, download size remains a concern. A web-based alternative was preferred for ease of access, though privacy concerns were noted. As [1] highlights, soft biometrics may lead to re-identification, necessitating secure design for web platforms.

**Active Learning based Semi-Automatic Annotation:** The current retrieval method relies on a pre-trained model with initial manual annotations.

A more efficient approach, based on active learning [5], was proposed. This would iteratively select the most informative samples, potentially reducing annotation effort while maintaining model performance.

## 6 Conclusions and Future Works

Annotation remains a demanding task, but dedicated tools can significantly reduce annotation time and improve quality. Features like semi-automatic labeling, dependency-based selections, and graphical controls proved especially helpful. Thus, investing in tool development or adapting existing ones for new datasets is a worthwhile step in dataset creation.

Drawing from our experience and expert discussions, we highlight several desirable features for future annotation tools. Given the diverse input data in HAR, synchronisation across modalities (e.g., IMU, MoCap, video) and flexible time-series visualisation are essential. Supporting varied MoCap formats (e.g., C3D, BVH, FBX) through flexible data ingestion or mapping methods is also recommended, as current tools like SARA and LARa handle only specific formats. Online learning is another promising direction. Enabling real-time model updates could support annotators more effectively during retrieval-based annotation. Similarly, offering multiple export options—beyond CSV—to accommodate both accessibility and research needs (e.g., bit-wise storage or batch exports) is desirable.

Future developments for SARA could include OBD data integration, enhanced labeling schemes (e.g., nested categories), and automated or unsupervised annotation support. Active learning techniques like uncertainty sampling [27,47] could reduce annotation load by prioritising uncertain samples [6,17,18,34]. Once annotators address these uncertain regions, predictions for the remaining data may be accepted with high confidence, thereby accelerating the process. Ultimately, broadening input/output format compatibility and enabling project-level organisation of annotations could further streamline annotation workflows.

**Acknowledgments.** This study was funded by the Federal Ministry of Research, Technology and Space of Germany and the state of North Rhine-Westphalia as part of the Lamarr Institute for Machine Learning and Artificial Intelligence.

## References

1. Abdelwhab, A., Viriri, S.: A survey on soft biometrics for human identification. Mach. Learn. Biometrics **37** (2018)
2. Altermann, E., Moya Rueda, F., Rusakov, E., Fink, G.A.: Retrieval-based annotation of multi-channel time-series data for HAR. In: 2022 IEEE International Conference on Pervasive Computing and Communications Workshops and other Affiliated Events (PerCom Workshops), to appear. Pisa, Italy (2022)

3. Avsar, H., Altermann, E., Reining, C., Moya Rueda, F., Fink, G.A.: Benchmarking annotation procedures for multi-channel time series HAR dataset. In: 2021 IEEE International Conference on Pervasive Computing and Communications Workshops and other Affiliated Events (PerCom Workshops), pp. 453–458. Kassel, Germany (2021). https://doi.org/10.1109/PerComWorkshops51409.2021.9431062
4. Baeza-Yates, R., Ribeiro-Neto, B.: Modern Information Retrieval: The Concepts and Technology behind Search, 2nd edn. Addison-Wesley Publishing Company, USA (2011)
5. Bi, H., Perello-Nieto, M., Santos-Rodriguez, R., Flach, P.: Human activity recognition based on dynamic active learning. IEEE J. Biomed. Health Inform. **25**(4), 922–934 (2020)
6. Blundell, C., Cornebise, J., Kavukcuoglu, K., Wierstra, D.: Weight uncertainty in neural network. In: International Conference on Machine Learning, pp. 1613–1622. PMLR (2015)
7. Bordel, B., Alcarria, R., Robles, T.: Recognizing human activities in industry 4.0 scenarios through an analysis-modeling-recognition algorithm and context labels. Integrated Comput. Aided Eng. **29**(1), 83–103 (2022)
8. Chen, W., et al.: Deep image retrieval: a survey (2021). https://arxiv.org/abs/2101.11282
9. Cheng, H.T., Sun, F.T., Griss, M., Davis, P., Li, J., You, D.: Nuactiv: recognizing unseen new activities using semantic attribute-based learning. In: Proceeding of the 11th Annual International Conference on Mobile Systems, Applications, and Services, pp. 361–374 (2013)
10. Ciliberto, M., Roggen, D., Morales, F.J.O.: Exploring human activity annotation using a privacy preserving 3d model. In: Proceedings of the 2016 ACM International Joint Conference on Pervasive and Ubiquitous Computing: Adjunct, pp. 803–812 (2016)
11. Cui, Y., Hiremath, S.K., Ploetz, T.: Reinforcement learning based online active learning for human activity recognition. In: Proceedings of the 2022 ACM International Symposium on Wearable Computers, pp. 23–27 (2022)
12. Demrozi, F., Turetta, C., Machot, F.A., Pravadelli, G., Kindt, P.H.: A comprehensive review of automated data annotation techniques in human activity recognition. arXiv preprint arXiv:2307.05988 (2023)
13. Diete, A., Sztyler, T., Stuckenschmidt, H.: A smart data annotation tool for multi-sensor activity recognition. In: 2017 IEEE International Conference on Pervasive Computing and Communications Workshops (PerCom Workshops), pp. 111–116 (2017). https://doi.org/10.1109/PERCOMW.2017.7917542
14. Dua, N., Singh, S.N., Challa, S.K., Semwal, V.B., Sai Kumar, M.: A survey on human activity recognition using deep learning techniques and wearable sensor data. In: Machine Learning, Image Processing, Network Security and Data Sciences: 4th International Conference, MIND 2022, Virtual Event, January 19–20, 2023, Proceedings, Part I, pp. 52–71. Springer (2023)
15. Farhadi, A., Endres, I., Hoiem, D., Forsyth, D.: Describing objects by their attributes. In: 2009 IEEE Conference on Computer Vision and Pattern Recognition, pp. 1778–1785 (2009). https://doi.org/10.1109/CVPR.2009.5206772
16. Feldhorst, S., Aniol, S., Ten Hompel, M.: Human activity recognition in der kommissionierung–charakterisierung des kommissionierprozesses als ausgangsbasis für die methodenentwicklung. Logistics J. Proc. **2016**(10) (2016)
17. Gal, Y., Ghahramani, Z.: Bayesian convolutional neural networks with bernoulli approximate variational inference. In: 4th International Conference on Learning

Representations, ICLR 2016, San Juan, Puerto Rico, May 2-4, 2016, Workshop Track Proceedings (2016)
18. Hendrycks, D., Gimpel, K.: A baseline for detecting misclassified and out-of-distribution examples in neural networks. In: 5th International Conference on Learning Representations, ICLR 2017, Toulon, France, April 24-26, 2017, Conference Track Proceedings. OpenReview.net (2017). https://openreview.net/forum?id=Hkg4TI9xl
19. Hu, N., Englebienne, G., Lou, Z., Kröse, B.: Learning to recognize human activities using soft labels. IEEE Trans. Pattern Anal. Mach. Intell. **39**(10), 1973–1984 (2016)
20. Issa, T., Isaias, P.: Usability and human–computer interaction (HCI). In: Sustainable design, pp. 23–40. Springer (2022)
21. Jiu, M., Sahbi, H., Qi, L.: Deep context networks for image annotation. In: 2018 24th International Conference on Pattern Recognition (ICPR), pp. 2422–2427. IEEE (2018)
22. Kipp, M.: ANVIL: The video annotation research tool, pp. 420–436 (2014). https://doi.org/10.1093/oxfordhb/9780199571932.013.024
23. Korpela, J., Akiyama, T., Niikura, T., Nakamura, K.: Reducing label fragmentation during time-series data annotation to reduce annotation costs. In: Adjunct Proceedings of the 2021 ACM International Joint Conference on Pervasive and Ubiquitous Computing and Proceedings of the 2021 ACM International Symposium on Wearable Computers, pp. 328–333 (2021)
24. Krippendorff, K.: Computing krippendorff's alpha-reliability (2011)
25. Krüger, F., Heine, C., Bader, S., Hein, A., Teipel, S., Kirste, T.: On the applicability of clinical observation tools for human activity annotation. In: 2017 IEEE International Conference on Pervasive Computing and Communications Workshops (PerCom Workshops), pp. 129–134. IEEE (2017)
26. Kwon, H., Abowd, G.D., Plötz, T.: Handling annotation uncertainty in human activity recognition. In: Proceedings of the 2019 ACM International Symposium on Wearable Computers, pp. 109–117 (2019)
27. Lewis, D.D., Gale, W.A.: A sequential algorithm for training text classifiers. In: Croft, W.B., van Rijsbergen, C.J. (eds.) Proceedings of the 17th Annual International ACM-SIGIR Conference on Research and Development in Information Retrieval. Dublin, Ireland, 3-6 July 1994 (Special Issue of the SIGIR Forum), pp. 3–12. ACM/Springer (1994). https://doi.org/10.1007/978-1-4471-2099-5_1
28. Luedtke, S., Moya Rueda, F., Fink, G.A., Kirste, T.: Human activity recognition using attribute-based neural networks and context information. In: 3RD Int. Workshop on Deep Learning for Human Activity Recognition(to appear). Montreal, Canada (2021). https://arxiv.org/abs/2111.04564
29. Martindale, C.F., Roth, N., Hannink, J., Sprager, S., Eskofier, B.M.: Smart annotation tool for multi-sensor gait-based daily activity data. In: 2018 IEEE International Conference on Pervasive Computing and Communications Workshops (PerCom Workshops), pp. 549–554 (2018). https://doi.org/10.1109/PERCOMW.2018.8480193
30. McHugh, M.L.: Interrater reliability: the kappa statistic. Biochem. Med. 276–282 (2012). https://doi.org/10.11613/BM.2012.031
31. Moya Rueda, F., Fink, G.A.: Learning attribute representation for human activity recognition. In: 2018 24th Int. Conf. on Pattern Recognition (ICPR), pp. 523–528. IEEE (2018). https://doi.org/10.1109/ICPR.2018.8545146
32. Moya Rueda, F., Grzeszick, R., Fink, G., Feldhorst, S., Hompel, M.: Convolutional neural networks for human activity recognition using body-worn sensors. MDPI Inform. (2018). https://doi.org/10.3390/informatics5020026

33. Niemann, F., et al.: LARa: creating a dataset for human activity recognition in logistics using semantic attributes. Sensors **20**(15) (2020)
34. Oberdiek, P., Fink, G., Rottmann, M.: UQGAN: a unified model for uncertainty quantification of deep classifiers trained via conditional GANs. In: Koyejo, S., Mohamed, S., Agarwal, A., Belgrave, D., Cho, K., Oh, A. (eds.) Advances in Neural Information Processing Systems. vol. 35, pp. 21371–21385. Curran Associates, Inc. (2022). https://proceedings.neurips.cc/paper_files/paper/2022/file/8648e249887ccb0fe8c067d596e35b40-Paper-Conference.pdf
35. Ollenschläger, M., et al.: Mad GUI: an open-source python package for annotation and analysis of time-series data. Sensors **22**(15), 5849 (2022)
36. Ponnada, A., et al.: Signaligner pro: a tool to explore and annotate multi-day raw accelerometer data. In: 2021 IEEE International Conference on Pervasive Computing and Communications Workshops and other Affiliated Events (PerCom Workshops), pp. 475–480. IEEE (2021)
37. Pustejovsky, J., Stubbs, A.: Natural language annotation for machine learning: a guide to corpus-building for applications. O'Reilly Media, Inc. (2012)
38. Quan, H., Bonarini, A.: Havptat: a human activity video pose tracking annotation tool. Softw. Impacts **12**, 100278 (2022)
39. Rasmussen, C.B., Kirk, K., Moeslund, T.B.: The challenge of data annotation in deep learning-a case study on whole plant corn silage. Sensors **22**(4), 1596 (2022)
40. Reining, C., Rueda, F.M., Niemann, F., Fink, G.A., t. Hompel, M.: Annotation performance for multi-channel time series HAR dataset in logistics. In: 2020 IEEE International Conference on Pervasive Computing and Communications Workshops (PerCom Workshops), pp. 1–6. PERCOM Workshops (2020). https://doi.org/10.1109/PerComWorkshops48775.2020.9156170
41. Reining, C., Nair, N.R., Niemann, F., Moya Rueda, F., Fink, G.A.: A tutorial on dataset creation for sensor-based human activity recognition. In: 2023 IEEE International Conference on Pervasive Computing and Communications Workshops and other Affiliated Events (PerCom Workshops), pp. 453–459 (2023). https://doi.org/10.1109/PerComWorkshops56833.2023.10150401
42. Reining, C., Niemann, F., Moya Rueda, F., Fink, G.A., ten Hompel, M.: Human activity recognition for production and logistics-a systematic literature review. Information **10**(8), 245 (2019)
43. Reining, C.S.: Attributbasierte Erkennung menschlicher Aktivitäten in industriellen Prozessen am Beispiel der Logistik. Praxiswissen Service (Jul 2021)
44. Reiss, A.: Personalized mobile physical activity monitoring for everyday life. Ph.D. thesis, Technische Universität Kaiserslautern (2014)
45. Roggen, D., et al.: Collecting complex activity datasets in highly rich networked sensor environments. In: 2010 Seventh International Conference on Networked Sensing Systems (INSS), pp. 233–240. IEEE (2010)
46. Rusakov, E., Rothacker, L., Mo, H., Fink, G.A.: A probabilistic retrieval model for word spotting based on direct attribute prediction. In: 16th International Conference on Frontiers in Handwriting Recognition (ICFHR), pp. 38–43. IEEE, Niagara Falls, NY, USA (2018). https://doi.org/10.1109/ICFHR-2018.2018.00016
47. Settles, B.: Active learning literature survey (2009)
48. Song, S., Lichtenberg, S.P., Xiao, J.: SUN RGB-D: a RGB-D scene understanding benchmark suite. In: 2015 IEEE Conference on Computer Vision and Pattern Recognition (CVPR), pp. 567–576. IEEE, Boston, MA, USA (2015). https://doi.org/10.1109/CVPR.2015.7298655
49. Sudholt, S., Fink, G.A.: Attribute CNNs for word spotting in handwritten documents. Int. J. Document Anal. Recogn. **21**(3), 159–160 (2018)

50. Tonkin, E.L., et al.: Talk, text, tag? understanding self-annotation of smart home data from a user's perspective. Sensors **18**(7), 2365 (2018)
51. Vondrick, C., Patterson, D., Ramanan, D.: Efficiently scaling up crowdsourced video annotation: a set of best practices for high quality, economical video labeling. Int. J. Comput. Vision **101**, 184–204 (2013)
52. Woznowski, P., Tonkin, E., Laskowski, P., Twomey, N., Yordanova, K., Burrows, A.: Talk, text or tag? In: 2017 IEEE International Conference on Pervasive Computing and Communications Workshops (PerCom Workshops), pp. 123–128. IEEE (2017)
53. Yordanova, K.: Towards automated generation of semantic annotation for activity recognition problems. In: 2020 IEEE International Conference on Pervasive Computing and Communications Workshops (PerCom Workshops), pp. 1–6. IEEE (2020)
54. Yordanova, K., Krüger, F.: Creating and exploring semantic annotation for behaviour analysis. Sensors **18**(9), 2778 (2018)

# Towards Standardized Dataset Creation for Human Activity Recognition: Framework, Taxonomy, Checklist, and Best Practices

Friedrich Niemann[1](✉), Fernando Moya Rueda[2], Moh'd Khier Al Kfari[3], Nilah Ravi Nair[1], Stefan Lüdtke[3], and Alice Kirchheim[1,4]

[1] Chair of Material Handling and Warehousing, TU Dortmund University, Dortmund, Germany
{friedrich.niemann,nilah.nair,alice.kirchheim}@tu-dortmund.de
[2] MotionMiners GmbH, Dortmund, Germany
fernando.moya@motionminers.com
[3] Institute for Visual and Analytic Computing, University of Rostock, Rostock, Germany
{mohd.kfari,stefan.luedtke}@uni-rostock.de
[4] Fraunhofer Institute for Material Flow and Logistics IML, Dortmund, Germany
alice.kirchheim@iml.fraunhofer.de

**Abstract.** Well-annotated and consistent datasets are essential for training supervised and self-supervised models, especially in human activity recognition (HAR). However, unlike research areas such as image recognition, HAR datasets vary widely in sensor types, environments, subjects, and presentation formats, often reflecting the individual practices of their creators. This inconsistency hinders usability, reproducibility, and long-term value. In this paper, we propose a standardized framework for creating HAR datasets, including taxonomies, a detailed checklist, and best practices to guide dataset development. We retrospectively apply this checklist to benchmark datasets HDM05, HDM12 Dance, HuGaDB, UMAFall, LARa, OpenPack, CAARL, and DaRA and compare them with industry-focused datasets to illustrate common gaps and opportunities for improvement.

**Keywords:** Dataset Creation · Human Activity Recognition (HAR) · Framework · Taxonomy · Checklist · Annotation

## 1 Introduction

Recent advancements in artificial intelligence (AI) and generative models have highlighted the importance of having large corpora of data, efficient data processing, and curated datasets. However, as said by [39], "Paradoxically, data is the most under-valued and deglamorized aspect of AI." Even though data is the

The original version of the chapter has been revised. In page 84 image has been revised. A correction to this chapter can be found at
https://doi.org/10.1007/978-3-032-09117-8_12


E. L. Tonkin et al. (Eds.): ARDUOUS 2025, CCIS 2706, pp. 74–93, 2026.
https://doi.org/10.1007/978-3-032-09117-8_5

core aspect that facilitates AI, the focus is often on computing power [10], neural network design [46], and training methodology [42]. A similar trend can also be seen in using AI for human activity recognition (HAR). HAR is the process of identifying the activity performed by a human at a particular point in time with the help of sensor data such as RGB video or inertial measurement units (IMUs) [22] that record the motion of the human body. Neural networks such as the convolutional neural network (CNN) and graph neural network [22] have facilitated activity recognition when trained on datasets of daily living with annotation labels such as running, walking, sitting and jumping. However, human motions are varied and depending on the field of application, the activity labels are prone to changes, such as in the case of logistics, where activities such as pushing a cart and handling items are required [34]. As a result, new datasets pertaining to the field of application, such as logistics, robotics or manufacturing, are required.

Unlike neural network training and architectures, dataset creation is rarely discussed explicitly [4,22,25]. The majority of the popular human motion datasets consist of activities of daily living such as walking, jogging, and cooking [25]. Few datasets are focused on industrial applications [11]. Along with the activities that are covered, the modality of the recording and the metadata provided for the dataset, the available annotation varies depending on the intended use. For example, the Epic Kitchen dataset [18] provides activity labels and bounding boxes for object detection, while poses are represented in the HumanEVA dataset [41]. In this paper, we focus on human motion datasets with activity class labels, additionally exploring further labels like semantic attributes or logistic processes [4,12,25].

The lack of standardized procedures for the creation of HAR datasets, coupled with a disproportionate emphasis on model development, can lead to biased and unreliable outcomes. Even the most sophisticated models fail to perform adequately when trained on poor-quality data. Inconsistent labels, insufficient dataset documentation, and restricted data accessibility further compromise comparability, generalizability, reproducibility, and limit practical applicability. These challenges are also common in other research areas such as social sciences, psychology, and medicine. To address these challenges, this work proposes to standardize dataset creation, with a particular focus on generating class-label annotated human activity datasets. We introduce a comprehensive **dataset creation framework** (Sect. 3) that outlines **best practices** for recording and annotation, provides **recommendations** and **taxonomies**. From this framework, we derive a **checklist** that serves as a practical tool for researchers in the creation of HAR datasets (Sect. 4). The checklist is retrospectively evaluated by the authors of benchmark datasets to assess its applicability and relevance. Furthermore, we compare these findings with practices in **industrial scenarios** to analyze how data quality impacts applied HAR methods (Sect. 5).

## 2 Related Work

Frameworks for the creation of HAR datasets have received little attention in the scientific literature. Existing reviews, surveys, and related contributions predominantly focus on AI methods and, to some extent, on summarizing existing datasets. To the best of our knowledge, no publication explicitly addresses the structured creation of HAR datasets. Some works do propose general conceptual models within the HAR domain, such as frameworks [24], pipelines [23], chains [13], taxonomies [8,20], architectures [40], or workflows [3]. However, these contributions primarily focus on model development, i.e., the stages following dataset creation. Only isolated aspects of dataset creation, such as annotation, are addressed, as seen in [20].

Beyond HAR, the importance of enhancing dataset quality in machine learning has been increasingly acknowledged. Drawing from interviews with 18 leading dataset creators, [36] propose seven recommendations to improve responsible dataset creation.

The lack of standardized procedures for dataset creation and the overall scarcity of high-quality data are clearly reflected in the challenges and limitations identified in the literature. For instance, four of the five challenges listed in [8] directly relate to dataset creation, ranging from data collection and preprocessing to hardware considerations and annotation inconsistencies (e.g., misalignment of activities). Many existing HAR datasets exhibit shortcomings such as incomplete or missing labels, unsynchronized recordings, limited or missing metadata, inconsistent or undocumented label categories, and restricted accessibility. Low annotation quality can significantly reduce the accuracy of HAR models. Furthermore, the lack of large-scale, high-quality datasets, the need for reliable data, and the general shortage of labeled samples are key challenges in the field [24,48].

In response to this research gap, the first approach to standardizing HAR dataset creation was introduced by [37]. The framework proposed therein is taken up, extended, and operationalized in the present work in the form of a user-friendly checklist. A review of existing medical checklists revealed that institutions engaged in human studies commonly provide their own checklists. These checklists outline key considerations that dataset collectors should account for when designing data collection protocols [2]. In some cases, such checklists are issued by institutional ethics committees and focus primarily on the types of data permitted for collection and the policies governing data retention [9]. Moreover, these checklists are intended to ensure that all ethical requirements are considered throughout the processes of data creation, analysis, and storage. However, they typically do not provide guidance on the dataset creation process itself.

## 3 HAR Dataset Creation Framework

The framework for creating a HAR dataset (Fig. 1) described herein is informed by the lessons learnt from our datasets LARa [34], CAARL [33], and DaRA, from application of datasets, as well as by general best practices derived from extensive literature and dataset reviews.

The framework is divided into four aspects: Planning, Data Recording (Preparation and Execution), Data Processing (Preparation and Execution), and Dataset Publication. Each of these aspects consists of several steps, which are explained in the following. It is important to note that these steps of the framework are not specifications in the strict sense, but rather suggestions that can be adapted to the specific needs of the dataset.

### 3.1 Dataset Creation Planning

Steps 1 to 9 of the framework define general parameters of the study and identify challenges and limitations. They should be planned and carried out prior to data recording.

**1. Dataset Purpose:** The dataset's purpose should be clearly defined from the outset, aligning it with a specific research or industrial application. This includes the dataset's goals, its intended audience, and how it will be used.

**2. Recording Scope:** The scope should reflect the dataset's purpose while aligning with available resources like time, personnel, and budget. Annotation and revision typically require more time than data acquisition, especially for complex label sets. Planning must account for this workload. For example, in the LARa dataset, capturing 14 hours of material (12.63 hours published) required 197 person-hours, whereas annotation of 8 classes and 19 attributes demanded 474 person-hours and revision required an additional 143 person-hours.

**3. Recording Environment Definition:** The recording environment in the development of HAR datasets can be classified into three categories: *controlled environments* (e.g., laboratories, and motion capture (MoCap)-studios), *semi-controlled environments* (e.g., simulated apartments, rehabilitation centers, and

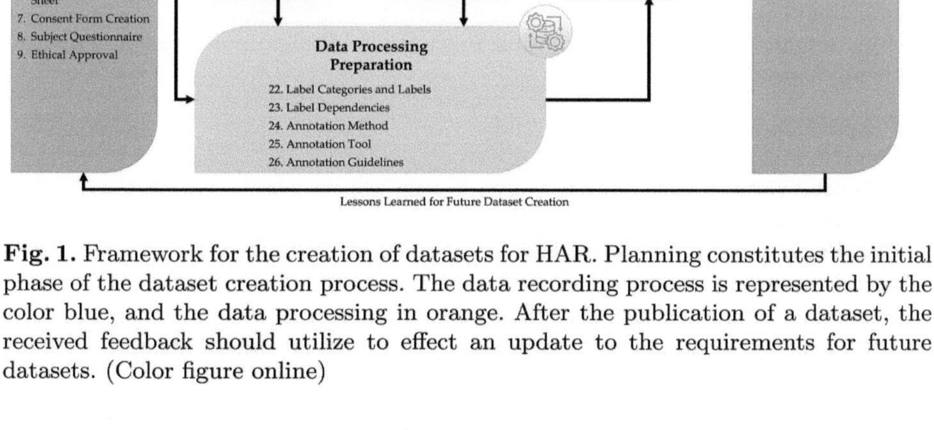

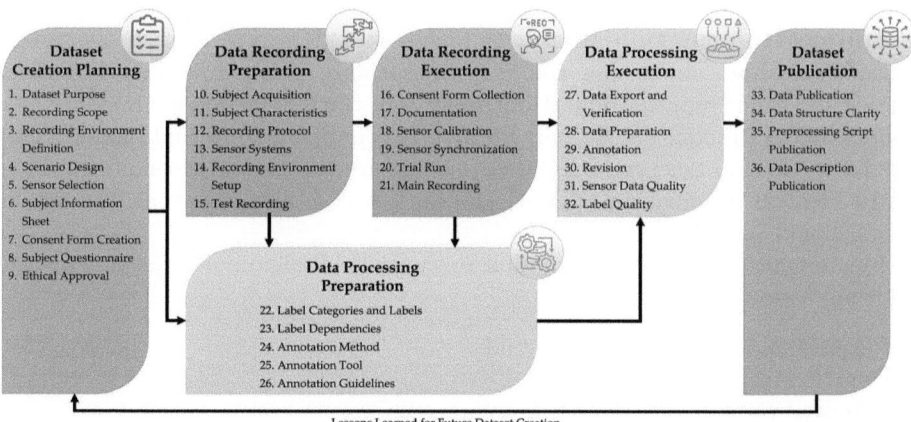


**Fig. 1.** Framework for the creation of datasets for HAR. Planning constitutes the initial phase of the dataset creation process. The data recording process is represented by the color blue, and the data processing in orange. After the publication of a dataset, the received feedback should utilize to effect an update to the requirements for future datasets. (Color figure online)

simulated warehouse), and *real-world environments* (e.g., private homes, workplaces, and industrial facilities). They each offering different levels of ecological validity and complexity. While labs offer precision and reproducibility, real environments yield more natural behavior but introduce unpredictability. Choosing the right setting depends on the desired balance between realism and control.

**4. Scenario Design:** Scenarios may be *scripted*, *free-living*, or *hybrid*. Scripted designs offer control and comparability through a predefined sequence of tasks (protocol), but they may constrain natural behavior. Free-living scenarios support realism and generalization, allowing subjects to perform activities in their daily or occupational environments without structured guidance or intervention; however, they are more difficult to annotate. Hybrid scenarios strike a balance between structure and flexibility: subjects are given general tasks, such as household chores or fitness routines, while retaining freedom in the order and manner of execution.

**5. Sensor Selection:** Sensor choice depends on the dataset's goals, infrastructure, and budget. IMUs are widely used for their cost-effectiveness and availability, being integrated in consumer devices such as smartphones and smartwatches [3]. Other sensors such as positioning sensors (GPS, Bluetooth beacons), heart rate sensors [38] or tactile and force sensors [27]) are additional options that can be considered. In the context of sensor-based human activity recognition, RGB cameras are typically used to aid annotation. Combining multiple modalities can improve accuracy but requires careful calibration and synchronization. A review of 61 HAR datasets [34] showed that 51 employed IMUs with accelerometer, magnetometer, gyroscope. Other frequently used modalities included RGB cameras (n = 18), MoCap systems (n = 16), microphones (n = 6), and depth sensors (n = 5).

**6. Subject Information Sheet:** Subjects should receive a clear, accessible information sheet explaining the study's purpose, risks, and data handling. Guidelines from International Conference on Harmonisation's Guideline for Good Clinical Practice (ICH-GCP E6 R2) [1], Council for International Organizations of Medical Sciences (CIOMS) [17] and Declaration of Helsinki from the World Medical Association (WMA) [45] outline core elements that such documents should include.

In summary, a subject information sheet for HAR should at least include the following aspects:

- Purpose and procedure of the study
- Duration of participation
- Potential risks or burdens
- Expected benefits and, if applicable, financial compensation
- Collection, processing, and publication of data
- Inclusion and exclusion criteria
- Potential advantages or limitations of participation
- Data protection measures (e.g., anonymization or pseudonymization)
- Identity of the organization funding or conducting the research
- Contact persons for further inquiries

**7. Consent Form Creation:** Informed consent is essential for any study involving human subjects, from ethical, legal, and scientific standpoints. Consent must be obtained before data collection and include permissions for specific data types and use cases. This protects subject rights and ensures research integrity. These principles are codified in international guidelines such as the Declaration of Helsinki [45]. From a legal perspective, informed consent constitutes a necessary legal basis for data processing under regulations such as the EU General Data Protection Regulation (GDPR).

**8. Subject Questionnaire:** Standardized questionnaires should be prepared to systematically collect both subject characteristics and information relevant to the study to support data interpretation and ensures compliance with inclusion/exclusion criteria.

**9. Ethical Approval:** Ethical approval by an institutional review board is a critical prerequisite for studies involving human subjects. It ensures the protection of subjects and is often required for data publication. While obtaining ethics approval has long been standard practice in the medical and sports sciences, its importance has only recently gained broader recognition within the HAR community.

### 3.2 Data Recording Preparation

The subsequent segment of the framework encompasses Steps 10 to 15, pertaining to the preparation of the data recording. We would like to specifically highlight the importance of the test recording in Step 15.

**10. Subject Acquisition:** A sufficient number of subjects is crucial to ensure variability and reduce bias. At least 15 subjects are recommended to cover core demographics. Recruiting external subjects as backups helps mitigate cancellations and logistical disruptions. A review of HAR datasets revealed an average of 21.1 subjects, ranging from 1 to over 200 [34]. Over 65% of the datasets included 15 or fewer subjects.

**11. Subject Characteristics:** A sufficiently large number of subjects is essential to capture a wide range of soft-biometric characteristics. A balanced distribution of these characteristics is crucial to improve model accuracy [31], enhance generalizability [32], and reduce bias [29]. Beyond age and sex, documenting the handedness, body size and weight, experience, and relevant qualifications improves the utility and fairness of the dataset. These details support better model generalization and minimize bias. Characteristics should be selected based on the application domain. Furthermore, application-specific characteristics such as physical impairments, fitness level and possibly cultural background or language should be considered, depending on the use case of the dataset.

**12. Recording Protocol:** A structured protocol enhances reproducibility and helps identify procedural issues. It should include detailed steps for the experimental setup, subject instructions, calibration routines, and contingencies. Protocols should be used consistently across all sessions.

**13. Sensor Systems and 14. Recording Environment Setup:** Sensors should be tested for reliability, synchronization, calibration, and data quality as well as data transmission and storage. The recording environment must be prepared based on the defined scenarios, ensuring all technical components function properly. This setup should be completed well in advance to allow for troubleshooting.

**15. Test Recording:** The test recording (pilot study) represents a preliminary implementation of the main data recording procedure [7]. It serves as a crucial step for validating the experimental setup, systems, and workflows. Another important function of the test recording is the training of study staff in technical handling, procedural execution, and subject interaction [26]. It should be conducted after the successful testing of sensors and the setup of the recording environment, but prior to the commencement of the main data recording phase.

### 3.3 Data Recording Execution

After the preparation stage, the data is recorded on one or more days. The process of data recording starts with signing the consent forms (Step 16) and concludes with the execution of the main recording (Step 21).

**16. Consent Form Collection:** Consent forms must be signed before data recording begins. A final briefing and confirmation of understanding should occur on the day of recording. Collecting consent afterward is considered ethically unacceptable [45].

**17. Documentation:** All aspects of the setup and session should be documented. This includes sensor placement, session schedules, environmental conditions, and any irregularities.

**18. Sensor Calibration:** Sensor system, like MoCap systems, might requires calibration. This includes confirming sampling rates, positional accuracy, and device connectivity.

**19. Sensor Synchronization:** Synchronization aligns different data streams temporally. Typically, synchronization is ensured by having the subject perform a specific, controlled movement such as raising the arm or stamping a foot. Annotators subsequently mark the start time of this synchronization activity for each sensor or IMU channel. Accurate synchronization is essential for sensor fusion and valid annotation. To achieve a consistent temporal alignment, all recordings should be re-sampled to a unified time axis, e.g., using piecewise spline interpolation.

**20. Trial Run:** Trial runs help subjects familiarize themselves with the tasks and reduce variability in behavior due to unfamiliarity. They should closely mirror the main recording procedures. A consistent trial structure across subjects ensures comparability.

**21. Main Recording:** During the main recording, researchers should minimize interventions to promote natural behavior. The study team should communicate using standardized and consistent instructions. Improvised guidance must be avoided. Training of the study staff, as carried out during preparatory test recordings (see Step 15), is essential for ensuring protocol adherence. Staff must monitor sensor status and maintain logs of any deviations.

### 3.4 Data Processing Preparation

As illustrated in Fig. 1, the data processing preparation (Steps 22 to 26) should be conducted concurrently with the data recording preparation and execution.

**22. Label Categories and Labels:** Labels define the activities and contexts represented in the dataset. They can be organized into categories like postures, object interactions, or environmental context (see Table 1). Annotation can be *frame-wise*, *segment-wise* (flexible durations), or *window-based* (fixed-length). Another salient dimension is label exclusivity: In *single-label* annotation, exactly one mutually exclusive label is assigned per time interval—either from a *flat*, non-hierarchical set or independently within each level of a hierarchical scheme. Conversely, *multi-label* annotation allows multiple concurrent labels, optionally weighted by relevance, and often benefits from *hierarchical* structures despite increased annotation effort. Finally, annotation typically uses *hard labels* (definitive label assignments, like "100% Step"), but can also employ *probabilistic labels* indicating likelihoods or *confidence-annotated labels* reflecting annotator certainty.

**Table 1.** Label categories taxonomy for HAR with example labels based on [15,30,35,43].

| Label Categories | Labels |
|---|---|
| Postures/Static Activities | sitting, standing, lying, squatting, kneeling |
| Gestures/Fine-motor Act. | waving, pointing, grasping, tapping, writing, raising hands |
| Human-to-Object Interaction | carrying, lifting, pushing, opening, packing, putting away, pouring, placing, throwing, folding, unscrewing |
| Activities of Daily Living (ADL) | brushing teeth, washing, eating, drinking, dressing, cooking, making beds, vacuum cleaning, ironing, folding laundry, house cleaning, watching TV, walking the dog, dishwashing |
| Sports | dance, gymnastics, acrobatics, martial arts, soccer, boxing, running, basketball, football, swimming, CrossFit |
| Health Events | fall, slip, trip, collapse, near-fall, stumble, loss of balance, freeze, hesitation, seizure, shivering, coughing, abnormal gait |
| Composite/High-Level Act. | cooking, office work, relaxing, cleanup, dance, yoga |
| Environmental/Procedural Context | location, process, picking order, coffee time, early morning |
| Behavior | smiling, crying, being angry, thinking |

**23. Label Dependencies:** Dependencies define valid and invalid combinations of labels. For instance, a subject cannot be labeled as both "Walking" and "Standing Still" simultaneously. Dependencies may exist not only within a single annotation level but also across multiple levels such as activity, location, and process. Encoding these dependencies in annotation tools improves consistency and reduces errors.

**24. Annotation Method:** Annotators and revisers must be recruited and trained; they may include *domain experts*, *trained internal staff*, *study subjects*, or *non-experts*.

Annotation method vary depending on how annotators are involved. In *single annotator labeling*, a recording is labeled by exactly one individual, which requires a subsequent revision to ensure label quality. *Multiple annotator labeling* involves two or more annotators labeling the same recording independently, allowing for assessment of consistency. In *consensus labeling*, two or more annotators jointly discuss each recording to agree on a unified label.

Annotation methods can be classified into *manual*, *fully automatic*, *semi-automatic*, *sensor fusion-based*, and *crowdsourced methods* [20]. Each has trade-offs between quality and efficiency. Manual methods ensure accuracy, while hybrid or automatic techniques offer scalability with reduced oversight.

**25. Annotation Tool:** Annotation tools facilitate the labeling process for the annotators. For example, to annotate a time-series motion capture data, the annotator would need to see the recorded motion data to understand the start and end of an activity. Furthermore, they may require additional support, such as RGB video data, to understand the scene or the objects being interacted with. Finally, the annotators may need a list of class labels or an interpretation of the annotation required for the dataset. Choosing the annotation tool, thus, is dependent on the visualization and annotation requirements of the annotator. Established tools such as ELAN, ANVIL, Signaligner Pro, NOVA, SAT-GDAD, SDAT-mSAR, Advene, WDK, MaD GUI, and SARA should be preferred when appropriate, although customization may be required.

**26. Annotation Guidelines:** Annotation guidelines ensure consistency and reduce subjectivity in the annotation process [20]. By having all annotators follow the same criteria, inter-rater reliability can be improved. Clear and thorough instructions also shorten onboarding time and minimize the need for clarification from new annotators. Additionally, well-documented guidelines enhance the reproducibility. They should include label definitions, tool instructions, and edge-case examples. Supplementing written materials with videos or annotated examples is highly recommended.

### 3.5 Data Processing Execution

After the recording of the data, it is exported and prepared for annotation and revision (Step 27 to 30). The final stage of the data processing procedure is the quality control of sensor data (Step 31) and labels (Step 32).

**27. Data Export and Verification:** Exporting data in widely supported formats (e.g., CSV, C3D) ensures long-term usability and compatibility. Proprietary formats that require niche tools should be avoided. Always verify that exported files are complete, accessible, and correctly formatted.

**28. Data Preparation:** Files should be named and organized consistently, e.g. by subject, session, scenario, etc. This is essential for efficient data handling. Proper file management supports reproducibility and reduces errors in analysis. The structure should align with the overall data collection protocol.

**29. Annotation:** In this step, annotation is performed according to the previously defined labels (Step 22), the selected annotation method (Step 24), the annotation tool (Step 25), and the annotation guidelines (Step 26). To ensure label quality, either standardized test annotations should be performed by all annotators or each recording should be annotated by at least two individuals (multiple annotator labeling). During annotation, responsibilities must be clearly assigned, and regular spot checks should be conducted. These can be automated (e.g., checking for label gaps) or manual (short reviews of recent labels). Large projects benefit from structured workflows and cloud-based collaboration.

**30. Revision:** Revision ensures annotation quality by verifying consistency, accuracy, and completeness, especially in single annotator labeling. Common methods include *manual revision*, *automated plausibility checks*, and *comparison of multiple annotations*. Automated plausibility checks typically include the detection of label gaps and implausible label sequences (e.g., a sitting posture immediately followed by pushing a picking cart). These checks can be performed both during annotation and as part of the final revision phase. They significantly improve annotation quality while requiring only minimal effort.

**31. Sensor Data Quality:** Sensor recordings should be reviewed for issues like dropouts, noise, or device failure. Erroneous segments may need to be corrected or excluded.

**32. Label Quality:** Label consistency should be assessed using metrics like Cohen's kappa, which accounts for agreement beyond chance. Performing consistency tests helps identify ambiguous labels or annotator-specific biases. This improves label reliability and model training outcomes.

### 3.6 Dataset Publication

In the final phase of the framework, the data, the existing code and the data description are published (see Steps 33 to 36).

**33. Data Publication:** Following FAIR [44] and FORCE11 [19] principles, datasets should be published via repositories with persistent identifiers (e.g., DOI) to ensure findability and long-term accessibility. All materials—sensor data, annotations, and documentation—must be provided in standardized, machine-readable formats, with clear licensing and metadata to support reuse [8].

**34. Data Structure Clarity:** A well-organized dataset with consistent file naming, clear folder hierarchies, and synchronized data streams greatly enhances

| Categories | Realization Options | |
|---|---|---|
| HAR Application Domains | healthcare / rehabilitation / nursing | exercise and athletic performance |
| | traffic and mobility | smart homes and AAL |
| | entertainment and gaming | behavioral research / psychology |
| | robotics/human-machine interaction | industry (production / logistics) |
| | security and surveillance | other |
| Recording Environments | controlled | semi-controlled |
| | real-world | |
| Scenarios | scripted | free-living |
| | hybrid | |
| Sensor Types | inertial sensors | visual sensors |
| | physiological/biosensors | acoustic sensors |
| | environmental sensors | positioning sensors |
| | tactile and force sensors | other |
| Label Categories | postures / static activities | locomotion |
| | gestures / fine-motor activities | human-to-object interaction |
| | activities of daily living (ADL) | sports |
| | composite / high-level activities | health events |
| | environmental / procedural context | behavior |
| Label Time Structure | frame-wise labeling | segment-wise labeling |
| | window-based labeling | |
| Exclusivity of the Labels | single-label | multi-label |
| Label Hierarchy | flat labels | hierarchical labels |
| Label Certainty / Uncertainty | hard labels | probabilistic labels |
| | confidence-annotated labels | |
| Automation Methods | manual | fully automatic |
| | semi-automatic | sensor fusion-based |
| | crowd-sourced | |
| Annotators | domain expert | trained internal annotator |
| | study subject | non-expert |
| Annotator Labeling | single annotator labeling | multiple annotator labeling |
| | consensus labeling | |
| Revision Methods | manual review by experts | automated plausibility checks |
| | comparison of multiple annotations | |

**Fig. 2.** Dataset taxonomy with HAR dataset DaRA highlighted in green as an example (AAL = Ambient Assisted Living). (Color figure online)

usability. Metadata on time, subjects, sensors, sensor placement, and activities should be included.

**35. Preprocessing Script Publication:** Preprocessing scripts should be provided to help users convert raw data into analysis-ready form. Scripts should cover steps like synchronization, segmentation, normalization, and handling missing values. Preprocessing scripts should be well documented and provide configuration files. 67.7% of surveyed users reported the need for preprocessing [5], highlighting the benefit of providing scripts. Furthermore, sample code for data access, visualization, and a basic model improves usability and helps users understand structure, synchronization, and handling of missing data. Information on effective augmentation strategies is also recommended.

**36. Data Description Publication:** Clear and structured dataset descriptions are key for transparency, interpretability, and reuse. Gebru et al. [21] propose datasheets to document context, content, and intended use. Poor metadata often hinders reuse [8]. Descriptions should be freely accessible in English (ideally with DOI) and include technical details on sensor setup, data collection methods, hardware, and software. For HAR datasets, provide information on subject demographics and physiology, label structure, annotation procedures and quality (including criteria, methods, agreement metrics), and sensor data quality. For the publication of the dataset description, we recommend classifying the dataset according to the taxonomy shown in Fig. 2, where an exemplary classification has been illustrated.

## 4 Checklist with Benchmark Datasets as Examples

The checklist (see Table 2) is derived from the 36 Steps of the framework. The primary objective of its development was to provide researchers with a tool to facilitate the creation of a dataset for HAR. Errors or omissions of significant criteria must be identified and precluded at an early stage in order to guarantee the highest possible quality of the resulting dataset.

In order to evaluate the completeness and practical applicability of the checklist, a retrospective evaluation of existing datasets was conducted on the basis of a self-assessment by their respective authors. In the context of an online survey, authors of datasets were presented with the information contained in the checklist and asked to apply it to classify the creation process of their dataset. It is important to note that more comprehensive information, such as that provided in Sect. 3, was not made available as part of the survey.

In total, the authors of eight benchmark datasets participated in the survey:

- HDM05 [28]: MoCap data covering locomotion, static postures, and sports.
- HDM12 Dance [6]: Argentine Tango sequences performed by 11 dance couples.
- HuGaDB [16]: Locomotion and posture activities for gait and activity analysis.
- UMAFall [14]: Daily activities and falls for fall detection research.

- LARa [34]: Packaging and picking activities labelled with classes and attributes.
- OpenPack [47]: Packaging data recorded via IMUs, RGB, and depth cameras.

**Table 2.** Checklist for dataset creation. Individual numbers are listed more than once, as several criteria should be taken into account for these steps of the framework (e.g., Step 11 has five criteria: $11_a$–$11_f$). In the last eight columns, datasets are evaluated retrospectively by their authors according to the criteria. Evaluation is conducted on a scale ranging from ○ not satisfied to ● fully satisfied.

| Checklist for each Step of the Dataset Creation Framework | | Datasets for Evaluation | | | | | | | |
|---|---|---|---|---|---|---|---|---|---|
| | | HDM05 2005 | HDM12 2012 | HuGaDB 2017 | UMAFall 2018 | LARa 2020 | OpenPack 2022 | CAARL 2022 | DaRA 2025 |
| **Dataset Creation Planning** | | | | | | | | | |
| 1 | Define the *benefit* and *purpose* of the dataset. | ● | ◕ | ● | ◕ | ● | ◕ | ● | ● |
| 2 | Specify the *scope* (length and amount) of the recording before starting. | ● | ◕ | ○ | ◕ | ◕ | ◕ | ● | ● |
| 3 | Determine the *recording environment*. | ● | ● | ● | ◕ | ● | ● | ● | ● |
| 4 | Define the *scenarios* clearly. | ● | ◑ | ● | ◕ | ◑ | ● | ◕ | ● |
| 5 | Select the *sensors* (type, number, positioning) to be used. | ● | ● | ● | ● | ● | ● | ● | ● |
| 6 | Prepare a *subject information sheet* about the study, recordings, and use of the data. | ○ | ● | ○ | ◕ | ◑ | ● | ● | ● |
| 7 | Prepare a *consent form* for subjects. | ○ | ● | ○ | ◕ | ◑ | ● | ● | ● |
| 8 | *Create a questionnaire* to collect personal data (e.g., age, weight) from the subjects. | ◔ | ● | ○ | ◕ | ◕ | ● | ◕ | ● |
| 9 | Obtain *ethical approval* for the planned study/recording. | ○ | ○ | ○ | ◕ | ○ | ● | ○ | ● |
| **Data Recording Preparation** | | | | | | | | | |
| $10_a$ | Acquire *enough subjects* to reflect demographic variability in the field. | ◔ | ◔ | ○ | ◑ | ● | ◕ | ◔ | ● |
| $10_b$ | Recruit *backup subjects* who are not part of the study team. | ○ | ○ | ○ | ○ | ○ | ◕ | ○ | ● |
| $10_c$ | Send *subject information sheet, questionnaire* and a *consent form* to all subjects. | ○ | ● | ○ | ◑ | ○ | ● | ● | ● |
| $11_a$ | Ensure *age distribution* matches the *target group*. | ◑ | ◕ | ○ | ◔ | ◕ | ◔ | ○ | ◕ |
| $11_b$ | Ensure *sex distribution* matches the *target group*. | ○ | ◕ | ◑ | ● | ◕ | ◔ | ◑ | ◕ |
| $11_c$ | Ensure *handedness* is balanced within the *target group*. | ○ | ◑ | ○ | ◑ | ● | ◑ | ○ | ◕ |
| $11_d$ | Ensure *occupational qualifications* reflect the *target group*. | ○ | ◑ | ○ | ◔ | ○ | ● | ○ | ◔ |
| $11_e$ | Ensure *activity-related experience* reflect the *target group*. | ◑ | ◕ | ◔ | ◔ | ◔ | ● | ○ | ◑ |
| $11_f$ | Ensure *body size* and *weight* are representative of the *target group*. | ◑ | ◕ | ◕ | ◑ | ● | ◕ | ◔ | ● |
| 12 | Create *protocols* for recording and documentation (e.g., assignment of subject IDs to sensor IDs, session start times, disturbances, sensor placements). | ● | ◕ | ○ | ◕ | ● | ● | ● | ● |
| 13 | Procure and test the *sensor systems*. | ◕ | ● | ● | ◕ | ● | ◕ | ● | ● |
| 14 | Set up the *recording environment*. | ● | ● | ● | ◕ | ● | ● | ● | ● |
| 15 | Perform *test recordings* to validate the recording pipeline before the main session. | ● | ◕ | ● | ◕ | ◑ | ◑ | ◕ | ● |
| **Data Recording Execution** | | | | | | | | | |
| 16 | Ensure all subjects have signed the *consent form* before the recording. | ○ | ● | ○ | ◑ | ○ | ● | ● | ● |
| $17_a$ | Fill in the *protocol* before, during and after data recording. | ● | ◕ | ○ | ◑ | ● | ● | ● | ● |
| $17_b$ | Ensure all subjects have completed the *questionnaire*. | ● | ● | ● | ◕ | ● | ● | ● | ● |
| 18 | Perform *calibration* to minimize measurement errors. | ● | ● | ● | ◑ | ● | ◑ | ● | ● |
| 19 | Ensure *synchronization* across all sensors for multi-sensor datasets. | ○ | ◑ | ● | ◕ | ● | ◑ | ● | ● |
| 20 | Conduct *trial runs* for all subjects. | ● | ◕ | ● | ◑ | ◕ | ◕ | ● | ● |
| $21_a$ | *Minimize interventions* by the study team to allow subjects to behave naturally. | ◔ | ◕ | ● | ◕ | ◕ | ◑ | ◕ | ● |
| $21_b$ | Regularly *check* if all *sensors* are recording correctly during and between sessions. | ● | ● | ● | ◕ | ◕ | ◑ | ◕ | ● |
| **Data Processing Preparation** | | | | | | | | | |
| 22 | Clearly define the *label categories/labels*. | ● | ◑ | ● | ● | ● | ● | ● | ● |
| 23 | Specify *dependencies* between label categories. | ◑ | ◑ | ● | ● | ◕ | ◕ | ◕ | ● |
| $24_a$ | *Recruit annotators* and revisers. | ◔ | ○ | ◑ | ○ | ● | ● | ● | ● |
| $24_b$ | *Onboard annotators* and revisers. | ◔ | ◔ | ◑ | ○ | ● | ● | ● | ● |
| 25 | Select and test the *annotation tool*. | ◕ | ◑ | ● | ◕ | ● | ● | ● | ● |
| 26 | Create clear *annotation guidelines*. | ◑ | ◑ | ● | ◑ | ● | ◑ | ● | ● |
| **Data Processing Execution** | | | | | | | | | |
| 27 | Process, format, and visually verify the *sensor data*. | ● | ● | ● | ● | ● | ◕ | ● | ● |
| $28_a$ | *Synchronize* all *sensor data*. | ● | ◑ | ● | ● | ● | ◕ | ● | ● |
| $28_b$ | *Name the sensor data* based on subject, session, scenario, and/or recording number. | ● | ● | ● | ● | ● | ◕ | ● | ● |
| $29_a$ | Conduct *test annotations* with annotators and revisers to verify label quality. | ◕ | ● | ◑ | ◑ | ● | ● | ● | ● |
| $29_b$ | Perform regular *label spot checks of each annotator's work* during recording. | ◕ | ◔ | ● | ◑ | ○ | ○ | ○ | ◔ |
| $29_c$ | Ensure *complete annotation* of the sensor data. | ● | ◕ | ● | ● | ◕ | ◑ | ● | ● |
| 30 | *Revise all annotations* from few experts. | ◕ | ◔ | ◑ | ○ | ◑ | ○ | ◑ | ◕ |
| $31_a$ | *Correct errors* (asynchronous data, missing data) in the dataset. | ● | ◔ | ○ | ● | ◑ | ◕ | ◑ | ◕ |
| $31_b$ | *Correct imbalances* (label imbalance) in the dataset. | ◑ | ○ | ○ | ◑ | ◑ | ○ | ○ | ○ |
| $31_c$ | Perform *quality control* on the *sensor data*. | ● | ○ | ○ | ◑ | ● | ◑ | ● | ● |
| 32 | Ensure final *label quality* is sufficient. | ● | ○ | ○ | ◑ | ◕ | ◕ | ◕ | ● |

*(continued)*

**Table 2.** (*continued*)

| | | | | | | | | | |
|---|---|---|---|---|---|---|---|---|---|
| **Dataset Publication** | | | | | | | | | |
| $33_a$ | Publish the **data** in a *repository* with a globally unique and persistent *identifier*. | ◕ | ◑ | ● | ● | ● | ● | ● | ● |
| $33_b$ | Ensure that the data is *open* and *accessible free* of charge. | ● | ● | ● | ● | ● | ● | ● | ● |
| $33_c$ | Provide *sensor data* and *labels* in a formal, accessible, and *widely usable format*. | ● | ◕ | ● | ● | ◕ | ● | ◕ | ● |
| $33_d$ | Ensure all *data designations, labels* and *Meta-informations* are *in English*. | ● | ● | ● | ● | ● | ● | ● | ● |
| $33_e$ | Specify the data with a clear and accessible usage *license*. | ◔ | ◑ | ● | ◕ | ● | ● | ● | ● |
| $33_f$ | Link the data to its *provenance information* (country, city). | ◑ | ○ | ● | ● | ● | ○ | ● | ● |
| $33_g$ | Include *references* to data description, the framework under which the dataset was created. | ◑ | ◑ | ● | ● | ● | ◕ | ● | ● |
| $33_h$ | *Register* or *index the data* in a searchable resource. | ◑ | ○ | ○ | ● | ● | ○ | ● | ● |
| $34_a$ | Ensure *sensor data* is *synchronized* if possible. | ● | ◑ | ● | ◕ | ○ | ◕ | ○ | ● |
| $34_b$ | Ensure all *sensor data* is *labeled*. | ● | ◑ | ● | ● | ● | ◑ | ● | ● |
| $34_c$ | Include a *code example* that demonstrates *how to access the data*. | ● | ◕ | ● | ◑ | ● | ● | ● | ● |
| $34_d$ | Ensure that the *annotation tool* is available in a *repository*. | ◑ | ◔ | ○ | ◑ | ● | ○ | ● | ● |
| 35 | Publish the *preprocessing code*. | ◑ | ◔ | ○ | ○ | ○ | ● | ○ | ● |
| $36_a$ | Publish a **description of the data** in English. | ● | ● | ● | ● | ● | ● | ● | ● |
| $36_b$ | Publish a description of the data in the repository itself. | ● | ● | ● | ● | ● | ● | ● | ● |
| $36_c$ | Publish a description of the data in an open-access publication with a persistent *identifier*. | ◕ | ○ | ● | ● | ● | ● | ● | ● |
| $36_d$ | Ensure that the description of the data is *open* and *accessible free* of charge. | ● | ● | ● | ● | ● | ● | ● | ● |
| $36_e$ | Provide a description of the *sensor setup*. | ● | ● | ● | ● | ◑ | ● | ◕ | ● |
| $36_f$ | Describe the *data recording pipeline*. | ◑ | ◕ | ● | ● | ● | ● | ● | ● |
| $36_g$ | Describe the *subject characteristics* (e.g., age, qualifications, body size). | ◑ | ◑ | ● | ● | ● | ● | ● | ● |
| $36_h$ | Describe the *annotated* and *revised labels* in detail. | ◕ | ◕ | ● | ● | ● | ◑ | ● | ● |
| $36_i$ | Document the *annotation* and *revision process*. | ◑ | ◕ | ● | ◑ | ◔ | ◑ | ◔ | ● |
| $36_j$ | Document the *annotation* and *revision results*. | ◑ | ◕ | ● | ◑ | ● | ◑ | ● | ● |
| $36_k$ | Describe the *quality* of *final labels*. | ◕ | ◔ | ● | ● | ○ | ○ | ○ | ● |
| $36_l$ | Describe the *quality* of the *sensor data*. | ◕ | ◔ | ● | ● | ○ | ● | ○ | ● |
| $36_m$ | Include the *data identifier in its description*. | ● | ○ | ● | ● | ● | ○ | ● | ● |

- CAARL [33]: Motion and positions of subjects and objects in intralogistics.
- DaRA: Human movement and context in intralogistics, annotated on 13 levels.

The results reveal a heterogeneous implementation of the recommended steps. While there are notable similarities in dataset preparation and data acquisition phases, the analysis indicates that, despite increasing maturity in the HAR field, a consistently standardized procedure for dataset creation is still lacking. Notable gaps exist particularly in the "Preparing Data Recording" and in "Performing Data Processing" such as annotation and revision. Deficiencies in documentation further limit transparency and reproducibility, emphasizing the need for clearly defined guidelines for HAR dataset development and revision.

Despite this heterogeneity, the analysis shows that all criteria included in the developed checklist are generally addressed or regarded as relevant. This supports the checklist's practical applicability as a structured framework for systematic HAR dataset creation. Especially for researchers new to the field, the checklist offers guidance across the full development pipeline, from planning to publication. However, it also became evident that condensing individual steps into single-sentence descriptions can lead to varying interpretations. It is therefore advisable to consult the detailed descriptions provided in Sect. 3 when applying the checklist in practice. Accordingly, the tabular assessment of existing datasets serves less as a comparative quality benchmark and more as a means of evaluating and validating the checklist itself. The findings suggest that the checklist is a useful reference tool for promoting standardization and transparency in HAR dataset creation.

The applicability of the checklist may be limited in use cases involving synthetically generated data, such as through simulation, motion capture re-synthesis, or AI-based methods. In these cases, steps like preparing and performing data recording are not relevant. Instead, aspects such as model validation and alignment with real recording data become central, yet are not covered by the checklist.

## 5 Dataset Creation in the Industry

In industrial applications, machine learning models are expected to perform consistently, reliably, and able to predict the exact same results. This assumption relies on the availability of high-quality data. However, the costs associated with manual annotation—such as the need for thorough review, re-annotation, and consistency checks—pose significant challenges. Consequently, in HAR applications, these processes are often minimized or skipped altogether.

Using MotionMiners GmbH as an example—whose work centers on HAR in logistics—dataset creation is largely client-driven. As shown in Fig. 1, new scenarios typically follow these steps:

- **Dataset Creation Planning:** This stage is highly pragmatic, with the dataset purpose and recording scope directly derived from the client's industrial problem. For instance, MotionMiners adapts its HAR models to meet specific client needs within warehouse environments.
- **Data Recording Preparation:** Recording sessions are arranged with the client, during which one or two workers are filmed for approximately one hour while performing their tasks. Ethical considerations, such as the visibility of faces or the presence of uninvolved individuals, are carefully addressed.
- **Data Recording Execution:** Calibration recordings are conducted, typically spanning around one hour with one or two workers, capturing IMU and Bluetooth Low Energy data streams.
- **Data Processing Preparation and Execution:** MotionMiners ensures high-quality data from a hardware perspective by guaranteeing synchronization of all sensors during recording, storing data locally on the sensors until transmission, and providing multiple sensor sets to bypass malfunctioning units. However, these steps are costly and are passed on to clients, which may not be feasible for low-cost or research-focused projects. Video data is annotated by an in-house expert without external supervision. This annotated dataset serves as a reference to evaluate the performance of the current HAR model in the new scenario. If the model's performance is insufficient, the new data is integrated into the training set. However, for generating annotated data in no time, there is no possibility for revision; nor consistency evaluation.
- **Dataset Publication:** Due to contractual obligations, privacy concerns, and company policies, the datasets are not published or shared externally. All data remains proprietary to MotionMiners, ensuring compliance with privacy legislation and safeguarding sensitive information.

Minimizing the effort required for model adaptation and data collection is crucial for developing deployable models that can be tailored to diverse client-specific scenarios. However, ensuring high-quality data remains essential for effective model adaptation. The steps outlined in Fig. 1 cannot be bypassed, as they involve substantial effort in data creation—particularly in terms of costly recordings and time-consuming annotation processes.

## 6 Discussion and Conclusions

This work developed a framework for the structured creation of HAR datasets, based on consistent taxonomies and best practices from the HAR community. The main outcome is a checklist that serves as a practical tool to enhance the quality and standardization of dataset creation.

We surveyed publicly available datasets using a checklist that covers each step of the dataset creation framework. The retrospective application to eight benchmark datasets confirmed the checklist's applicability and relevance, but also revealed limitations, particularly in addressing synthetically generated motion data. Furthermore, it became evident that many existing datasets suffer from insufficient documentation, hindering reproducibility. These findings highlight the need for continuous refinement to better accommodate future developments and the diverse requirements of different application domains.

Additionally, we examined an industry case from a company that develops and employs HAR models to analyze manual processes, focusing on their data creation practices. In general, most of the proposed steps are bypassed, with an emphasis instead on the rapid generation of datasets to meet client demands—often at the expense of cost efficiency or model quality.

We recommend the widespread adoption and iterative enhancement of the checklist within the HAR community. Additionally, we advocate for the establishment of a culture that not only promotes best practices but also systematically documents common mistakes. Such a collection could serve as a valuable resource for researchers creating new datasets and sustainably improve the quality and comparability of HAR research.

**Acknowledgments.** This study was funded by Federal Ministry for Economic Affairs and Climate Action (grant numbers KK5072230MA3, KK5110002MA3, KK5526202MA3) and the Federal Ministry of Research, Technology and Space of Germany and the state of North Rhine-Westphalia as part of the Lamarr Institute for Machine Learning and Artificial Intelligence.

**Disclosure of Interests.** The authors have no competing interests to declare that are relevant to the content of this article.

## References


1. ICH Harmonised Guideline: Integrated Addendum to ICH E6(R1): Guideline for Good Clinical Practice E6(R2). Report E6(R2), International Council for Harmonisation of Technical Requirements for Pharmaceuticals for Human Use (ICH), Geneva (2016). https://database.ich.org/sites/default/files/E6_R2_Addendum.pdf
2. Enhanced Collaborative Model (ECM) Anti-Human Trafficking Task Force Protocol Development Checklists, July 2020. https://www.theiacp.org/resources/document/enhanced-collaborative-model-ecm-anti-human-trafficking-task-force-protocol
3. Aguileta, A.A., Brena, R.F., Mayora, O., Molino-Minero-Re, E., Trejo, L.A.: Multi-sensor fusion for activity recognition—a survey. Sensors **19**(17), 3808 (2019). https://doi.org/10.3390/s19173808. https://www.mdpi.com/1424-8220/19/17/3808
4. Ahad, M.A.R., Antar, A.D., Ahmed, M.: IoT Sensor-Based Activity Recognition. ISRL, vol. 173. Springer, Cham (2021). https://doi.org/10.1007/978-3-030-51379-5
5. Alam, G., McChesney, I., Nicholl, P., Rafferty, J.: Open datasets in human activity recognition research—issues and challenges: a review. IEEE Sens. J. **23**(22), 26952–26980 (2023). https://doi.org/10.1109/JSEN.2023.3317645. https://ieeexplore.ieee.org/document/10272298/
6. Vögele, A., Krüger, B.: HDM12 dance - documentation on a data base of tango motion capture. techreport CG-2016-1, University of Bonn, Bonn (2016)
7. Arain, M., Campbell, M.J., Cooper, C.L., Lancaster, G.A.: What is a pilot or feasibility study? A review of current practice and editorial policy. BMC Med. Res. Methodol. **10**(1), 67 (2010). https://doi.org/10.1186/1471-2288-10-67. https://bmcmedresmethodol.biomedcentral.com/articles/10.1186/1471-2288-10-67
8. Arshad, M.H., Bilal, M., Gani, A.: Human activity recognition: review, taxonomy and open challenges. Sensors **22**(17), 6463 (2022). https://doi.org/10.3390/s22176463. https://www.mdpi.com/1424-8220/22/17/6463
9. Behnke, M., Saganowski, S., Kunc, D., Kazienko, P.: Ethical considerations and checklist for affective research with wearables. IEEE Trans. Affect. Comput. **15**(1), 50–62 (2024). https://doi.org/10.1109/TAFFC.2022.3222524. https://ieeexplore.ieee.org/document/9953318/
10. Bello, H., Geißler, D., Suh, S., Zhou, B., Lukowicz, P.: TSAK: two-stage semantic-aware knowledge distillation for efficient wearable modality and model optimization in manufacturing lines. In: Antonacopoulos, A., Chaudhuri, S., Chellappa, R., Liu, C.L., Bhattacharya, S., Pal, U. (eds.) Pattern Recognition. LNCS, vol. 15325, pp. 201–216. Springer, Cham (2025). https://doi.org/10.1007/978-3-031-78389-0_14. https://link.springer.com/10.1007/978-3-031-78389-0_14
11. Benmessabih, T., Slama, R., Havard, V., Baudry, D.: Online human motion analysis in industrial context: a review. Eng. Appl. Artif. Intell. **131**, 107850 (2024). https://doi.org/10.1016/j.engappai.2024.107850. https://linkinghub.elsevier.com/retrieve/pii/S0952197624000083
12. Bhola, G., Vishwakarma, D.K.: A review of vision-based indoor HAR: state-of-the-art, challenges, and future prospects. Multimedia Tools Appl. **83**(1), 1965–2005 (2024). https://doi.org/10.1007/s11042-023-15443-5. https://link.springer.com/10.1007/s11042-023-15443-5
13. Bock, M., Hoelzemann, A., Moeller, M., Laerhoven, K.V.: Tutorial on deep learning for human activity recognition (2021). https://doi.org/10.48550/arXiv.2110.06663. http://arxiv.org/abs/2110.06663. arXiv:2110.06663 [cs]

14. Casilari, E., Santoyo-Ramón, J.A., Cano-García, J.M.: UMAFall: a multisensor dataset for the research on automatic fall detection. Procedia Comput. Sci. **110**, 32–39 (2017). https://doi.org/10.1016/j.procs.2017.06.110. https://linkinghub.elsevier.com/retrieve/pii/S1877050917312899
15. Chatterjee, S.: The review of human activity recognition survey, September 2023. https://doi.org/10.20944/preprints202309.1939.v1. https://www.preprints.org/manuscript/202309.1939/v1
16. Chereshnev, R., Kertész-Farkas, A.: HuGaDB: human gait database for activity recognition from wearable inertial sensor networks. In: van der Aalst, W.M.P., et al. (eds.) AIST 2017. LNCS, vol. 10716, pp. 131–141. Springer, Cham (2018). https://doi.org/10.1007/978-3-319-73013-4_12
17. Council for International Organizations of Medical Sciences (CIOMS): International Ethical Guidelines for Health-related Research involving Humans. Technical report, Council for International Organizations of Medical Sciences (CIOMS) (2016). https://doi.org/10.56759/rgxl7405. https://cioms.ch/publications/product/international-ethical-guidelines-for-health-related-research-involving-humans/
18. Damen, D., et al.: Rescaling egocentric vision: collection, pipeline and challenges for EPIC-KITCHENS-100. Int. J. Comput. Vis. **130**(1), 33–55 (2022). https://doi.org/10.1007/s11263-021-01531-2. https://link.springer.com/10.1007/s11263-021-01531-2
19. Data Citation Synthesis Group, Martone, M.: Joint declaration of data citation principles. Technical report, Force11 (2014). https://doi.org/10.25490/A97F-EGYK. https://www.force11.org/group/joint-declaration-data-citation-principles-final
20. Demrozi, F., Turetta, C., Machot, F.A., Pravadelli, G., Kindt, P.H.: A comprehensive review of automated data annotation techniques in human activity recognition (2023). https://doi.org/10.48550/ARXIV.2307.05988. https://arxiv.org/abs/2307.05988. Version Number: 1
21. Gebru, T., et al.: Datasheets for datasets. Commun. ACM **64**(12), 86–92 (2021). https://doi.org/10.1145/3458723. https://dl.acm.org/doi/10.1145/3458723
22. Hossen, M.A., Abas, P.E.: Machine learning for human activity recognition: state-of-the-art techniques and emerging trends. J. Imaging **11**(3), 91 (2025). https://doi.org/10.3390/jimaging11030091. https://www.mdpi.com/2313-433X/11/3/91
23. Huang, Y., Zhou, Y., Zhao, H., Riedel, T., Beigl, M.: A survey on wearable human activity recognition: innovative pipeline development for enhanced research and practice (2024). https://doi.org/10.5445/IR/1000169626. https://publikationen.bibliothek.kit.edu/1000169626. Medium: PDF Publisher: Institute of Electrical and Electronics Engineers (IEEE)
24. Kaur, H., Rani, V., Kumar, M.: Human activity recognition: a comprehensive review. Exp. Syst. **41**(11), e13680 (2024). https://doi.org/10.1111/exsy.13680. https://onlinelibrary.wiley.com/doi/10.1111/exsy.13680
25. Kumar, P., Chauhan, S., Awasthi, L.K.: Human activity recognition (HAR) using deep learning: review, methodologies, progress and future research directions. Arch. Comput. Methods Eng. **31**(1), 179–219 (2024). https://doi.org/10.1007/s11831-023-09986-x. https://link.springer.com/10.1007/s11831-023-09986-x
26. Leon, A.C., Davis, L.L., Kraemer, H.C.: The role and interpretation of pilot studies in clinical research. J. Psychiatr. Res. **45**(5), 626–629 (2011). https://doi.org/10.1016/j.jpsychires.2010.10.008. https://linkinghub.elsevier.com/retrieve/pii/S002239561000292X

27. Maurice, P., et al.: AndyData-lab-onePerson, June 2019. https://doi.org/10.5281/ZENODO.3254403. https://zenodo.org/record/3254403
28. Meinard Müller, T.R., Clausen, M., Eberhardt, B., Krüger, B., Weber, A.: Documentation mocap database HDM05. Technical report. CG-2007-2, Institut für Informatik II, Universität Bonn, Germany (2007)
29. Mennella, C., Esposito, M., De Pietro, G., Maniscalco, U.: Promoting fairness in activity recognition algorithms for patient's monitoring and evaluation systems in healthcare. Comput. Biol. Med. **179**, 108826 (2024). https://doi.org/10.1016/j.compbiomed.2024.108826. https://linkinghub.elsevier.com/retrieve/pii/S0010482524009119
30. Morshed, M.G., Sultana, T., Alam, A., Lee, Y.K.: Human action recognition: a taxonomy-based survey, updates, and opportunities. Sensors **23**(4), 2182 (2023). https://doi.org/10.3390/s23042182. https://www.mdpi.com/1424-8220/23/4/2182
31. Nair, N.R., Schmid, L., Reining, C., Moya Rueda, F., Pauly, M., Fink, G.A.: Representation biases in time-series human activity recognition with small sample sizes. In: Antonacopoulos, A., Chaudhuri, S., Chellappa, R., Liu, C.L., Bhattacharya, S., Pal, U. (eds.) Pattern Recognition. LNCS, vol. 15315, pp. 33–48. Springer, Cham (2025). https://doi.org/10.1007/978-3-031-78354-8_3. https://link.springer.com/10.1007/978-3-031-78354-8_3
32. Napoli, O., et al.: A benchmark for domain adaptation and generalization in smartphone-based human activity recognition. Sci. Data **11**(1), 1192 (2024). https://doi.org/10.1038/s41597-024-03951-4. https://www.nature.com/articles/s41597-024-03951-4
33. Niemann, F., Lüdtke, S., Bartelt, C., Ten Hompel, M.: Context-aware human activity recognition in industrial processes. Sensors **22**(1), 134 (2021). https://doi.org/10.3390/s22010134. https://www.mdpi.com/1424-8220/22/1/134
34. Niemann, F., et al.: LARa: creating a dataset for human activity recognition in logistics using semantic attributes. Sensors **20**(15), 4083 (2020). https://doi.org/10.3390/s20154083. https://www.mdpi.com/1424-8220/20/15/4083
35. Oleh, U., Obermaisser, R., Ahammed, A.S.: A review of recent techniques for human activity recognition: multimodality, reinforcement learning, and language models. Algorithms **17**(10), 434 (2024). https://doi.org/10.3390/a17100434. https://www.mdpi.com/1999-4893/17/10/434
36. Orr, W., Crawford, K.: Building better datasets: seven recommendations for responsible design from dataset creators, August 2024. https://doi.org/10.48550/arXiv.2409.00252. http://arxiv.org/abs/2409.00252. arXiv:2409.00252 [cs]
37. Reining, C., Nair, N.R., Niemann, F., Rueda, F.M., Fink, G.A.: A tutorial on dataset creation for sensor-based human activity recognition. In: 2023 IEEE International Conference on Pervasive Computing and Communications Workshops and other Affiliated Events (PerCom Workshops), pp. 453–459. IEEE, Atlanta, GA, USA, March 2023. https://doi.org/10.1109/PerComWorkshops56833.2023.10150401. https://ieeexplore.ieee.org/document/10150401/
38. Reiss, A., Stricker, D.: Introducing a new benchmarked dataset for activity monitoring. In: 2012 16th International Symposium on Wearable Computers, pp. 108–109. IEEE, Newcastle, United Kingdom, June 2012. https://doi.org/10.1109/ISWC.2012.13. http://ieeexplore.ieee.org/document/6246152/
39. Sambasivan, N., Kapania, S., Highfill, H., Akrong, D., Paritosh, P., Aroyo, L.M.: "Everyone wants to do the model work, not the data work": data cascades in high-stakes AI. In: Proceedings of the 2021 CHI Conference on Human Factors in

Computing Systems, pp. 1–15. ACM, Yokohama, Japan, May 2021. https://doi.org/10.1145/3411764.3445518. https://dl.acm.org/doi/10.1145/3411764.3445518

40. Sedaghati, N., Ardebili, S., Ghaffari, A.: Application of human activity/action recognition: a review. Multimedia Tools Appl. (2025). https://doi.org/10.1007/s11042-024-20576-2. https://link.springer.com/10.1007/s11042-024-20576-2
41. Sigal, L., Balan, A.O., Black, M.J.: HumanEva: synchronized video and motion capture dataset and baseline algorithm for evaluation of articulated human motion. Int. J. Comput. Vis. **87**(1-2), 4–27 (2010). https://doi.org/10.1007/s11263-009-0273-6. http://link.springer.com/10.1007/s11263-009-0273-6
42. Thukral, M., Haresamudram, H., Plötz, T.: Cross-domain HAR: few-shot transfer learning for human activity recognition. ACM Trans. Intell. Syst. Technol. **16**(1), 1–35 (2025). https://doi.org/10.1145/3704921. https://dl.acm.org/doi/10.1145/3704921
43. Vrigkas, M., Nikou, C., Kakadiaris, I.A.: A review of human activity recognition methods. Frontiers Rob. AI **2** (2015). https://doi.org/10.3389/frobt.2015.00028. http://journal.frontiersin.org/Article/10.3389/frobt.2015.00028/abstract
44. Wilkinson, M.D., Dumontier, M., Aalbersberg, I.J.: The FAIR guiding principles for scientific data management and stewardship. Sci. Data **3**(1), 160018 (2016). https://doi.org/10.1038/sdata.2016.18. https://www.nature.com/articles/sdata201618
45. World Medical Association (WMA): Declaration of Helsinki: Ethical Principles for Medical Research Involving Human Subjects. Technical report, World Medical Association (WMA), Fortaleza, Brazil (2013). https://www.wma.net/policies-post/wma-declaration-of-helsinki-ethical-principles-for-medical-research-involving-human-subjects/
46. Wu, Z., Ding, Y., Wan, L., Li, T., Nian, F.: Local and global self-attention enhanced graph convolutional network for skeleton-based action recognition. Pattern Recogn. **159**, 111106 (2025). https://doi.org/10.1016/j.patcog.2024.111106. https://linkinghub.elsevier.com/retrieve/pii/S0031320324008574
47. Yoshimura, N., Morales, J., Maekawa, T., Hara, T.: OpenPack: a large-scale dataset for recognizing packaging works in IoT-enabled logistic environments. In: 2024 IEEE International Conference on Pervasive Computing and Communications (PerCom), pp. 90–97. IEEE, Biarritz, France, March 2024. https://doi.org/10.1109/PerCom59722.2024.10494448. https://ieeexplore.ieee.org/document/10494448/
48. Zhang, S., et al.: Deep learning in human activity recognition with wearable sensors: a review on advances. Sensors **22**(4), 1476 (2022). https://doi.org/10.3390/s22041476. https://www.mdpi.com/1424-8220/22/4/1476

# Towards Practical, Best Practice Video Annotation to Support Human Activity Recognition

Hoan Tran(✉), Veronika Potter, Umberto Mazzucchelli, Dinesh John, and Stephen Intille

Northeastern University, Boston, MA 02115, USA
{tran.hoan1,potter.v,mazzucchelli.u,s.intille}@northeastern.edu, dineshjohn@yahoo.com

**Abstract.** Researchers need ground-truth activity annotations to train and evaluate wearable-sensor-based activity recognition models. Oftentimes, researchers establish ground truth by annotating the video recorded while someone engages in activity wearing sensors. The "gold-standard" video annotation practice requires two trained annotators independently annotating the same footage with a third domain expert resolving disagreements. Such annotation is laborious, and so widely-used datasets have often been annotated using only a single annotator per video. Because the research community is moving towards collecting data of more complex behaviors from free-living people 24/7 and annotating more granular, fleeting activities, the annotation task grows even more challenging; the single-annotator approach may yield inaccuracies. We investigated a "silver-standard" approach: rather than using two independent annotation passes, a second annotator *revises* the work of the first annotator. The proposed approach reduced the total annotation time by 33% compared to the gold-standard approach, with near-equivalent annotation quality. The silver-standard label was in higher agreement with the gold-standard label than the single-annotator label, with Cohen's $\kappa$ of 0.77 and 0.68 respectively on a 16.4 h video. The silver-standard labels also had higher inter-rater reliability than the single-annotator labels, with the respective mean Cohen's $\kappa$ across six videos (92 h of total footage) of 0.79 and 0.68.

**Keywords:** Video · Annotation · Taxonomy · Human Activity Recognition

## 1 Motivation

Accurate measurement of physical activity and other everyday behavior supports research in many fields. An "objective" and non-burdensome approach is to use wearable motion sensors such as accelerometers to continuously measure behaviors [13]. This approach has been used to measure sedentary and physical activity behaviors in national health surveillance studies [5,13], and research


E. L. Tonkin et al. (Eds.): ARDUOUS 2025, CCIS 2706, pp. 94–118, 2026.
https://doi.org/10.1007/978-3-032-09117-8_6

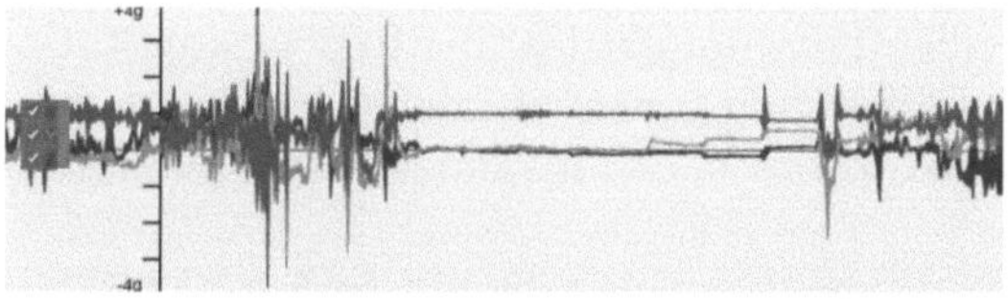

(a) A (about 2 min) snippet of CAPTURE-24 data [4], where the ground-truth label is *walking* [16].

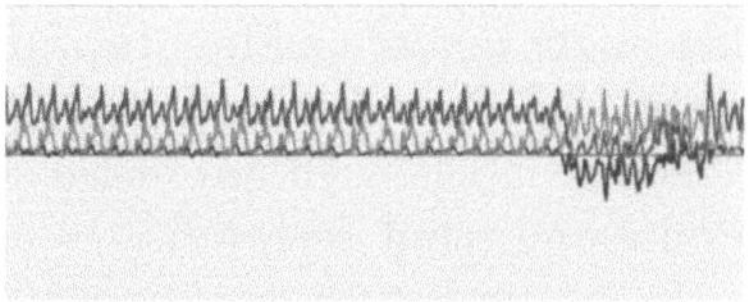

(b) A (about 1 min) snippet of *walking* activity in our to-be-released dataset.

**Fig. 1.** Examples of wrist-worn accelerometer signals from two different free-living datasets with the same *walking* label, but the actual accelerometer signals differ. Non-movement (flat-line) in Fig. 1a suggests *non-walking*, meaning the provided ground-truth may be inaccurate.

is ongoing in the field of human activity recognition (HAR) to develop models that can detect not only activity levels, but also specific types of activities with high fidelity. To do so, researchers must train and validate machine learning models with annotated activity datasets with wearable sensors where accurate ground-truth labels of physical activity have been obtained. Annotation of video where people are filmed performing activities of interest is considered the best approach to establish such reliable labels [7]. Studies to date have been mostly limited to small amounts of annotated data with simple activity taxonomies (i.e., a small set of possible labels for activities). Scaling up algorithm training and validation to improve algorithm performance, however, will require labeling larger amounts of video data (using more complex activity taxonomies) as people engage in unconstrained, free-living activity. This is an arduous task.

When labeling video for research, the "gold-standard" approach is to have two trained annotators independently label each video segment, and then to have a third trained domain expert resolve disagreements [17,18]. While manageable for a few hours of video, this approach does not scale to larger annotation tasks required for training and evaluating robust machine learning models. In practice, for HAR datasets, often only one trained annotator labels each video segment [17]. An alternative method that researchers have explored to control cost and increase speed is crowd-sourced annotation [2], but video footage obtained from free-living volunteers in research studies is often private and thus not suitable for crowd-sourcing.

Not only are researchers interested in compiling datasets of free-living activity from larger cohorts for longer periods of time, they also desire richer activity taxonomies to be labeled to develop and evaluate future state-of-the-art algorithms for detecting novel activities. When labeling video footage acquired from the laboratory, annotators are likely aware of the entire small set of possible activities and the timing of all activities performed in the video. Additionally, lab-controlled data collection allows for a dedicated assistant to film the entire data collection session from a third-person perspective. In contrast, labeling activity of people in unconstrained free-living settings will generally require a larger activity taxonomy and labeling video acquired from a front-facing camera that might not adequately capture all activity details, leading to poor annotation quality [1]. Poor-quality annotations, including incorrect labels (Fig. 1), missing labels, or labels with imprecise start/stop times, can invalidate HAR evaluation results and stunt research.

In our own work, we are confronting the daunting task of labeling 22,000 h of free-living behavior from front-facing video at the second-by-second level using an activity/posture taxonomy including 49 unique activity types and 13 different postures. Motivated by this task, we investigated the merits of the gold-standard annotation approach, single-annotator approach, and the proposed "silver-standard approach" that could be used to reduce labor and related costs relative to the gold standard method and improve annotation over a single annotator. Based on our annotation experiments described in the remainder of this paper and our ongoing efforts to label our large dataset, we demonstrate the proposed silver-standard protocol can:

- Reduce the person-hours required for annotation by 33% compared to the gold-standard approach and can further eliminate the need for a trained expert to review.
- Improve the agreement rate (from the single-annotator approach) against the gold-standard approach from Cohen's $\kappa$ of 0.68 to 0.77.
- Result in more reliable annotations (compared to the commonly used single-annotator approach), improving Cohen's $\kappa$ from 0.68 (for single-annotator annotations) to 0.79 (for silver-standard annotations).

**Table 1.** Summary of annotation details described in a sample of existing HAR datasets where researchers mentioned using video or image annotation to obtain ground truth. Some researchers did not discuss components of their annotation approaches in detail (marked ✗), which include training annotators (Training), computing post-training inter-rater reliability (Reliability), and describing a post-annotation quality-control protocol (QC).

| Dataset | Setting | Footage | Annotators | Training | Reliability | QC |
|---|---|---|---|---|---|---|
| CAPTURE-24 [4] | FL | 2,562 hrs | A | ✓ | ✗ | ✗ |
| HARTH [9] | FL | 37 hrs | A | ✗ | ✓ | ✓ |
| Opportunity [3] | Lab | 5.3 hrs | A | ✓ | ✗ | ✓ |
| SPHERE [14] | Lab | ✗ | A | ✗ | ✗ | ✗ |
| Clemson [10] | Lab | 15 hrs | A | ✗ | ✗ | ✗ |
| OxWalk [11] | FL | 39 hrs | E | – | ✗ | ✓ |
| Hang-Time [6] | FL | 38 hrs | A | ✗ | ✗ | ✗ |

A: Trained annotators; E: Domain experts; FL: Free-living collection; Lab: Lab collection

## 2 Video Annotation for Human Activity Recognition

Researchers annotating datasets have often relied on a single-annotator approach [17]. We searched on Google Scholar using combinations of these keywords to identify publicly available HAR datasets: "datasets," "human activity recognition," and "wearable sensors." We reviewed the relevant references to identify related citations for publicly available datasets. Studies where the data are not available publicly for download were excluded. We identified only seven datasets, summarized in Table 1, where the researchers explicitly mentioned using video or image data to obtain ground-truth annotations. Ideally, reports on datasets would include descriptions that allow assessment of annotation quality, specifically information on training protocol, annotation protocol, inter-rater reliability, and quality-control procedures. In practice, HAR researchers often omit such information required to understand the provenance of the datasets they have released.

In the sample of relevant datasets we analyzed, only one dataset was annotated by trained domain experts and had an explicit quality control protocol; the two primary researchers in the OxWalk study [11] independently annotated the same 39 h of footage, but the paper does not include details on how disagreements were resolved. Other researchers have employed trained annotators, but researchers for only two such studies (CAPTURE-24 [4] and Opportunity [3]) mentioned their annotation training protocols. For example, the Opportunity study researchers organized sessions among annotators to discuss annotation edge cases in order to obtain reliable and consistent annotations. The CAPTURE-24 research team ensured that annotators were highly in agreement with an expert on example footage prior to annotating new data. Neither team reported post-training annotator reliability. Only one of the seven identified datasets includes data on post-training annotator reliability [9]. This sample of

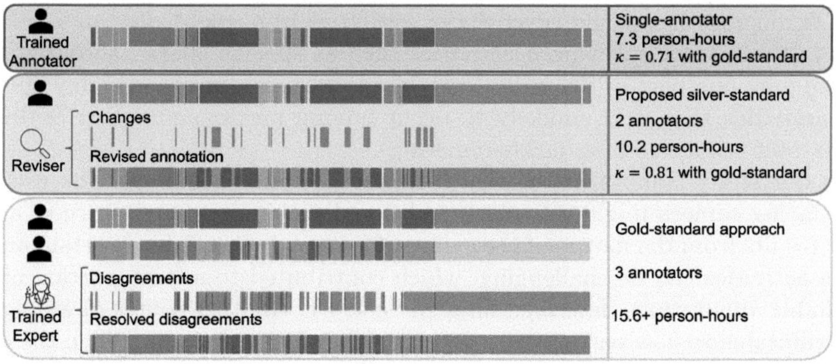


**Fig. 2.** Comparisons between the single-annotator, silver-standard, and gold-standard approach (top to bottom). Annotation timelines were visualized using an hour of actual annotation data. Person-hours were calculated based on analyses using 16 h footage covering a waking day.

datasets suggests that even when collecting relatively small datasets, the gold-standard annotation protocol may not be used—likely due to the cost and burden involved—and details on how annotation was accomplished may not be available. Nevertheless, because annotated data are in short supply, such publicly available datasets are heavily used.

# 3 Method

Our own challenging annotation task led us to explore a middle-ground approach between the single-annotator approach and the gold-standard annotation approach, because gold-standard annotation is financially out of reach. Instead of having a second, completely independent annotator and a third domain expert resolving differences between annotators 1 and 2, we explored having a second trained annotator *review and revise* annotations from the first annotator (Fig. 2). In this section, we describe the annotation training protocols and annotation method. Then we describe the experiments we used to assess the labor cost and annotation quality improvements of the proposed "silver-standard" annotation approach.

## 3.1 Annotation Scheme and Annotation Software

Our taxonomy is designed to enable labeling of contextualized free-living activity and posture. Each annotation consists of at least two labels: the participant's posture (one of 13 mutually exclusive options, see Appendix Table 6) and physical activity type (one of 49 mutually exclusive options, see Appendix Table 7). Although we wanted our taxonomy to encompass both major HAR activities from prior research and fine-grained free-living behaviors, we balanced this comprehensiveness with practical constraints because annotators might have been overwhelmed by a taxonomy with a substantially larger set of labels. We opted for a taxonomy that would cover major activities from the American Time Use survey [15] but not specialized activities such as specific sports, activities that involve only one part of the body (e.g., hand gestures), or other highly specialized activities that were unlikely to occur among participants contributing to the dataset (e.g., sledding, jackhammering).

In our study, annotators labeled front-facing camera footage. The use of a front-facing camera might introduce additional ambiguity. One source of ambiguity results from the nature of the camera footage; distinguishing certain ambulation activities can be challenging, which contributed to a large portion of the unreliable annotations described later in Sect. 4.1. Another source of ambiguity is attributable to how participants wore the front-facing camera. When the cameras were partially covered, annotators sometimes cannot accurately decipher the current activity or posture. Thus, it is also important that the taxonomy allows annotators to indicate when labeling is not possible. In our annotation taxonomy, annotators can describe such cases with the use of *PA_ Type_ Indecipherable/ Video_ Unavailable* and *Posture_ Type_ Indecipherable/Video_ Unavailable.*

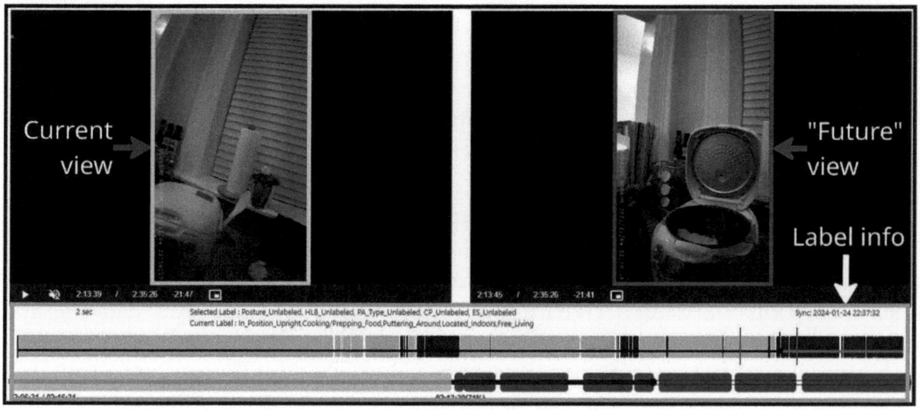


**Fig. 3.** A screenshot of the annotation software interface.

Researchers using our dataset will not be able to view the original front-facing camera video used for annotation because we must protect participants' privacy. To help researchers using the dataset interpret their results, our annotations also include non-mutually exclusive labels about the participant's "high-level behavior" (HLB) and additional context that may impact the participant's physical activity. The HLB and context labels are meant to provide helpful information but are not used for model training or evaluation directly, nor are they provided by any other datasets in Table 1, and thus we will not discuss quality assessment of these data in this work.

Our annotators use custom software designed for efficient free-living annotation using our taxonomy (Fig. 3). Annotators can watch the video sped up when there are no changes in behavior, stopping at transitions to label. The "future" video view allows the annotator to anticipate changes in annotation complexity and dynamically change the video speed in response without overshooting, thus saving time. Annotators use the interface, with keyboard commands, to add new activity labels, merge two consecutive labels, split a label at the current frame, or edit the current labels. The software also flags behaviors that may be incompatible (e.g., a posture that is incompatible with an activity), provides suggestions of compatible posture or HLB labels (with the selected activity), and pre-populates selections with recent activities (Appendix Fig. 4).

### 3.2 Annotation Training Protocol

We recruited annotators from the undergraduate student body of Northeastern University. Each completed a standardized training protocol. First, all annotators completed the required human subject research certification required by our institutional review board. Annotators then reviewed material on general data handling practices and the annotation process, including hands-on annotation practice under the supervision of a trained expert. After reviewing the material, they had to pass a quiz on the material. Finally, to demonstrate annotation proficiency, annotators were required to achieve at least 90% second-by-second agreement in both the physical activity and posture label categories on a set of ten 10-minute videos annotated by a domain expert. Annotators were allowed to re-annotate these videos until they achieved the required benchmark. After reaching this benchmarking, annotators labeled two two-hour clips. The first consisted of a relatively common and obvious set of activities such as clear *Walking* or *Standing_ With_ Movement*; the second consisted of some less common activities such as *Doing_ Resistance_ Training_ Free_ Weights* and quick transitions between activities (e.g., short transitions between *Walking* and *Standing_ With_ Movement* while doing household activities such as cooking). Using the resulting annotations, we calculated post-training inter-rater reliability among all annotators. For the physical activity category, the newly trained annotators achieved an overall Fleiss' $\kappa = 0.76$ for the simple scenario and 0.61 for the complex scenario. While the resulting inter-rater reliability scores can both be interpreted as "substantial" agreement [8], the $\kappa = 0.61$ score for the complex scenario is closer to the "moderate" level agreement and demonstrates the complexity of our annotation task. The "moderate" level agreement on complex scenarios must be considered by future researchers as they develop HAR models using such data; ground-truth annotation will always contain some inaccurate or imprecise labels. These fast-changing scenarios, however, are not common in daily activities and should not hinder traditional HAR research aiming at recognizing more common daily ambulation activities, such as *Walking* or *Sitting_ With_ Movement.*

More intense or longer training might improve annotator reliability [1], but it also may be impractical. The entire annotation training protocol in our study, including the post-annotation reliability evaluation, requires about 20 h of effort for each annotator to complete. Further, our annotators are undergraduate students who are only available for a few months per semester and have limited working hours. The annotation task is also such a tedious task that many students do not want to continue annotating long-term. Thus, increasing annotation training time even more is not desirable, given that we do not anticipate large improvement gains.

### 3.3 Experiments

We explored three research questions (RQs) given our activity/posture taxonomy, front-facing video, and annotation software:

- **RQ1**: Can the silver-standard protocol produce annotations that are similar (i.e., high inter-rater agreement) to the gold-standard protocol?
- **RQ2**: Are the silver-standard annotations more reliable than single-annotator annotations?
- **RQ3**: Can annotators review and revise labels faster than annotating from scratch?

To explore these questions, we selected six videos covering six waking days totaling to 92 h of footage (from Monday until Saturday) from the first participant in our to-be-released dataset. During the entire waking day, this participant wore a front-facing camera (recording at 30 fps and 480p resolution) on their chest and only took the camera off for privacy reasons or during nighttime sleep.

**Experiment 1: Silver-Standard Annotations Versus Gold-Standard Annotations.** To answer RQ 1 , we calculated the agreement rate between the silver-standard annotation and the gold-standard annotation. We selected one day with 16.4 h of footage; this is the day the participant performed the most activities.

First, to obtain the gold-standard annotation, independent annotators labeled each second of this video to obtain two independent annotation sets. Because the video is long and the annotation is laborious, multiple annotators were used for each set, but the result was two different independent annotations of the same day. A domain expert, also trained in annotation, then resolved disagreements from the two sets of annotations. The resolved annotations could contain activities that were not in either of the original annotation passes. The resulting annotation is considered the gold-standard annotation of the day. The domain expert required about 2 h of effort to resolve disagreements and obtain the final set of labels for 16.4 h of video.

To obtain the single-annotator annotation, a new set of independent annotators—*who were not involved in the process of generating the gold-standard annotation*—labeled the footage. We then obtained two sets of silver-standard annotations by selecting two trained annotators with varying experience levels annotating other data to be the "revisers." The less-experienced reviser had three months of experience, and the more experienced reviser had eight months of experience. All annotators work approximately 8–10 h per week for $15 USD per hour.

**Experiment 2: Silver-Standard Annotations Versus Single-Annotator Annotations.** To answer RQ 2 and to assess whether the silver-standard approach is more reliable than the single-annotator approach, we evaluated the inter-rater reliability of silver-standard annotations compared to the single-annotator annotations on 92 h of data. Two independent annotator groups annotated all six days of videos resulting in two complete single-annotator annotation sets. We then recruited an additional group of revisers from our trained annotators–*who were not involved in the first pass of annotation*—to each individually revise these two sets of annotations. We then calculated inter-rater reliability between each of the single-annotator annotations as well as between each of the silver-standard annotations.

**Analysis: Agreement Metrics.** We considered each second of the video as a discrete segment for labeling. To evaluate inter-rater agreement, we used Cohen's

$\kappa$ as the primary metric and additionally reported percent agreement. The widely accepted interpretation of agreement ranges for Cohen's $\kappa$ are $< 0.20$ as "none to slight" agreement, 0.21–0.40 as "fair" agreement, 0.41–0.60 as "moderate" agreement, 0.61–0.80 as "substantial" agreement, and $> 0.8$ as "almost perfect" agreement [8]. There is no equivalent interpretation for percent agreement. We used the Python implementation of Cohen's $\kappa$ and percent agreement provided by scikit-learn version 1.6.

**Analysis: Annotator Productivity Rate.** To answer RQ 3, we measured annotators' productivity rate while they were either annotating or revising. We define the *productivity rate* as the duration of footage annotated or revised divided by the total time spent working. Because annotators can work in multiple short shifts, we calculated and reported the mean productivity rate across all working shifts in that annotation set.

## 4 Results

For RQ 1 and RQ 2, we report inter-rater agreement on both the mutually exclusive physical activity and mutually exclusive posture types in Sect. 4.1 and 4.2, respectively. As mentioned previously, although annotators record additional high-level behavior and contextual information as they label, those labels are provided as part of the dataset only for additional understanding of the primary physical activity and posture labels and thus are not included in this analysis.

For RQ 3, we report the overall annotation and revision productivity rate in Sect. 4.3.

**Table 2.** Cohen's $\kappa$ and percent agreement from the single-annotator and silver-standard annotations by less experienced (less-exp) and more experienced (more-exp) revisers against the gold-standard annotation in the physical activity category. To account for an unlikely error in the gold-standard annotation resulting from the two independent annotators both incorrectly labeling a segment of *PA_ Type_Indecipherable/Video_ Unavailable* as *Sitting_ With_ Movement*, we calculated an adjusted $\kappa$ and percent agreement while excluding this incorrect segment.

| Annotation Set | Cohen's $\kappa$ | Adjusted $\kappa$ | % Agree | Adjusted % |
|---|---|---|---|---|
| Single-annotator annotation | 0.68 | 0.71 | 80% | 82% |
| Silver-standard (less-exp) | 0.73 | 0.76 | 83% | 85% |
| Silver-standard (more-exp) | 0.77 | 0.81 | 86% | 88% |

### 4.1 Silver-Standard Annotations Versus Gold-Standard Annotations

For the physical activity category, the single-annotator annotation was in "substantial" agreement with the gold-standard annotation with Cohen's $\kappa = 0.68$ (80% agreement). The silver-standard protocol further improved annotation quality, resulting in higher agreement rate with the gold-standard annotation. The more experienced reviser produced the better revised labels (i.e., higher agreement with gold-standard labels) with Cohen's $\kappa = 0.77$ (86% agreement), compared to our less experienced reviser with $\kappa = 0.73$ (82% agreement). While these agreement scores can all be interpreted as "substantial" agreement, the revised annotations were generally in better agreement with the gold-standard annotation (Table 2).

One noticeable difference between the single-annotator, silver-standard, and gold-standard annotations was a long 1,600 s segment where the correct label was *PA_ Type_ Indecipherable/Video_ Unavailable*. In the gold-standard annotation, this portion was labeled as *Sitting_ With_ Movement*. The independent annotators likely inferred that the participant was *Sitting_ With_ Movement* because the participant was doing that activity immediately before and after the *PA_ Type_ Video_ Unavailable/Indecipherable* footage. Unfortunately, both our annotators introduce an incorrect but agreed upon label to the gold-standard annotation. Because we want to compare the silver-standard approach against the "best possible" annotation approach, we recomputed the "adjusted" Cohen's $\kappa$ while excluding this 1,600 s segment from all annotation sets. The recomputed Cohen's $\kappa$ was 0.71, 0.76, and 0.81 for single-annotator annotation, revision by less-experienced reviser, and revision by more-experienced reviser, respectively.

For the posture category, there were fewer available labels to choose from and there were less frequent posture changes. Labeling posture might be a simpler task. In fact, the single-annotator annotation and both silver-standard annotations by the two revisers were in "almost perfect" agreement with the gold-standard annotation (Appendix Table 8).

**Changes Made by the Revisers.** Both revisers added details and new activities to the original annotation (Table 3). Both revisers added 16 min of the *Vacuuming* activity and 2 min of the *Washing_ Hands* activity. Both revisers also added more detailed bouts for ambulation activities that are frequently studied in HAR research. For example, the more experienced reviser added seven more bouts of *Walking_ Down_ Stairs*; even though this was only 25 s of changed annotations. Similarly, this reviser added 19 more bouts of *Walking*, but reduced the total *Walking* duration by 1,445 s; in some health studies, measuring bouts of activity may be as important as volume of activity. The added bouts suggests that revisers were identifying, adding, or even refining the precision of quick ambulation activities.

The more experienced reviser added more new activities than the less experienced reviser, such as *Folding_ Clothes* (14.4 min), *Sweeping* (6.4 min), *Watering_ Plants* (2 min), and *Loading/Unloading_ Washing_ Machine/Dryer* (2 min). In total, the more experienced reviser added 43 min of new activities that were

**Table 3.** Changes made by the less experienced (Less E.) reviser and more experienced (More E.) reviser compared to the original (Orig.) annotation.

| Activity | Total Duration (s) | | | Number of Bouts | | |
|---|---|---|---|---|---|---|
| | Orig. | Less E. | More E. | Orig. | Less E. | More E. |
| *Putting_ Clothes_ Away* | 0 | 218 | 0 | 0 | 2 | 0 |
| *Walking_ Down_ Stairs* | 82 | 82 | 107 | 11 | 13 | 18 |
| *Watering_ Plants* | 0 | 0 | 110 | 0 | 0 | 3 |
| *Loading_ Unloading_ Washer_ Dryer* | 0 | 0 | 122 | 0 | 0 | 3 |
| *Walking_ Up_ Stairs* | 138 | 140 | 149 | 15 | 15 | 17 |
| *Washing_ Hands* | 20 | 154 | 174 | 1 | 7 | 6 |
| *Kneeling_ With_ Movement* | 426 | 209 | 315 | 17 | 8 | 12 |
| *Sweeping* | 0 | 0 | 383 | 0 | 0 | 6 |
| *Folding_ Clothes* | 0 | 0 | 863 | 0 | 0 | 5 |
| *Vacuuming* | 0 | 982 | 967 | 0 | 1 | 1 |
| *Puttering_ Around* | 0 | 139 | 2,633 | 0 | 1 | 31 |
| *Walking* | 6,288 | 4,942 | 4,843 | 125 | 125 | 144 |
| *Standing_ With_ Movement* | 10,135 | 10,307 | 6,582 | 92 | 98 | 103 |
| *PA_ Type_ Unavailable* | 8,167 | 8,174 | 8,129 | 22 | 21 | 22 |
| *Sitting_ With_ Movement* | 33,324 | 33,349 | 33,323 | 25 | 25 | 27 |

not included in the original annotation; the less experienced reviser added 22 min. The set of new activities added was different, with the less experienced reviser adding the *Putting_ Clothes_ Away* label but the more experienced reviser simply used the *Folding_ Clothes* label instead.

**Changes Not Aligned with the Gold-Standard Annotation.** Thirty-two percent of changes made by the reviser were not aligned with the adjusted gold-standard annotation. For example, the more experienced reviser made 1,903 s of changes that did not match (Appendix Table 10). Most of the differences (836 s) were due to the differences in the usage of two physical activity labels that represent different levels of motion: *Puttering_ Around* and *Standing_ With_ Movement.* In the taxonomy, *Puttering_ Around* is described as intermittently moving around and standing, while *Standing_ With_ Movement* is defined as being in a standing position where movements, such as shuffling feet or shifting body weight might occur. More precise annotators would label each individual movement bout instead of clustering them into *Puttering_ Around.* The experienced annotator was *more detailed* than the gold-standard annotation for a total of 196 s. Vice versa, the more experienced reviser used *Puttering_ Around* instead of using precise ambulation labels for 640 s. There were also 210 s of total non-aligned changes due to the reviser using precise activity labels (e.g., *Vacuuming* for 39 s) instead of generic ambulation labels. Finally, there were 60 s

**Table 4.** Inter-rater reliability (Cohen's $\kappa$) computed using physical activity labels for single-annotator annotations and silver-standard annotations.

| Day (video length) | Single-annotator $\kappa$ | Silver-standard $\kappa$ | Improvement ($\Delta\kappa$) |
|---|---|---|---|
| Day 1 (4.8 h) | 0.49 | 0.77 | +0.28 |
| Day 2 (16.5 h) | 0.83 | 0.83 | 0.00 |
| Day 3 (17.7 h) | 0.63 | 0.76 | +0.13 |
| Day 4 (19 h) | 0.73 | 0.77 | +0.04 |
| Day 5 (17.4 h) | 0.80 | 0.83 | +0.03 |
| Day 6 (16.4 h) | 0.63 | 0.78 | +0.15 |
| **Mean per day** | **0.68** | **0.79** | **+0.11** |

where the differences were from small boundary changes in activity start/stop times, or where the gold-standard annotation had a short gap in activity labels.

There were only 76 s of clear ambulation error between the silver-standard annotation (by the experienced reviser) and the gold-standard annotation. The experienced reviser also missed three activities: *Putting_Clothes_Away*, *Wet_Mopping*, and *Organizing_Shelf/Cabinet*, totaling 721 s. Notably, the reviser did change 5 min of *Standing_With_Movement* to *Folding_Clothes*, but the gold-standard label was *Putting_Clothes_Away*.

### 4.2 Silver-Standard Annotations Versus Single-Annotator Annotations

On average across six days, the silver-standard physical activity annotations were more reliable than the single-annotator annotations with $\kappa = 0.79$ (in the "substantial" agreement range and close to being in "almost perfect" agreement) and $\kappa = 0.68$ ("substantial" agreement) respectively (Table 4). The biggest difference was for Day 1 with $\Delta\kappa = 0.28$. Across all days, the poorest agreement between independent silver-standard annotations was $\kappa = 0.76$ on Day 3, but was still an improvement from the single-annotator annotations on the same day with $\kappa = 0.63$.

Similarly, the silver-standard approach had consistent labeling for the posture category with mean (across six days) $\kappa = 0.91$ ("almost perfect" agreement); the single-annotator approach was in the "substantial" agreement range and came close to being "almost perfect," with the mean (across six days) $\kappa = 0.79$ (Appendix Table 9). Notably, single-annotator reliability for Day 1 was only "moderate" with $\kappa = 0.56$. All silver-standard posture annotations were in the "almost perfect" agreement range, with the minimum agreement at $\kappa = 0.88$. Given the higher agreement score across the board in both the physical activity and posture categories, we concluded that the silver-standard approach resulted in better annotation consistency over the single-annotator approach.

**Total Duration of All Changes.** The revisers made between 1,866–10,822 s of total changes per day in the physical activity category (Appendix Table 11). For certain days, revisers changed up to 10,822 s, or more than 3 h, worth of changes. These changes made by revisers improved annotation quality by adding some new activities and more detailed activity bouts to the original annotation (Appendix Tables 12 and 13).

### 4.3 Productivity Rate

Annotators revised annotations faster than they annotated from scratch (Table 5). Across our experiments, the average annotation rate was 2.2 h of annotation per hour worked (1 h of work resulted in 2.2 h of annotated video). Based on labeling efforts to date, including annotators who were not included in our experiments, the overall annotation rate is 2.8. In comparison, the mean revising rate was 5.6.

**Table 5.** Annotation rate (AR) and revision rate (RR), hours annotated/revised per hour worked, for annotators (of varying experience levels measured in months) in our experiments.

| **Annotator (experience)** | **AR** | **RR** |
|---|---|---|
| Annotator 1 (3 mon) | 1.1 | 3.5 |
| Annotator 2 (8 mon) | 3.1 | 7.6 |
| Annotator 3 (3 mon) | 1.5 | 4.4 |
| Annotator 4 (3 mon) | 2.1 | 5.9 |
| Annotator 5 (3 mon) | 2.6 | 5.9 |

| **Annotator (experience)** | **AR** | **RR** |
|---|---|---|
| Annotator 6 (3 mon) | 2.0 | 7.5 |
| Annotator 7 (8 mon) | 2.9 | 4.4 |
| All annotators (N/A) | 2.8 | N/A |
| **Mean (4.4 mon)** | 2.2 | 5.6 |

Based on the computed productivity rate, we estimated that, on average, it would take one annotator 7.3 h to annotate a typical video of a waking day (16 h). To achieve the gold-standard annotation, 15.6 h are required—14.6 h for two annotators to individually annotate, and 1–2 h for the domain expert to resolve disagreements (assuming 20% disagreement and a productivity rate of 2.8). The proposed silver-standard protocol would cut that time to 10.2 h, saving about 33% of total person-hours compared with the gold-standard approach.

## 5 Discussion

Demand for high-quality labeled data with increasingly large taxonomies that can be used to support machine learning and AI model training and validation is growing. As a result, a compromise between single-annotator annotation and the gold-standard method may be warranted. We are currently annotating a wearable sensor dataset with 22,000 h of front-facing video of free-living activity. Based on labeling to date, our trained annotators annotate at a mean annotation rate of 2.8 h of video annotated for every 1 h of annotation work. At this rate, we estimate that two independent annotation passes would take 15,800 person-hours. Additionally, a domain expert would need to resolve disagreements. Given a 20% disagreement rate (with $\kappa = 0.68$), this corresponds to 4,400 h of footage that the domain expert would need to resolve, which would take 1,600 h minimum. Overall, we estimate the gold-standard approach would require 17,400 person-hours of effort. In our study, the single-annotator inter-rater reliability can be as low as $\kappa = 0.61$ on more complex scenarios, which led us to explore the "silver-standard" method proposed here.

The complexity of our taxonomy contributes to the annotation challenge. In fact, our annotators were more accurate labeling postures because the annotation taxonomy only involves 13 postures, some of which are clearly distinguishable from the front-facing video. Furthermore, postures usually do not change as frequently as physical activities. In one minute, a person can be *Standing_ With_ Movement*, then *Sweeping*, then *Walking*, but still remain in the posture *In_ Position_ Upright* throughout. If our physical activity taxonomy were simplified (e.g., using a generic label to describe household ambulations), then annotation reliability might increase; yet, to improve HAR algorithms, the community needs more detailed labels for activities.

The nature of front-facing recording also contributes to the overall annotation challenge. Consider the *Puttering_ Around* label, which was created to account for short, quick, and frequent changes between *Standing_ With_ Movement* and *Walking* for which precise annotation is not possible in a reasonable amount of time. In our training, we discouraged the use of *Puttering_ Around*, but there are edge cases where participants moved their feet and shifted the weight of their body such that annotators felt the activity was in a gray area (such as when a person is moving around in a small kitchen for cooking). Also, sometimes it is not clear from the front-facing camera the degree to which feet are moving. In our result described in Sect. 4.1, there were some differences in how this *Puttering_ Around* label was used for labeling these edge cases; these differences likely contributed to the lower inter-rater agreement.

These unique annotation challenges led us to explore a compromised annotation approach between the single-annotator and the gold-standard approach. We decided to explore the silver-standard annotation strategy because the revision task might be inherently easier than the annotation task. When annotating from scratch, annotators have to look at both the "current" and "future" views (Fig. 3) to identify when the current activity stops and a new activity starts. Juggling both views at the same time might require additional mental strain, on top of normal operations to add a new label. Revisers only need to look at the "current" view and determine if the provided label matches the current footage. Revising is, therefore, likely a simpler task, which is why revisers can pay more attention to finer details. In our experiments, the revisers improved the annotation by adding novel activities and more precise details that were missed using the single-annotator approach. These additional details and activities were small (in duration compared to the entire day), but for some studies might be important. Conventional ambulation activities, such as *Walking* or *Standing*, are already well-studied using lab data. Thus, the new frontier of activity recognition should be on detecting activities in free-living and detecting finer activities, including precisely detecting ambulation bouts. Currently, HAR algorithms are rarely evaluated on finer activities (e.g., *Putting_ Clothes_ Away*, or short bouts of *Walking_ Up_ Stairs*); high-quality annotated data are required to train and evaluate novel HAR algorithms that can precisely detect fleeting or uncommon activities in free-living individuals.

### 5.1 Limitations and Implications

We conducted the experiments testing the silver-standard method on a week of front-facing video from a single participant (92 h). Our experiments required a combined total of 200 h of footage to be annotated and required 131 h of human labor. Although expensive, ideally, our experiments should be repeated on additional participants to further validate our results. Our investigation could further be enhanced with the collection and analysis of qualitative data from annotators explaining their thought processes as they revise annotations (e.g., were the revisers primarily fixing inaccurate annotations, or were they adding finer details that were originally missed? What strategies do they develop as they work?). Furthermore, our experiments did not evaluate how changes to the annotation taxonomy (e.g., larger taxonomies or taxonomies that include objects or hand gestures) might impact the utility of our proposed approach. The proposed revision strategy appears promising, but more work with a larger video sample set is warranted.

As one might expect, we found that more experienced annotators were more likely to produce better revisions. Unlike the gold-standard annotation approach, where the initial two annotations are independent, the revisers can be biased toward the original annotation when revising, thus producing poor-quality revisions. These poor-quality revisions, although unlikely to contain inaccurate annotations (i.e., using the wrong label to describe physical activity or posture), can fail to include finer activity details. More experienced annotators, who likely have a better understanding of the annotation scheme, might be more aware of fleeting activities. All revisions, however, were still better than the original single-annotator annotations. The revised annotations yielded much higher inter-rater agreement and were in high agreement with the gold-standard annotation. Therefore, the silver-standard approach, although partially limited by the annotator's skill, is still likely to result in improved annotations over the original annotation.

One way to achieve better annotation might be longer, or more intensive, training [1,18], but our training already involves 20 h of effort. In practice, most researchers delegate annotation to student annotators earning minimum wage [3,18] who may have a high turnover rate that an onerous training process might further exacerbate. Another way to ensure better annotation quality might be to employ annotators long-term, because annotation quality might improve with practice [12], but the annotation task is tedious and not a task that many people want to continue long-term. A middle-ground approach may be to select a subset of high-performing annotators (e.g., annotators who performed well during the initial training) as revisers and to provide them with additional training specifically focused on optimizing annotation via revision.

Our annotators are paid $15/h USD, and a domain expert (doctoral student) is paid $40/h. Therefore, annotation of Day 6 of our test (16.4 h of footage) at actual annotation rates would run as follows: single-annotator annotation ($109.50 USD), silver-standard annotation ($153 USD), and gold-standard annotation ($299 USD). For our entire dataset, costs would be: single-annotator annotation ($118,500 USD), silver-standard annotation ($177,000 USD), and gold-standard annotation ($301,000 USD).

We have concluded that gold-standard annotation is out of reach for our project because of limited funding and resources. Had we sufficient resources, based on this work, we would use silver-standard annotation. Unfortunately, in practice, even achieving single-annotator annotation (using best practices for extensive annotator training) is proving challenging. We are now exploring additional strategies using computer-assisted annotation and revision.

## 6 Conclusion

We find that a "silver-standard" annotation strategy, using a single-pass annotation followed by a "revising" pass fix can yield annotation quality approaching the gold-standard level while saving 33% of total annotation time. The silver-standard annotation improved the agreement rate (compared to single-annotator annotation) against the gold-standard annotation from Cohen's $\kappa$ of 0.77 up from 0.68. Furthermore, the silver-standard annotations had higher inter-rater reliability than single-annotator annotations, with Cohen's $\kappa = 0.79$ and 0.68, respectively. As demand for high-quality physical activity annotation data increases, researchers may want to consider strategies that augment single-annotator labeling and intensify efforts to report details of how annotation was accomplished and the effort that was required.

**Acknowledgments.** Research reported in this publication was supported, in part, by the National Cancer Institute of the National Institutes of Health under award number R01CA252966. The content is solely the responsibility of the authors and does not necessarily represent the official views of the National Institutes of Health.

**Disclosure.** The authors have no competing interests to declare that are relevant to the content of this article

# A Appendix or Supplemental Material

**Table 6.** The posture taxonomy

| Label | Description (The participant is definitely ...) |
|---|---|
| *In_ Position_ Kneeling* | In the position of kneeling, either still or with some other body movement. Could be with one knee or two. |
| *In_ Position_ Reclining/Slouching* | In the position of reclining or slouching back (typically on a chair, recliner, or couch). This would include reclining in bed if someone is propped up, but not *Lying_ On_ Back.* |
| *In_ Position_ Sitting* | In the position of sitting (includes sitting in a normal chair, barstool, swing, etc.). |
| *In_ Position_ Upright* | Upright, either still or moving. This posture includes both standing and ambulatory activities unless there is a distinct bending at the hip that substantially alters the upright position (e.g., bending to pick something up). |
| *Lying_ On_ Back* | In the position of lying on the back. |
| *Lying_ On_ Left_ Side* | In the position of lying on the left side. |
| *Lying_ On_ Right_ Side* | In the position of lying on the right side. |
| *Lying_ On_ Stomach* | In the position of lying on the stomach. |
| *Posture_ Video_ Unavailable/Indecipherable* | The video is missing, too blurry, or at too poor of a camera angle to label the posture at this time. |
| *Posture_ Other* | In a specific and well-understood posture that would not be accurately described as being in a sitting, upright, lying (on back, left, right, stomach) or reclining/slouching posture. Examples might be well-defined Yoga or exercise postures (e.g., tree, hero, handstand) or on oneâĂŹs knees and doing something. |
| *Posture_ Too_ Complex* | The posture of the participant is deemed to be changing too fast or with too much complexity to label accurately during this time. |
| *Posture_ Unlabeled* | Posture for this segment of video has not been labeled. This is the default condition. |

**Table 7.** The physical activity taxonomy

| Label | Description (The participant is definitely ...) |
|---|---|
| *Applying_ Makeup* | Applying makeup to the face. |
| *Bathing* | Bathing in a tub. This does not include showering in a standing shower. |
| *Blowdrying_ Hair* | Using a hand-held blow dryer to dry hair. This does not involve hair drying at a parlor by a hairdresser. |
| *Brushing_ Teeth* | Cleaning teeth using a manual or electric brush. |
| *Brushing/Combing/Tying_ Hair* | Untangling/styling hair using a brush or a comb. |
| *Cycling_ Active_ Pedaling_ Regular_ Bicycle* | Pedaling while riding a non-stationary regular bicycle that facilitates the forward propulsion of the bicycle. This does not include coasting on the bicycle after pedaling or going downhill. |
| *Cycling_ Active_ Pedaling_ Stationary_ Bike* | Using cycle ergometer- e.g., commercially available exercise bikes such as a Peloton bike. Includes both seated and standing while pedaling. This does not include sitting on the bike at rest. |

*(continued on next page)*

(continued from previous page)

| Label | Description (The participant is definitely ...) |
|---|---|
| *Doing_ Resistance_ Training_ Free_ Weights* | Muscular training specifically involving the lifting of free weights. This label only applies to when the actual lifting (up/down) is occurring, not if the person is standing and resting. |
| *Doing_ Resistance_ Training_ Other* | All forms of resistance training other than lifting free weights. This includes using weight lifting machines and resistance bands or body weight. |
| *Dry_ Mopping* | Using a dry mop as an alternative to sweeping (e.g., Swiffer sweeper or other dry mop). |
| *Dusting* | Using a handheld duster to clean a surface. This ranges from using a cloth to other forms of modified dusters (e.g., a feather duster or Swiffer duster). |
| *Flossing_ Teeth* | Flossing teeth using string-based floss. |
| *Folding_ Clothes* | Folding clothes by hand. This includes laundered clothes and other cloth materials. |
| *Ironing* | Using a handheld iron or steamer to iron clothes. |
| *Kneeling_ Still* | In a kneeling position, still. |
| *Kneeling_ With_ Movement* | In a kneeling position but not still. may include upper or lower extremity movement while performing a task, fidgeting,or deliberate upper body movement (e.g., sway). |
| *Loading/Unloading_ Washing_ Machine/Dryer* | Manually placing/removing clothes from a washing machine. |
| *Lying_ Still* | In the lying posture with no limb or body movement. |
| *Lying_ With_ Movement* | In the lying posture with some limb or body movement. This may typically involve limb movement that occurs when doing an activity while lying, e.g, flipping pages when reading a book, or gesturing while speaking on the phone with someone. |
| *Organizing_ Shelf/Cabinet* | Arranging/rearranging items in a shelf/cabinet/bookcase to organize or tidy up. |
| *PA_ Type_ Other* | A specific, well-understood PA_Type that would not be accurately described as any of the others on this list. |
| *PA_ Type_ Too_ Complex* | The behavior of the participant is deemed to be changing too fast or with too much complexity to label accurately during this time. |
| *PA_ Type_ Unlabeled* | PA_Type for this segment of video has not been labeled. This is the default condition. |
| *PA_ Type_ Video_ Unavailable/ Indecipherable* | The video is missing, too blurry, or at too poor of a camera angle to label the posture at this time. |
| *Playing_ Frisbee* | Playing with a flying disc with someone else, or outside with a dog. |
| *Puttering_ Around* | Upright and intermittently moving around/standing, such as often happens when cooking. If in the middle of *Puttering_ Around* there is a clear, extended bout of another activity that should be explicitly labeled. |
| *Putting_ Clothes_ Away* | Stowing clothes in a closet, cabinet, or other storage area. |
| *Running_ Non-Treadmill* | Running outdoors or on an indoor track or in any other context that is not a treadmill. |
| *Running_ Treadmill* | Running on a treadmill. |
| *Showering* | Showering in a standing shower. This does not include bathing in a tub. |
| *Shoveling_ Mud/Snow* | Using a hand-held shovel to manually move snow or mud for any purpose. |

(continued on next page)

*(continued from previous page)*

| **Label** | **Description (The participant is definitely ...)** |
|---|---|
| *Sitting_Still* | In a seated position, still. Includes sitting at rest on a stationary bicycle. |
| *Sitting_With_Movement* | In a seated position but not still. may include upper or lower extremity movement while performing a task, fidgeting,or deliberate upper body movement (e.g., sway). Includes coasting on a bicycle while seated. |
| *Standing_Still* | In a standing position, still. |
| *Standing_With_Movement* | In a standing position but not still. Movement may include upper or lower extremity movement while performing a task, fidgeting, or deliberate upper body swaying. Normal shuffling of feet while standing in the same place (e.g., to shift weight or move forward slowly in a line) may occur. |
| *Sweeping* | Using a handheld broom to sweep the floor. |
| *Synchronizing_Sensors* | Performing the sensor and camera time syncing activity specific to the Datasets Project. This involves clapping of hands and flexing the hip joint such that each knee is raised with the help of one's hands. |
| *Vacuuming* | Using an electric vacuum to clean a floor/carpet. This does not include small portable handheld vacuums. |
| *Walking_Down_Stairs* | Going downstairs. This may involve a break in descending that occurs when walking on a level surface for brief bouts between consecutive flights of stairs. It could involve the use of handrails for support. |
| *Walking_Fast* | Walking faster than a normal pace that is deliberate. E.g., purposefully increasing walking speed to make sure one can catch a train, or to get somewhere on time. A normal walking speed is between 3 and 3.5 mph for most people. This is a judgment call and should be used only if you are convinced that this is deliberate. |
| *Walking_Slow* | Walking slower than a normal pace that is deliberate. E.g., strolling in a park and chatting with someone. A normal walking speed is between 3 and 3.5 mph for most people. This is a judgment call and use only if you are convinced that this is deliberate. Use unless it is not discernibly uphill. If so, label as <Walking>. |
| *Walking_Treadmill* | Walking on a treadmill. |
| *Walking_Up_Stairs* | Going up stairs. This may involve a break in ascending that occurs when walking on a level surface for brief bouts between consecutive flights of stairs. It could involve the use of handrails for support. |
| *Walking* | Walking naturally. |
| *Washing_Face* | Washing one's face using water, soap, or face wash. This includes removing makeup. |
| *Washing_Hands* | Deliberately washing one's hands using water, soap, or hand sanitizer. |
| *Watering_Plants* | Watering household plants using a watering can or hose. |
| *Wet_Mopping* | Using a handheld mop or cloth to clean the floor. Includes manually mopping the floor using a cloth, mop and bucket, electronic handheld mops such as Swiffer Wetjet. These are different from dry mopping as the latter involves more activities (e.g., dipping mop in bucket, wringing, mopping) and requires significantly higher effort. |

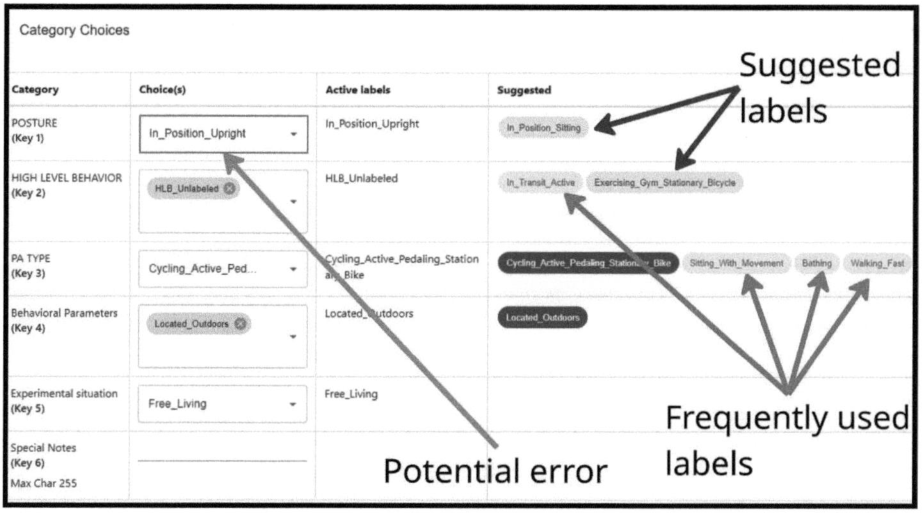


**Fig. 4.** A screenshot of the label edit dialogue.

**Table 8.** Cohen's $\kappa$ and percent agreement from the single-annotator and silver-standard annotations by less experienced (less-exp) and more experienced (more-exp) revisers against the gold-standard annotation in the posture category. To account for an unlikely error in the gold-standard annotation resulting from the two independent annotators both incorrectly labeling a segment of *Posture_Indecipherable/Video_Unavailable* as *In_Position_Sitting*, we calculated an adjusted $\kappa$ and percent agreement while excluding this incorrect segment.

| Annotation Set | Cohen's $\kappa$ | Adjusted $\kappa$ | % Agree | Adjusted % |
|---|---|---|---|---|
| Single-annotator annotation | 0.86 | 0.94 | 94% | 96% |
| Silver-standard (less-exp) | 0.90 | 0.95 | 94% | 97% |
| Silver-standard (more-exp) | 0.86 | 0.90 | 92% | 94% |

**Table 9.** Inter-rater reliability (Cohen's $\kappa$) computed using posture labels for single-annotator annotations and silver-standard annotations.

| Day (video length) | Single-annotator $\kappa$ | Silver-standard $\kappa$ | Improvement |
|---|---|---|---|
| Day 1 (4.8 h) | 0.56 | 0.88 | +0.32 |
| Day 2 (16.5 h) | 0.94 | 0.95 | +0.02 |
| Day 3 (17.7 h) | 0.70 | 0.90 | +0.20 |
| Day 4 (19 h) | 0.93 | 0.95 | +0.02 |
| Day 5 (17.4 h) | 0.84 | 0.88 | +0.04 |
| Day 6 (16.4 h) | 0.78 | 0.89 | +0.11 |
| **Mean per day** | **0.79** | **0.91** | **+0.12** |

**Table 10.** Details of all non-aligned changes made by the more experienced reviser discussed in Sect. 4.1

| Changed From | Changed To | Should Be | Duration (s) |
|---|---|---|---|
| *Reviser Less Detailed and Used Puttering_Around (Total: 640 s)* | | | |
| Standing_With_Movement | Puttering_Around | Standing_With_Movement | 458 |
| Walking | Puttering_Around | Standing_With_Movement | 161 |
| Walking | Puttering_Around | Walking | 15 |
| PA_Type_Unlabeled | Puttering_Around | Standing_With_Movement | 6 |
| *Actual Ambulation Disagreement (Total: 76 s)* | | | |
| Standing_With_Movement | Walking | Standing_With_Movement | 60 |
| Walking | Standing_With_Movement | Walking | 8 |
| Standing_With_Movement | Walking | Sitting_With_Movement | 3 |
| Sitting_With_Movement | Walking | Sitting_With_Movement | 3 |
| PA_Type_Unlabeled | Standing_With_Movement | Walking | 2 |
| *Annotator Did Not Use Puttering_Around and Was More Detailed (Total: 196 s)* | | | |
| Standing_With_Movement | Walking | Puttering_Around | 111 |
| Walking | Standing_With_Movement | Puttering_Around | 37 |
| Sitting_With_Movement | Walking | Puttering_Around | 14 |
| PA_Type_Unlabeled | Walking | Puttering_Around | 12 |
| Kneeling_With_Movement | Walking | Puttering_Around | 10 |
| Walking_Up_Stairs | Walking | Puttering_Around | 7 |
| PA_Type_Unlabeled | Standing_With_Movement | Puttering_Around | 5 |
| *Used Detail Activity Instead of Ambulation Related (Total: 210 s)* | | | |
| Standing_With_Movement | Sweeping | Puttering_Around | 37 |
| Walking | Vacuuming | Standing_With_Movement | 29 |
| Standing_With_Movement | Washing_Hands | Standing_With_Movement | 26 |
| Standing_With_Movement | Sweeping | Standing_With_Movement | 23 |
| Standing_With_Movement | Washing_Hands | Puttering_Around | 16 |
| Walking | Walking_Down_Stairs | Walking | 12 |
| Walking | Watering_Plants | Standing_With_Movement | 12 |
| Standing_With_Movement | Watering_Plants | Puttering_Around | 8 |
| Walking | Vacuuming | Puttering_Around | 7 |
| Walking | Watering_Plants | Puttering_Around | 7 |
| Standing_With_Movement | Loading/Unloading_Washer_Dryer | Standing_With_Movement | 7 |
| Standing_With_Movement | Folding_Clothes | Walking | 7 |
| Kneeling_With_Movement | Sweeping | Puttering_Around | 5 |
| Walking | Walking_Down_Stairs | Puttering_Around | 4 |
| Standing_With_Movement | Folding_Clothes | Standing_With_Movement | 3 |
| Walking | Kneeling_With_Movement | Puttering_Around | 3 |
| PA_Type_Unlabeled | Vacuuming | Puttering_Around | 2 |
| Kneeling_With_Movement | Loading/Unloading_Washer_Dryer | Standing_With_Movement | 2 |
| *Annotator Missed a Detailed Activity (Total: 721 s)* | | | |
| Standing_With_Movement | Folding_Clothes | Putting_Clothes_Away | 310 |
| Standing_With_Movement | Puttering_Around | Organizing_Shelf/Cabinet | 159 |
| Standing_With_Movement | Walking | Putting_Clothes_Away | 92 |
| Walking | Puttering_Around | Putting_Clothes_Away | 82 |

(*continued*)

**Table 10.** (*continued*)

| Changed From | Changed To | Should Be | Duration (s) |
|---|---|---|---|
| Standing_With_Movement | Puttering_Around | Putting_Clothes_Away | 61 |
| Standing_With_Movement | Puttering_Around | Washing_Hands | 8 |
| Walking | Puttering_Around | Folding_Clothes | 7 |
| PA_Type_Unlabeled | Walking | Putting_Clothes_Away | 2 |
| *Missing Label or Boundary Related Error (Total: 60 s)* | | | |
| Standing_With_Movement | Puttering_Around | PA_Type_Unlabeled | 9 |
| Standing_With_Movement | Walking | PA_Type_Unlabeled | 8 |
| Walking | Puttering_Around | PA_Type_Video_Unavailable | 8 |
| Standing_With_Movement | Folding_Clothes | PA_Type_Video_Unavailable | 7 |
| Sitting_With_Movement | Walking | PA_Type_Unlabeled | 5 |
| PA_Type_Unlabeled | Walking | PA_Type_Unlabeled | 3 |
| PA_Type_Unlabeled | Puttering_Around | PA_Type_Unlabeled | 3 |
| Standing_With_Movement | Sweeping | PA_Type_Unlabeled | 2 |
| Kneeling_With_Movement | Loading/Unloading_Washer_Dryer | PA_Type_Video_Unavailable | 2 |
| Standing_With_Movement | Walking | PA_Type_Video_Unavailable | 2 |
| Standing_With_Movement | Walking | Kneeling_With_Movement | 1 |
| PA_Type_Unlabeled | Walking | Walking_Up_Stairs | 1 |
| Walking_Up_Stairs | Walking | Walking_Up_Stairs | 1 |
| Standing_With_Movement | Vacuuming | Standing_With_Movement | 1 |
| Walking | PA_Type_Unlabeled | Sitting_With_Movement | 1 |
| Standing_With_Movement | Puttering_Around | Walking | 1 |
| Standing_With_Movement | Washing_Hands | PA_Type_Unlabeled | 1 |
| PA_Type_Unlabeled | Sitting_With_Movement | Sitting_Still | 1 |
| PA_Type_Unlabeled | Sitting_With_Movement | Walking | 1 |
| Walking_Down_Stairs | Walking_Up_Stairs | Walking | 1 |
| Standing_With_Movement | PA_Type_Unlabeled | Puttering_Around | 1 |
| **Total Duration of All Incorrect Fixes** | | | **1,903 s** |

**Table 11.** Duration of changes made by revisers (in seconds) across the two independent annotator groups.

| Day (video length) | First annotator group (s) | Second annotator group (s) |
|---|---|---|
| Day 1 (4.8 h) | 254 | 4,417 |
| Day 2 (16.5 h) | 1,866 | 3,285 |
| Day 3 (17.7 h) | 6,784 | 4,254 |
| Day 4 (19 h) | 2,130 | 7,687 |
| Day 5 (17.4 h) | 4,839 | 10,822 |
| Day 6 (16.4 h) | 7,621 | 10,355 |

**Table 12.** Changes made by the reviser compared to the original annotation by the first annotator group.

| Activity | Total Duration (s) | | Number of Bouts | |
|---|---|---|---|---|
| | Original | Revised | Original | Revised |
| *Walking_Fast* | 20 | 0 | 1 | 0 |
| *Walking_Slow* | 10 | 10 | 1 | 1 |
| *Standing_Still* | 73 | 51 | 2 | 1 |
| *PA_Type_Too_Complex* | 0 | 55 | 0 | 1 |
| *PA_Type_Other* | 116 | 122 | 8 | 6 |
| *Watering_Plants* | 242 | 230 | 1 | 1 |
| *Brushing_Teeth* | 251 | 242 | 3 | 3 |
| *Synchronizing_Sensors* | 236 | 264 | 9 | 10 |
| *Walking_Down_Stairs* | 187 | 301 | 25 | 41 |
| *Loading/Unloading_Washing_Machine/Dryer* | 334 | 334 | 4 | 4 |
| *Walking_Up_Stairs* | 208 | 391 | 29 | 47 |
| *Lying_Still* | 411 | 411 | 1 | 1 |
| *Ironing* | 436 | 436 | 1 | 1 |
| *Sweeping* | 447 | 507 | 2 | 3 |
| *Organizing_Shelf/Cabinet* | 549 | 549 | 2 | 2 |
| *Putting_Clothes_Away* | 667 | 644 | 6 | 5 |
| *Folding_Clothes* | 657 | 689 | 7 | 7 |
| *Kneeling_With_Movement* | 667 | 696 | 14 | 16 |
| *Washing_Hands* | 727 | 823 | 25 | 33 |
| *PA_Type_Unlabeled* | 844 | 844 | 4 | 4 |
| *Vacuuming* | 1,035 | 1,035 | 1 | 1 |
| *Cycling_Active_Pedaling_Stationary_Bike* | 9,448 | 9,448 | 2 | 2 |
| *Walking* | 13,745 | 13,143 | 214 | 242 |
| *Puttering_Around* | 26,860 | 22,252 | 319 | 487 |
| *Standing_With_Movement* | 16,271 | 22,288 | 267 | 444 |
| *PA_Type_Video_Unavailable/Indecipherable* | 52,854 | 62,704 | 71 | 101 |
| *Sitting_With_Movement* | 199,094 | 190,279 | 229 | 229 |

**Table 13.** Changes made by the reviser compared to the original annotation by the second annotator group.

| Activity | Total Duration (s) | | Number of Bouts | |
|---|---|---|---|---|
| | Original | Revised | Original | Revised |
| *Cycling_Active_Pedaling_Regular_Bicycle* | 0 | 27 | 0 | 1 |
| *Standing_Still* | 31 | 31 | 1 | 1 |
| *Synchronizing_Sensors* | 70 | 70 | 2 | 2 |
| *Folding_Clothes* | 0 | 156 | 0 | 1 |
| *PA_Type_Other* | 2,404 | 172 | 49 | 13 |
| *Loading/Unloading_Washing_Machine/Dryer* | 0 | 187 | 0 | 5 |
| *Brushing_Teeth* | 261 | 261 | 3 | 3 |
| *Putting_Clothes_Away* | 347 | 355 | 3 | 3 |
| *Walking_Down_Stairs* | 176 | 381 | 17 | 33 |
| *Walking_Up_Stairs* | 304 | 553 | 27 | 42 |
| *Washing_Hands* | 462 | 606 | 18 | 24 |
| *Kneeling_With_Movement* | 416 | 710 | 7 | 16 |
| *Vacuuming* | 0 | 971 | 0 | 1 |
| *Sitting_Still* | 989 | 989 | 5 | 5 |
| *Puttering_Around* | 24,805 | 4,660 | 372 | 111 |
| *Cycling_Active_Pedaling_Stationary_Bike* | 5,700 | 9,289 | 1 | 4 |
| *Walking* | 19,380 | 20,684 | 200 | 413 |
| *Standing_With_Movement* | 25,772 | 39,093 | 414 | 508 |
| *PA_Type_Video_Unavailable/Indecipherable* | 60,118 | 61,315 | 120 | 132 |
| *Sitting_With_Movement* | 188,371 | 189,223 | 444 | 441 |

## References


1. Bayerl, P.S., Paul, K.I.: What determines inter-coder agreement in manual annotations? A meta-analytic investigation. Comput. Linguist. **37**(4), 699–725 (2011). https://doi.org/10.1162/COLI_a_00074
2. Buhrmester, M., Kwang, T., Gosling, S.D.: Amazon's Mechanical Turk: a new source of inexpensive, yet high-quality, data? Perspectives on Psychol. Sci. **6**(1), 3–5 (2011). https://doi.org/10.1037/14805-009
3. Calatroni, A., Roggen, D., Tröster, G.: Collection and curation of a large reference dataset for activity recognition. In: 2011 IEEE Int'l Conf. on Sys., Man, and Cybernetics, pp. 30–35. IEEE (2011). https://doi.org/10.1109/ICSMC.2011.6083638
4. Chan, S., et al.: CAPTURE-24: a large dataset of wrist-worn activity tracker data collected in the wild for human activity recognition. Sci. Data **11**(1), 1135 (2024). https://doi.org/10.1038/s41597-024-03960-3
5. Doherty, A., et al.: Large scale population assessment of physical activity using wrist worn accelerometers: the UK Biobank study. PLoS ONE **12**(2), 1–14 (2017). https://doi.org/10.1371/journal.pone.0169649

6. Hoelzemann, A., Romero, J.L., Bock, M., Laerhoven, K.V., Lv, Q.: Hang-time HAR: a benchmark dataset for basketball activity recognition ISING wrist-worn inertial sensors. Sensors (Basel) **23**(13) (2023).https://doi.org/10.3390/s23135879
7. Keadle, S.K., Lyden, K.A., Strath, S.J., Staudenmayer, J.W., Freedson, P.S.: A framework to evaluate devices that assess physical behavior. Exerc. Sport Sci. Rev. **47**(4), 206–214 (2019). https://doi.org/10.1249/JES.0000000000000206
8. Landis, J.R., Koch, G.G.: The measurement of observer agreement for categorical data. Biometrics 159–174 (1977). https://doi.org/10.2307/2529310
9. Logacjov, A., Bach, K., Kongsvold, A., Bårdstu, H.B., Mork, P.J.: HARTH: a human activity recognition dataset for machine learning. Sensors (Basel) **21**(23) (2021). https://doi.org/10.3390/s21237853
10. Mattfeld, R., Jesch, E., Hoover, A.: A new dataset for evaluating pedometer performance. In: 2017 IEEE Int'l Conf. on Bioinformatics and Biomedicine (BIBM), pp. 865–869 (2017). https://doi.org/10.1109/BIBM.2017.8217769
11. Small, S.R., et al.: Self-supervised machine learning to characterize step counts from wrist-worn accelerometers in the UK Biobank. Med. Sci. Sports Exerc. **56**(10), 1945 (2024). https://doi.org/10.1249/MSS.0000000000003478
12. Stoev, T., Suravee, S., Yordanova, K.: Variability of annotations over time: an experimental study in the dementia-related named entity recognition domain. In: INFORMATIK 2024, pp. 473–486. Gesellschaft für Informatik eV (2024).https://doi.org/10.18420/inf2024_35
13. Troiano, R.P., Berrigan, D., Dodd, K.W., Mâsse, L.C., Tilert, T., McDowell, M.: Physical activity in the United States measured by accelerometer. Med. Sci. Sports Exerc. **40**(1), 181 (2008)https://doi.org/10.1249/mss.0b013e31815a51b3
14. Twomey, N., et al.: The SPHERE challenge: activity recognition with multimodal sensor data. arXiv preprint (2016). https://doi.org/10.48550/arXiv.1603.00797
15. U.S. Bureau of Labor Statistics: American Time Use Survey. Data file (2024). https://www.bls.gov/tus/. Accessed 28 July 2025
16. Willetts, M., Hollowell, S., Aslett, L., Holmes, C., Doherty, A.: Statistical machine learning of sleep and physical activity phenotypes from sensor data in 96,609 UK Biobank participants. Sci. Rep. **8**(7961) (2018). https://doi.org/10.1038/s41598-018-26174-1
17. Yordanova, K.: Challenges providing ground truth for pervasive healthcare system. IEEE Pervasive Comput. **18**(2), 100–104 (2019). https://doi.org/10.1109/MPRV.2019.2912261
18. Yordanova, K., Kruger, F.: Creating and exploring semantic annotation for behaviour analysis. Sensors (Basel) **18**(9) (2018). https://doi.org/10.3390/s18092778

# Annotation of Textual Data

# Large Language Models Rival Human Performance in Historical Labeling

Fabio Celli[1(✉)] and Valerio Basile[2]

[1] Gruppo Maggioli, Santarcangelo di Romagna, Italy
fabio.celli@maggioli.it
[2] University of Turin, Turin, Italy

**Abstract.** This study examines the application of Large Language Models to automatically annotate the phases of the Structural-Demographic Theory from short descriptions of historical decades. This task is useful for understanding social instability, but it is inherently subjective and challenging due to the temporal nature of labels. A single misalignment in phase labeling between annotators can cascade through subsequent time-steps, causing the inter-annotator agreement to decrease exponentially. Our results indicate that models with more than 400 billion parameters achieve very high agreement, while models with fewer than 100 billion parameters are prone to hallucinations. Moreover, the two largest models we tested (GPT4 and Lama3.1-405b) reach inter-annotator agreement comparable to pairs of human annotators, paving the way towards automated annotation. However, the need for very large models could hinder the democratization of automatic historical annotation due to the required computational resources. To mitigate this, we suggest collaborations between universities and companies, in order to share knowledge and computational power.

**Keywords:** Large Language Models · Structural Demographic Theory · Historical Phase Labeling

## 1 Introduction and Background

The Structural Demographic Theory (SDT) offers a computationally viable framework for understanding the long-term social pressures that can ignite socio-political instability, revolutions and civil wars [6]. This theory describes how demographic changes, economic inequalities, and the dynamics within the elite class cyclically create or alleviate pressures for instability [7,16]. In fact, when combined with data modeling, SDT allowed researchers to accurately predict the global crises of the 2020s [17]. It also proved to be useful to analyze many historical events, such as the French Revolution's causes; the American Civil War's elite rivalries [18], and the Qing Dynasty's collapse [10]. Moreover, researchers successfully used the SDT framework to understand contemporary outbreaks of instability, from the Egyptian revolution of 2011 [9] to the US political instability in 2021 [19]. This wide record of applications demonstrates the value of


E. L. Tonkin et al. (Eds.): ARDUOUS 2025, CCIS 2706, pp. 121–128, 2026.
https://doi.org/10.1007/978-3-032-09117-8_7

SDT for analyzing complex socio-political patterns in historical data [20], and recent research explored the possibility to annotate data with SDT. In particular, the SDT defines five cyclical historical phases: growth, population immiseration, elite overproduction, state stress and crisis. Despite it is possible to annotate SDT phases on textual data [1], the task proved to be very challenging. Crucially, the subjective nature of historical phase interpretation introduces significant inter-annotator variability, potentially influenced by personal bias, including Eurocentrism. While certain historical periods exhibit clear consensus (e.g., the French Revolution is a crisis), others, such as the French intervention in Mexico or the early Maoist era in China, reveal significant interpretive divergence, demonstrating the difficulty in establishing consistent phase boundaries. The predominant methodologies in historical data annotation involve the development of schemas and guidelines for event detection and categorization that are grounded in linguistic theory [14] or thesauri [12]. Literature on the application of these methodologies reports a fairy high Cohen's $k$ [3], around 0.7, with twenty labels and two annotators. In contrast, the annotation of SDT phases from short texts exhibits limited inter-annotator agreement. The reported inter-annotator agreement for identifying SDT phases from brief historical descriptions is a poor Fleiss' $k$ [4] of 0.206 [1]. Achieving high agreement on this specific task is inherently challenging due to the temporal nature of SDT phases, which introduces extra constraints than a normal annotation task. In practice, a single misalignment in phase labeling between two annotators can cascade through subsequent time-steps, causing the inter-annotator agreement to decrease exponentially. A fair agreement (Fleiss' $k$ 0.455) can be achieved by first assigning a default SDT sequence (e.g., two decades of growth, two of population impoverishment, two of elite overproduction, three of state stress, and one of crisis) and then having annotators assess and modify these labels for each decade [1]. However, we suggest that this approach artificially inflates agreement. This is because the fewer changes annotators make to the initial sequence, the higher their resulting agreement will be. For this reason, we will use $k$=0.206 as reference baseline. State-of-the-art methods, such as the use of generative AI, proved to be successful in supporting annotation workflows [15], hence we propose the use of Large Language Models (LLMs) as annotators to address SDT phase labeling. LLMs-as-Annotators proved to be promising [11], and literature shows that they possess historical knowledge that can be leveraged [2]. In order to exploit LLMs-as-annotators for this task, we turn existing guidelines on SDT annotation into a prompt, then we execute this prompt with different LLMs annotating the same data, then we compute the inter- and intra-annotator agreement. Finally, we compare the results against a human baseline. The paper is structured as follows: in Sect. 2 we describe the SDT labels and the annotation schema, in Sect. 3 we describe the data we use, in Sect. 4 we report the prompt and the results of the annotation evaluation, and finally in Sect. 5 we draw our conclusions.

## 2 Annotation Schema

The SDT posits that long-term societal instability and upheaval are driven by cyclical interactions between demographic, economic, and political factors. These cyclical interactions, called secular cycles [21], are typically 75–100 years in duration [8], and are characterized by the interplay of three core actors through five distinct phases. The actors are the population, elites and the State. Population constitutes approximately 90% of society, the population functions as the primary source of labor and resources, with limited consumption of generated wealth. Elites represent roughly 8% of society and are responsible for problem-solving and constitute the pool of potential State members. Elite composition and mobility are contingent upon the prevailing governance structure. State is approximately 2% of society. It enforces governance and manages resource allocation. It consists of one or more elite factions, and serves to codify and perpetuate societal culture. These actors engage in five sequential phases, marked by increasing socio-political instability and defined as follows:

- Growth Phase: characterized by robust cultural cohesion, increased state control and trade network expansion, this phase leads societies towards stability, albeit with sustainability concerns. Post-war reconstruction periods exemplify this phase.
- Population Immiseration Phase: population growth outpaces economic expansion, driven by the disparity between capital return and wage growth [13]. This results in heightened inequality and social unrest, as the state's extractive capacity reaches its limits.
- Elite Overproduction Phase: increased population access to elite ranks strains social mobility mechanisms, diminishing elite problem-solving capacity and increasing societal instability.
- State Stress Phase: State governance and elite-population cooperation deteriorate, leading to elite fragmentation and potential civil conflict. The financial instability of the state makes it vulnerable to destabilizing events.
- Crisis, Collapse, or Recovery Phase: the state undergoes reformation or overthrow, culminating in a new social equilibrium and the initiation of a subsequent cycle.

This schema describes a process. However, in order to operationalize the guidelines into a prompt (we will call it "annotation prompt"), we need to find recognizable cues from text associated to the different labels, and turn them into clear instructions. To do so, we use another prompt (we will call it "knowledge extraction prompt"), and generate instructions from data, as described in the next section.

## 3 Data and Prompts

For the sake of reproducibility, and to allow comparison with previous studies, we opted to use the Chronos dataset [1]. Chronos is a historical dataset containing short, decade-by-decade textual descriptions of 366 polities sampled from 18 sampling points equally distributed around the world, and spanning from prehistory to the 2010 s. It was compiled using Seshat [22] and Wikipedia, focusing on the collection of key historical events (wars, rulers, reforms, etc.) summarized within a 400-character limit. Chronos is manually annotated with SDT phases by an official human annotator, and evaluated by other two human raters on 93 examples, and 5 labels. Exploiting the existing SDT annotation, we extracted 60 examples of historical decades descriptions per label (for a total of 300 examples) and summarized them with the knowledge generation prompt [5] reported in Fig. 1. In this way we obtained clear instructions that we included in the annotation prompt, reported in Fig. 2.

> Summarize the following description/phase pairs into prompt instructions optimized to classify the phases and reducing potential overlaps:
> ⟨*data*⟩

**Fig. 1.** Knowledge Extraction Prompt for the generation of instructions related to SDT labels. Executed with GPT-4.

The data we use in our experiments are the same as those used for evaluating the annotation of the Chronos dataset. It comprises 93 decades from 6 polities from different places and times: the Mexican Republic, the Later Jin Dynasty, the Mongol Empire, the Yuan Dynasty, the Roman Kingdom and the Early Roman Republic. The dataset is freely available for replication studies[1]. Examples follows:

- Decade: 380 s b.C., polity: Early Roman Republic, description: The Romans were defeated by Brennus of Senones in the Battle of Allia River in 387 BC. The Senones besieged Rome but probably the health conditions were bad and accepted a ransom in gold and silver to leave the city. Brennus cheated when weighting the gold and Romans, helped by the returned Furius Camillus, defeated Brennus.
- Decade: 1170 s, polity: Later Jin Dynasty, description: Emperor Shizong (r. 1161–1189) confiscated unused land from Jurchen landowners and redistributed to Jurchen farmers, but they preferred to lease the work to Chinese farmers and engage in drinking instead. in 1175 paper factory in Hangzhou employed more than a thousand Chinese workers. Integration problems (language and customs).
- Decade: 1290 s, polity: Yuan dynasty, description: Kublai Kahn promoted commercial, scientific, and cultural growth. He supported the merchants of the Silk Road trade network by protecting the Mongol postal system he also cancelled the Confucian exhamination and managed power in autocratic way.

[1] https://huggingface.co/datasets/facells/chronos-llm-sdt-agreeement.

Act as an expert historian and consider the Structural Demographic Theory (SDT). Given a set of descriptions of historical decades for different polities, label each description with one of the following secular cycle phases (sdtphase):
*Start of knowledge-generated prompt*
0=crisis (in this phase may happen societal collapse patterns, power transitions, conflicts, administrative or social structure changes, and external influences. Look for signs of civil wars, military coups, environmental factors, population movements, reform of tax systems, trade network disruptions, class conflicts, and foreign invasions).
1=growth (a society recovers from a crisis finding a new fresh culture that creates social cohesion. to recognize this phase examine the power structure patterns, legitimacy of rule, social organization, cultural elements, military aspects, and social changes. Look for the presence of strong elite classes, religious legitimation of power, centralized administrative systems, trade networks, cultural practices, territorial expansion, and population movements);
2=population impoverishment (growth slows and inequalities begin to emerge. to recognize this phase evaluate the power dynamics, economic patterns, military aspects, cultural/religious elements, administrative features, and infrastructure development. Look for succession struggles, trade route development, territorial conquests, religious tolerance, bureaucratic reforms, and construction projects);
3=elite overproduction (the number elite aspirants rises and the social lift mechanisms deteriorate. To recognize this phase assess power dynamics, governance, economic patterns, social structures, cultural and technological development, and common catalysts for change. Look for power struggles, trade system developments, social unrest between elite and population, religious developments, and military conflicts),
4=state stress (elites struggle to institutionalize their advantages. to recognize this phase review political instability, power struggles, economic challenges, military conflicts, administrative changes, and social/religious tensions. Look for succession disputes, financial crises, territorial loss, reforms to advantage specific elite groups, social unrest and religious conflicts).
*End of knowledge-generated prompt*
A cycle cannot turn back and cannot skip phases. So if in 1940 there is a phase 0, in 1950 there should be a phase 1, in 1960 there can be a phase 1 or phase 2. If in 1960 there is a phase 2, in 1970 there can be a phase 2 or phase 3, not a phase 4. If in 1970 there is a phase 3, in 1980 there can be a phase 3 or 4, and if in 2000 there is phase 4, in 2010 there can be a phase 0 or another phase 4. The decade after phase 0 the cycle restarts from phase 1.
This is an example of the input (json): ⟨*example*⟩
and this is the desired output (csv): ⟨*example*⟩
set of descriptions to label (json): ⟨*data*⟩

**Fig. 2.** Annotation Prompt. The part generated with the Knowledge Extraction prompt is marked by tags. The secular cycle phases are defined as numeric labels: 1 = growth, 2 = population immiseration, 3 = elite overproduction, 4 = state stress, 0 = crisis.

## 4 Experiments

We performed three experiments: 1) to test the feasibility of the task; 2) to compare the inter-annotator agreement of humans and LLMs; 3) to test intra-annotator agreement of LLMs. We used LLMs of different size: Mistral-7b (7.25 billion parameters); Llama3.3-70b (70 billion parameters); Mistral-Large-2411 (123 billion parameters); Llama-3.1-405b (405 billion parameters) and GPT-4 (1.8 trillion parameters). We set the temperature to zero in order to perform a deterministic inference and enhance reproducibility.

**Table 1.** Evaluation of the Inter- and Intra-Annotator Agreement between LLMs and humans. The best result is marked in bold, the ones below the baseline are marked in italics.

| Inter-Annotator Agreement | raters | examples | Fleiss' K | Cohen's K |
|---|---|---|---|---|
| human baseline | 3 | 93 | 0.206 | – |
| all LLMs | 3 | 93 | *0.133* | – |
| mistral-large-2411 + gpt4 | 2 | 93 | *0.081* | *0.095* |
| mistral-large-2411 + llama3.1-405b | 2 | 93 | *0.049* | *0.076* |
| llama3.1-405b + gpt4 | 2 | 93 | **0.255** | **0.253** |
| human-official + human1 | 2 | 93 | *0.138* | *0.139* |
| human-official + human2 | 2 | 93 | 0.232 | 0.234 |
| human1 + human2 | 2 | 93 | 0.248 | 0.250 |
| llama3.1 + official-human | 2 | 93 | 0.206 | 0.206 |
| llama3.1 + human1 | 2 | 93 | **0.454** | **0.455** |
| llama3.1 + human2 | 2 | 93 | 0.262 | 0.263 |
| gpt4 + official-human | 2 | 93 | 0.211 | 0.214 |
| gpt4 + human1 | 2 | 93 | *0.104* | *0.109* |
| gpt4 + human2 | 2 | 93 | 0.278 | 0.280 |
| **Intra-Annotator Agreement** | **trials** | **examples** | **Fleiss' K** | **Cohen's K** |
| llama3.1-405b | 2 | 93 | **0.641** | **0.642** |
| llama3.1-405b | 3 | 93 | 0.572 | – |
| gpt4 | 2 | 93 | 0.525 | 0.525 |
| gpt4 | 3 | 93 | 0.331 | – |
| human-official | 2 | 93 | 0.519 | 0.510 |

The goal of experiment 1 is to correctly generate SDT labels formatted in csv. Some LLMs had input limitations, so we had to input one polity at a time. However, the smallest LLMs failed to produce the desired output. Mistral-7b and Llama3.3-70b, run on 4 NVIDIA A40 GPUs with 46GB VRAM, generated hallucinations, misaligned outputs or correct results only for some polities. In general, these smaller models tend to focus on the last few elements of the input data. Instead the larger models, running on Google cloud, correctly generated the output. We were able to run experiments 2 and 3 only with models larger than 100 billion parameters. The experimental setting for experiment 2 consists of the 5 SDT labels and 93 examples, the same used for evaluating the annotation in the Chronos dataset. We evaluated this experiment with both Fleiss' and Cohen's $k$ on the results generated by Mistral-large-2411 (123b), GPT4 (1.8t) and Llama3.1-405b.

The results, reported in Table 1, reveal that the Inter-Annotator agreement between the largest models (Llama3.1-405b and GPT-4) is comparable to the best human performance, while combinations with smaller LLMs yield poor agreement. This suggests that the number of parameters in the model greatly affects the ability of the LLM to evaluate a complex context and select a label. In order to have comparable results, We also tested the agreement between humans and LLMs, finding that this combination yields the best results. Experiment 3 on Intra-Annotator agreement revealed that Llama3.1-large has great consistency, higher than humans, while GPT-4 proved to have lower consistency, as reported in Table 1.

## 5 Discussion and Conclusion

The observed relation between model size and annotation agreement in the identification of SDT phases from short texts highlights the profound contextual demands of this task. Our findings suggest that models exceeding 400 billion parameters exhibit significantly improved Inter-Annotator agreement over smaller models, reaching human performance. We suggest that very large LLMs have access to more information than humans, and more work is needed to understand how LLMs use this information for label selection. We plan to address this issue in future work. In conclusion, our observations reinforce the notion that inherently subjective annotation tasks such as SDT phase recognition, necessitates a vast reservoir of learned knowledge. While larger models offer a great performance, their demand for high computational power raises concerns regarding cost, environmental impact, and accessibility. Unfortunately, smaller, locally deployable models, though potentially more sustainable and democratizing, are more prone to hallucinations and hardly achieve acceptable results in this task. This trade-off between performance and practicality underscores the critical need for further research into efficient knowledge representation and transfer within LLMs, particularly when balancing the need for accuracy with the goal of democratizing access to historical analysis. Under this perspective, universities and companies should collaborate, sharing know-how and computational power.

**Acknowledgments.** This research was supported by the European Commission, grant 10121294: Bankable by Design, Continuous, and Predictive Climate Adaptation Investments with Co-Benefits - CLIMINVEST.

**Disclosure of Interests.** The authors have no competing interests to declare that are relevant to the content of this article.

## References

1. Celli, F., Basile, V.: History repeats: historical phase recognition from short texts. In: Proceedings of the CLIC-it (2024)
2. Celli, F., Mingazov, D.: Knowledge extraction from llms for scalable historical data annotation. Electronics **13**(24), 4990 (2024)
3. Cohen, J.: Statistical Power Analysis for the Behavioral Sciences. Academic Press, New York (1977)
4. Fleiss, J.L., Levin, B., Paik, M.C.: The measurement of interrater agreement. Stat. Methods Rates Proportions **2**, 212–236 (1981)
5. Ge, Y., et al.: Implicit knowledge-augmented prompting for commonsense explanation generation. Knowl. Inf. Syst. 1–36 (2025)
6. Goldstone, J.A.: A theory of political demography. Polit. Demography: Popul. Changes Reshaping Int. Secur. Natl. Polit. 10–28 (2012)
7. Goldstone, J.A.: Demographic structural theory: 25 years on. Cliodynamics **8**(2) (2017)
8. Korotaev, A.V.: Introduction to social macrodynamics: secular cycles and millennial trends in Africa. Editorial URSS (2006)
9. Korotayev, A., Zinkina, J.: Egypt s 2011 revolution: a demographic structural analysis. In: Handbook of Revolutions in the 21st Century: The New Waves of Revolutions, and the Causes and Effects of Disruptive Political Change, pp. 651–683. Springer (2022)
10. Orlandi, G., et al.: Structural-demographic analysis of the qing dynasty (1644–1912) collapse in china. PLoS ONE **18**(8), e0289748 (2023)
11. Pavlovic, M., Poesio, M.: The effectiveness of llms as annotators: a comparative overview and empirical analysis of direct representation. LREC-COLING **2024**, 100 (2024)
12. Piao, S., et al.: A time-sensitive historical thesaurus-based semantic tagger for deep semantic annotation. Comput. Speech Lang. **46**, 113–135 (2017)
13. Piketty, T.: Capital in the Twenty-first Century. Harvard University Press (2014)
14. Sprugnoli, R., Tonelli, S.: Novel event detection and classification for historical texts. Comput. Linguist. **45**(2), 229–265 (2019)
15. Stoev, T., Tonkin, E.L., Yordanova, K., Tourte, G.J.: Tutorial: developing a data annotation protocol. In: Ubicomp/ISWC 2023 (2023)
16. Turchin, P.: Long-term population cycles in human societies. Ann. N. Y. Acad. Sci. **1162**(1), 1–17 (2009)
17. Turchin, P.: Political instability may be a contributor in the coming decade. Nature **463**(7281), 608–608 (2010)
18. Turchin, P.: A Structural-Demographic Analysis of American History. Beresta Books Chaplin (2016)
19. Turchin, P.: End times: elites, counter-elites, and the path of political disintegration. Penguin (2023)
20. Turchin, P., Korotayev, A.: The 2010 structural-demographic forecast for the 2010–2020 decade: a retrospective assessment. PLoS ONE **15**(8) (2020)
21. Turchin, P., Nefedov, S.A.: Secular Cycles. Princeton University Press (2009)
22. Turchin, P., et al.: An introduction to seshat: global history databank. J. Cogn. Historiography **5**, 115–123 (2020)

# Annotation and Label Validation of Upper-Tier Tribunal Decisions in Immigration Law

Laura Scheinert[1(✉)] and Emma L. Tonkin[2]

[1] Faculty of Environment, Science and Economy (Associate), University of Exeter, Exeter, UK
l.scheinert-idodo2@exeter.ac.uk
[2] Digital Health, University of Bristol, Bristol, UK
e.l.tonkin@bristol.ac.uk

**Abstract.** Upper tribunal decisions form a vital component of the immigration appeal system in the United Kingdom (UK), since these decisions often act as a 'corrective' to initial judicial decision-making by the first-tier tribunal. This paper describes the process of annotating a corpus drawn from the UK's Upper Tribunal Immigration and Asylum Chamber (UTIAC) decisions openly published by the tribunal, covering the years 2000 to 2021. A label taxonomy is developed and applied by two annotators for annotation of several types of features, including decision outcomes and the presence of and type of legal errors identified by the tribunal. Annotations were implemented via a low-cost, high-accessibility tool and validated calculating inter-annotator agreement. We discuss the pros and cons of our annotation tool and also critically reflect on annotator background. We successfully used the produced ground truth for supervised machine learning classification tasks, adding further confidence to the suitability of annotations for said tasks. We are considering ethics and data protection compliant ways to safely make the corpus and annotations available for future work.

**Keywords:** Corpus annotation · Judicial decisions · Immigration and asylum

## 1 Introduction

### 1.1 The Role of Tribunal Decisions in Immigration Law

The immigration and asylum appeals system exists to provide an opportunity for challenging administrative decision-making by the government body responsible for issuing immigration statuses. In the United Kingdom (UK), the First-tier Tribunal Immigration and Asylum Chamber (FtTIAC) is the first judicial instance to deal with immigration and asylum appeals. Administrative decisions by the UK's Home Office – the government department dealing with the various immigration and asylum applications – can be appealed to the FtTIAC by appellants (those making immigration or asylum applications). The Immigration and Asylum Chamber (IAC), which has UK-wide jurisdiction, has a


E. L. Tonkin et al. (Eds.): ARDUOUS 2025, CCIS 2706, pp. 129–146, 2026.
https://doi.org/10.1007/978-3-032-09117-8_8

two-tiered structure, being one of seven chambers in the First-tier Tribunal and one of four in the Upper Tribunal. Judging by numbers of received appeals, the FtTIAC is the third-largest tribunal, after the Social Security and Child Support (part of the Social Entitlement Chamber) and Employment Tribunals (see https://www.gov.uk/government/collections/tribunals-statistics#tribunal-statistics-quarterly, last accessed 2025/07/20). FtTIAC decisions can, in turn, be challenged by both the person bringing the initial appeal (usually called the *appellant*) as well as by the Home Office (usually in form of the Secretary of State for the Home Department (SSHD), an entry clearance officer (ECO), or immigration officer (IO)). If a so-called *permission to appeal* is granted (either by the FtTIAC or UTIAC), the UTIAC hears appeals on points of law (and conducts judicial review of Home Office decisions, i.e., an assessment into the lawfulness of such decisions; for details see, e.g., [18,19]). This means that UTIAC hearings focus on establishing whether the FtTIAC erred in law, as opposed to whether the FtTIAC reached the "right" decision. In a similar vein, UTIAC decisions can be appealed, with permission, to the Court of Appeal, and eventually the Supreme Court, the UK's highest judicial instance.

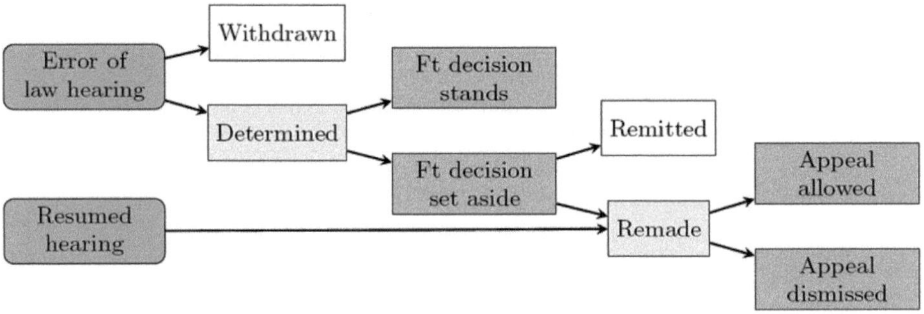


**Fig. 1.** Overview of UTIAC hearing and decision outcome types (Ft = First-tier).

Simply speaking, there are two major types of hearings and related decisions in the UTIAC: 1) an error of law (EOL) hearing and decision, and 2) a resumed hearing and remade decision (see Fig. 1). If an appeal does not get withdrawn, the error of law hearing and decision establish whether the FtTIAC decision under appeal needs to be overturned ("set aside") for error of law, or whether it is upheld ("can stand"). An overturned decision can either be sent back ("remitted") to the FtTIAC (or SSHD), or decided by the UTIAC itself in either the same EOL hearing or at a further substantive, so-called "resumed", hearing. Substantive hearings in the UTIAC can also be prompted by appeals remitted to it from the higher instance courts (Court of Appeal, Supreme Court), by judicial review, or by guidance cases. The latter are cases of particular importance and complexity for which the UTIAC wishes to issue binding guidance for the FtTIAC.

The UTIAC's function to detect errors of law means that upper tribunal decisions often result in a necessary corrective to initial judicial decision-making by the first-tier tribunal, and hence, published upper-tier decisions are a rich information source for several reasons. Beyond providing a corpus of legal decisions to which many of the established methods from the Artificial Intelligence (AI) and law and judicial analytics fields can be applied, including, for example, argument summarisation, citation extraction, and linguistic analysis, UTIAC decisions can also be employed in the evaluation of judicial training. From the perspective of judicial training evaluation, the following features of the immigration and asylum appeals system are of interest: firstly, the number of appeals approximate onward litigation, as do the number of remitted cases. Secondly, the *number* of overturned FtTIAC decisions can give insight into *how many* decisions there are needing correction, while thirdly, the *types of errors* identified as the basis for overturning FtTIAC decisions can explain *why* FtTIAC decisions get set aside – which, in turn, can feed into training effectiveness and needs analysis.

Previous work employing analysis of similar decisions mainly focuses on outcome prediction for US, European and Chinese courts, i.a. identifying decision outcomes such as, e.g., affirm/ reverse in US state court appellate decisions [10] or violation/non-violation of human rights in European Court of Human Rights (ECtHR) decisions [1,3,8]. A variety of techniques are applied to support these aims, ranging from simple supervised binary classifiers such as support vector machines [1,8,17] to more complex neural network models [3,10]. While similar approaches could be useful for decision classification for judicial training evaluation purposes as described above, none of these techniques have yet, to the best of our knowledge, been transferred to outcome classification or extraction of information about attested errors of law in second-instance (here: UTIAC) judicial decisions for that purpose.

### 1.2 Understanding Argument, Outcome, and Error: Establishing Effectiveness of Judicial Training

In our examination of the effectiveness of judicial training, we reach for UTIAC decisions to support appeals analysis. This analysis formed part of a wider social sciences PhD project completed by the first author, which developed, tested, and critically reflected on a mixed methods framework for judicial training evaluation at all levels drawing on training course observation, training materials analysis, qualitative interviews with judges and judicial trainers, and computational analysis of judicial decisions [12]. While judicial training – the induction and continuous training, learning and development undertaken by judges once in office – aims to build and maintain judicial competence so that judges may confidently take on their independent adjudication task, it is an ongoing research problem whether training does indeed support judges in this way, and whether it positively influences the quality of administered justice. Among other things, previous work in the judicial training evaluation field calls for greater attention to quantitative outcome measures of judicial performance at the systemic rather than individual level by drawing on analysis of judicial decisions and court management data [2,5,11,20].

In this way, appeal decisions (here: by the UTIAC) are conceptualised as a 'corrective' to first-instance (here: FtTIAC) decisions that make statements and provide information about attested accuracy of the first-instance decision-making process (though notably not the decision outcome itself, as explained above). UTIAC decisions understood in this sense yield at least two pieces of information relevant to judicial training evaluation in the immigration tribunals: 1) an assessment as to whether or not a FtTIAC decision can *stand* or needs to be *overturned* (i.e., whether or not the UTIAC upholds the FtTIAC decision), and 2) for overturned decisions, insight into so-called errors of law as the reasons for overturning a FtTIAC decision. While rates of overturned decisions can be calculated based on the published official Tribunal Statistics (https://www.gov.uk/government/collections/tribunals-statistics, last accessed 2025/07/20), these do not offer a breakdown into individual decisions, nor do they enable a follow-on analysis of error patterns (i.e., the identification of reasons for why FtTIAC decisions get overturned). This empirical problem clearly represents classical classification tasks, justifying and motivating the application of machine learning (ML) classifiers.

All supervised ML techniques rely on a labelled dataset, a so-called *ground truth*, against which classifiers can be trained and evaluated for performance. In most related previous work, such labels are available as part of decision meta-data as authors use texts from well-established and maintained judicial decisions corpora, such as the ECtHR's online decisions database (called HUDOC, available at https://hudoc.echr.coe.int/eng, last accessed 2025/07/20; e.g., [1,8]) or national databases, such as the French Supreme Court decisions database, meaning they can 'use the metadata provided as "natural" labels to be predicted by the machine learning system' [17, p. 2].

UTIAC decisions, however, do not come with meta-data that includes decision outcomes. For context, UTIAC decisions are publicly available on a dedicated Tribunals Decisions Website (https://tribunalsdecisions.service.gov.uk/utiac, last accessed 2025/07/20). The index page provides a high-level overview of published decisions, while decision-specific sub-pages contain case number and, for some decisions, further meta-data, incl. appellant name, decision status, hearing and decision dates, appellant country, and judge(s) hearing the case. The decision files and meta-data available on these sub-pages formed the basis for our corpus (for detail of its compilation, see [14]), which in its finalised and pre-processed form comprises a total of 33756 UTIAC decisions, published between 2000 and quarter 1 of 2021. The majority of decisions (31633 decisions or 93.71%) in the corpus are "unreported", i.e., do not constitute binding precedent for the FtTIAC. Unreported decisions can be differentiated into ten appeal types plus judicial review decisions. The appeal types are, in alphabetical order: Asylum, Deport(ation), Deprivation of Citizenship, European Economic Area (EEA) Free Movement, Entry Clearance, Family Visit Visa, Human Rights, Managed Migration, Protection, and Revocation of Protection.

Note that while these are the appeal types present in the corpus, not all of them are currently available as appeal routes: the Immigration Act 2014 significantly reduced appeal rights and thereby possible appeal types, from an initial nine to five. At the time of writing (July 2025), Home Office decision types that can be appealed to the immigration and asylum tribunals are Protection, Human Rights, EEA Free Movement, Deportation, and Deprivation of Citizenship (see https://www.gov.uk/immigration-asylum-tribunal, last accessed 2025/07/20).

As available meta-data for UTIAC decisions did not include decision outcomes, we were, like Petrova et al. [10, p. 137], 'faced with the so-called "cold start" problem' and needed 'to get some labelled data first'. This usually means manual annotation of a subset of the corpus. In this paper, we describe the annotation approach used to label a corpus suitable for our aims of training classifiers to identify decision outcomes of UTIAC decisions and error types attested to overturned FtTIAC decisions in support of judicial training evaluation, while working within the time and resource constraints of the wider PhD project. The paper presents the annotation toolkit, methodology, and results before critically discussing our approach, presenting recommendations, and concluding.

## 2 Defining an Annotation Toolkit

### 2.1 Designing an Annotation Scheme

To create a ground truth against which to train and evaluate ML classifiers employed for outcome and error type classification, we developed and implemented an annotation approach consisting of 1) defining an annotation scheme, 2) manually annotating a sample of decisions, and 3) linking the annotation information to the SQLite database that holds the corpus (see Fig. 2). To validate the approach, steps two and three were repeated with a second annotator on a sub-sample of annotations performed by the first author.

Defining the annotation scheme, firstly, followed the purpose of the annotations: understanding UTIAC decisions as 'corrective' to and making statements about FtTIAC decisions meant the training data had to accurately supply labels that highlight relevant statements (here, about whether or not an FtTIAC decision can stand or needs to be overturned and about types of errors of law attested to overturned FtTIAC decisions) so that they can be identified (i.e., what and where are these statements) and classified (i.e., what do these statements mean). The first author initially familiarised themselves with key statements and terminology relating to decision outcomes and error types during detailed reading of a small set of ten randomly selected decision documents. Detailed reading and highlighting with pen on paper supported a better understanding and general overview of salient features in UTIAC written decisions, such as, e.g., location of different types of information in the text and general structure of the decisions. These usually consist of a *header* containing (more or less) structured information about the appeal hearing, presiding judge(s), appeal parties, and hearing centre/setting, and a free-text *main body* which, despite considerable variation in the detailed structure and sub-headings used, is usually roughly set up to

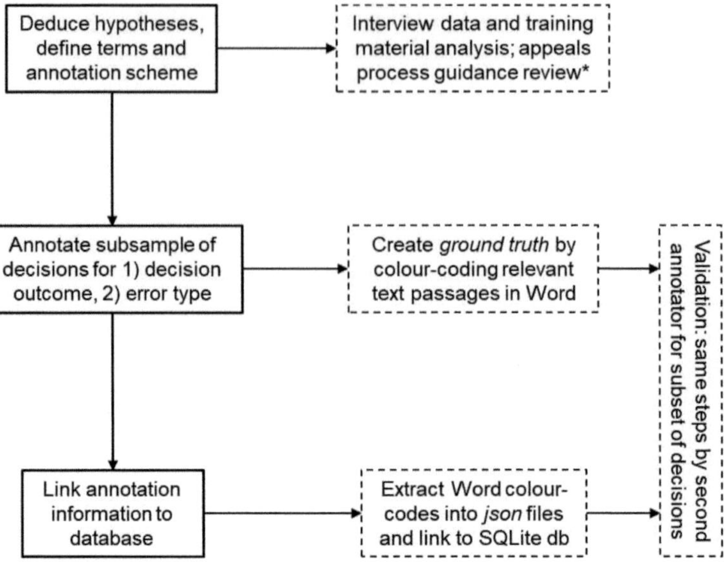


*Notes*: *applies to error type annotation only; db = database, UTIAC = Upper Tribunal Immigration and Asylum Chamber.

**Fig. 2.** Three-step annotation approach for creating a training set of labelled UTIAC decisions.

detail background of the appeal, submissions by appeal parties, discussion, and notice of decision.

For outcome annotation, the first author followed Petrova et al. [10] in assigning an overall outcome label (upheld/ overturned) to the decision as well as devising a sentence-level annotation scheme to identify sentences containing relevant outcome information. We did not limit these sentences to only those stating outcomes in the sense of "appeal outcome" – which would be either "allowed" or "dismissed" – but also included those sentences containing information about whether the FtTIAC decision could "stand", needed to be "set aside", "remade" or "remitted" to give us a relevant yet full source of sentences relating to the various outcomes associated with UTIAC hearings (see Fig. 1). Annotation of such outcome sentences allows for pre-filtering sentences on which to classify the actual outcome on, which can lead to increased classification accuracy: Petrova et al. [10, p. 137] report that 'at extraction time, pre-filtering outcome sentences leads to more accurate outcome extraction in our setting'. The first author identified possible appeal outcomes and relevant related information from engaging with the appeals process (see, e.g., https://righttoremain.org.uk/toolkit/ut/, last accessed 2025/07/20) and sense-checking their understanding in an informal chat with a domain expert. Relevant outcome markers include information about error of law findings (error/ no error), whether the FtTIAC decision under appeal gets upheld or overturned, if an overturned decisions gets remitted (i.e., sent back to the FtTIAC, the SSHD, or to another UTIAC judge) or remade, and what the overall outcome of the appeal is from an appeal party's perspective (allowed/ dismissed).

The first author followed an analogous approach for error type annotation: labelling the decision with the different error labels (error type X present/error type X not present) and labelling sentences and paragraphs that contained information about a specific error type (i.e., that explained why a particular error of law was attested to the FtTIAC decision) for enabling the pre-filtering of error information sentences. They identified possible error types from official guidance for bringing appeals to the UTIAC and drew on insights from the judicial interviews and training materials data collected and analysed for the wider PhD project. Official guidance lists three types of errors based on which a FtTIAC decision can be appealed to the UTIAC (see https://www.gov.uk/upper-tribunal-immigration-asylum/how-to-appeal, last accessed 2025/07/20): 1) legal, 2) procedural, and 3) evidential errors. Training material and judicial interviewee information details these three overarching error types further into: law and legal approach, procedure and fairness, and errors regarding evidence. The interviewee and training materials data also add errors around reasons or findings, the conclusion, mis-applied burden or standard of proof, and expression.

These initial labels were further refined through the annotation process into a set of 12 different error codes: law, legal approach, fairness, procedure, evidence, reasons, findings, conclusion, burden/ standard of proof, expression, facts, and no jurisdiction. Validation by a second annotator (see below) suggested these might be too fine-grained to adequately distinguish – as Hachey and Grover [4, p. 311] observe: 'In designing an annotation scheme, decisions must be made about how fine-grained the labels can be and an optimal balance has to be found between informational richness and human annotator reliability' (we report inter-annotator agreement below). We therefore condensed the 12 codes into a second version containing only five labels: legal, procedural, evidentiary, reasoning, and expression errors. This was done post-annotation as the condensed version subsumes the existing codes from the detailed annotations (see Table 1).

Once outcome and error type labels were defined, the first author manually annotated a subset of UTIAC decisions from the corpus to create a labelled dataset for classifier training and evaluation purposes. To reiterate, the information annotated for the two tasks was as follows:

1. Decision outcomes: at the sentence-level, information revealing error of law findings (error/ no error), determination (upheld/ overturned), further decisions (remitted/ remade), and appeal outcome (allowed/ dismissed).
2. Error types: at the sentence and paragraph levels, information that revealed the types of error of law attested to overturned FtTIAC decisions.

## 2.2 Creating an Annotation Tool

There exist a wide variety of tools for labelling texts with annotations. Examples include *GATE* (https://gate.ac.uk/), *Sublime Text* (https://www.sublimetext.

**Table 1.** Condensed and full codes used in labelling error types in UTIAC decisions that overturn FtTIAC decisions

| Condensed codes | Full codes | Code description |
|---|---|---|
| Legal errors | Law | did not apply law correctly, did not apply UTIAC (country) guidance (correctly), did not apply relevant law (at relevant date) |
| | Legal approach | did not follow structured approach, did not (correctly apply or follow) relevant tests/exercises, incl. inadequate proportionality assessment |
| | Burden/standard of proof | incorrectly identified/ applied burden/standard of proof |
| | No jurisdiction | FtTIAC did not have jurisdiction to decide appeal/case |
| Procedural errors | Fairness | errors in handling of hearing, procedural unfairness, no fair hearing |
| | Procedure | followed incorrect procedure/ "defect in procedure" |
| Evidentiary errors | Evidence | did not take all, or incorrect/irrelevant evidence (incl. post-decision evidence) into account, misunderstood evidence |
| | Facts | erred on the facts, facts not accurate/misunderstood/overlooked/ speculated about, incl. error of fact |
| Reasoning errors | Reasons | did not give adequate reasons/inadequately reasoned, not properly/clearly argued, irrelevant reasons, incl. reasoning |
| | Findings | made incorrect findings, incl. no basis for findings made, failure to make findings |
| | Conclusions | reached inadequate conclusion, conclusion (decision) not justified/ not supported by evidence/not open to the judge; incl. did not resolve issues in dispute |
| Expression errors | Expression | did not express themselves well; little structure, clarity; difficult to understand |

Source: Own compilation.

com/), and *brat* (https://brat.nlplab.org/. As [9] remarks, annotation is very often a bottleneck in dataset preparation, and the usability and suitability for purpose are key factors in timely completion.

Since in this particular instance, the annotation tool was to be used by legal professionals rather than by engineers or technically inclined staff, and had to account for the time and resource constraints of the wider PhD project, the requirements of the annotation aspect of the PhD were focused largely on accessibility and easy availability, as well as completeness (e.g., the capability to successfully label all of the points identified in the annotation scheme). Accessibility, in this sense, implies firstly that there is no complexity barrier to the use of the system, so that the individual can adapt to using the tool with minimal effort or additional installation requirements, and ideally that it employs skills that are already available to them; secondly, that there are no cost, availability, or functional barriers.

We therefore followed Petrova et al.'s [10] technical implementation of performing annotations via colour coding in Word. This approach has both advantages (user-friendliness, accessibility) and drawbacks (limited colour palette, needing additional processing steps). On the *pro* side, annotating in Word directly used the Word decision files scraped from the Tribunals decisions website in an easy-to-read format and could be performed without additional software, online tool logins, or specialist technical annotation training. On the *con* side, Word has a limited highlighting colour palette which might be too restricted for tasks with higher numbers of labels and which has colours that can be difficult to distinguish. In this regard, colour-based annotation might not be accessible to people with colour blindness or other visual impairments.

Yet, the overriding advantage is that this approach required no specialist software or online tool login on the annotator's part at all. Since their workflow was to open a .docx file, annotate relevant terms or phrases within the file, and return the file, we concluded that the most straightforward way to achieve this was to simply draw the annotations from the file itself. To this end, a colour-coding was agreed for labels, and an explanatory key sent to annotators. This had the beneficial effect that since all annotators already had word processing software in place capable of annotating a file in this manner, there was no setup cost for the annotators.

To obtain the annotations from these files, however, it was necessary to read the .docx programmatically with a tool capable of identifying and extracting these annotations. Fortunately, this problem is quite simple to solve using the .docx format, since the data is ultimately stored in XML. We wrote a corresponding tool using Python, able to extract the relevant labels and their positions and encode them in a json file format (source code for this tool can be found online at https://github.com/etonkin/docx_annotation, last accessed 2025/07/20). A key corresponding to the human-readable key provided to the annotators gives the tool the information that it requires to correctly encode marked sections with the relevant label.

While this might appear cumbersome to some, working with the challenge of XML manipulation rather than avoiding it by not using Word resulted in some useful outcomes. It helped reveal errors affecting the plain text extraction step of corpus building which we might have otherwise missed despite spot-checking extracted plain text files. Our thorough evaluation of the annotation tool therefore improved the wider corpus-building workflow (see below). This evaluation also allowed us to identify the use of shared templates in judicial decision-writing. As we discuss in the Recommendations section below, this observable judicial practice could be a useful starting point for suggesting recommendations towards standardisation that might simplify the process of and further reduce potential ambiguity in annotation, while preserving judicial independence.

### 2.3 Evaluating the Annotation Tool

The annotated text extraction step had two opposite challenges: one, not extracting highlighted text, and two, extracting more text than highlighted. Firstly, the json extraction incidentally revealed a special Word features issue, discovering embedded objects and macros, such as form-based drop-down menus and text fields for entering, e.g., hearing centre, appeal party or appeal outcome information in the decision. Manual inspection of json files uncovered that in some cases, certain words did not show up in the highlighted text information even though the words had been annotated with a highlighting colour. This was due to standard plain text extraction methods not being able to capture text in these embedded objects and macros. An example is "This appeal is dismissed" where all four words were highlighted in the Word decision file but only "This appeal is" was extracted into json, as "dismissed" was embedded in a drop-down field. As this potentially affected all Word decision files from which plain text was extracted to build the corpus, it was fortunate that this issue was discovered during annotation so it could be remedied for all files (see below).

Manual inspection of json files, secondly, showed that, in some cases, more text was extracted than highlighted. Such 'noise' included judges' signatures, or the words "image" and "media" indicating image insertion in the original Word documents: The word "signed" often comes directly after the decision outcome sentence and can be followed by a scanned image of a judge's signature which would explain why the words "image" or "media" were present in the paragraph context of a highlighted text passage. For example, the end of a decision document might look like this: "This appeal is dismissed. [Newline] Signed: Judge X [Newline] [Signature or image of signature]", which extracted to json as "This appeal is dismissed. Signed image 1". There was also a small number of other words unrelated to the annotation task. Examples are "Crown Copyright", "Fee Award", or "Upper Tribunal Judge", which all come at the end of a decision text, or even the footer of a decision document.

The first challenge was resolved by revising the plain text extraction preprocessing step, applying XML manipulation in Python to strip out special Word features, to ensure all relevant textual information labelled during annotation would be available in the SQLite database of the corpus (source code for this tool can be found online at https://github.com/etonkin/docx_deformer). The second challenge was left unmitigated as, while accepting it potentially added some 'noise' (i.e., unrelated or irrelevant information) to the classifier input, it was deemed a lesser issue than not having relevant text extracted.

## 3 Annotation and Evaluation Methodology

The steps of annotating decisions in Word and extracting annotation highlights into json files to add to the SQLite database were performed for two annotators. In a first round of annotations, the first author randomly selected a subset of 500 decisions for annotation as the full corpus is simply too large for manual annotation of all decisions. There is no standard figure stating the ideal percentage of annotations per corpus as required numbers of annotations vary depending on the classification approach. For the application of simple binary supervised learning classifiers for which the ground truth was created, 500 annotations seems reasonable – and feasible given the other demands and restraints of the PhD project – and compares to related work as follows: for a similar task of outcome detection, Petrova et al. [10] annotated 500 out of 350 000 decisions or 0.14 %% of their corpus; for information extraction purposes, Hachey and Grover [4] annotated a total of 69 out of 188 decisions, or 36.7% of their corpus. We annotated 1.6% decisions in our corpus, i.e., 500 out of 31 445 decisions (see next paragraph for an explanation of decision numbers). The percentage is larger than in Petrova et al.'s [10] work, while total annotation numbers are larger than in Hachey and Grover's [4] work, striking a balance between adequacy for classification requirements and feasibility within our available resources.

Recall that the full corpus contains both reported and unreported as well as judicial review decisions. To ensure that the format of decisions on which to train the classifiers would be as similar as possible, i.e., actually capturing mainly error of law decisions that make statements about the FtTIAC decision under appeal, we worked with unreported decisions from the ten appeal types only. The sampling frame from which we drew decisions for annotation therefore excluded reported decisions (due to them often being guidance or resumed decisions) and judicial review cases (as they do not make error of law assessments), and focused only on all other unreported appeal types. This gives a total of 31 445 unreported (minus judicial review) decisions, that span the years 2013 to quarter one of 2021. To account for the different appeal types into which unreported decisions fall, we used stratified random sampling so that the total of 500 randomly selected decisions spread proportionally across the 10 unreported appeal types represented in the corpus. Based on the 31 445 creview) decisions, the percentages of decisions in each of the appeal types are as follows (total numbers in parantheses): Asylum: 12.74% (64), Deport(ation): 5.22% (26), Deprivation of citizenship: 0.17% (1), EEA Freedom of Movement: 5.06% (25), Entry clearance: 6.87% (34), Family visit visa: 1.80% (9), Human rights: 17.23% (86), Managed migration: 28.50% (143), Protection: 21.78% (109), Revocation of protection: 0.59% (3).

As a first step, the first author annotated this stratified random sample of 500 unreported decisions for outcomes. In a second step, they annotated only those decisions of the previous 500 for error type information that had fully overturned the respective FtTIAC decision. These were a total of 292 decisions (note that in this step, the distribution of decisions across appeal types was no longer proportionate to the corpus). For both annotation steps, the first author compiled a spreadsheet each, respectively detailing the decision outcomes (upheld/ overturned) and error types for every annotated decision. These spreadsheets served as the decision-level *ground truth* against which to train and evaluate the

ML classifiers and were linked – along with the sentence-level annotation information extracted into json files as described above – to the tokenized decisions in the SQLite database via the decision file name.

To get a sense of the extent to which two human annotators agree on the labels (inter-annotator agreement), a sub-sample of the 500 decisions annotated in the first round were double-annotated in a second round. A second annotator annotated a stratified random sample of 102 decisions of the previously selected 500. This means 20.4% of annotated decisions were double-annotated. For comparison, out of the 69 decisions annotated in [4] corpus, 11 were double-annotated, or 15.94%. [10] do not report double annotation or inter-annotator agreement. As described for the first annotator, the selection of decisions for further annotation maintained the proportions of the appeal type distribution across all unreported minus judicial review decisions. Percentages of decisions in each of the ten appeal types are based on the 31,445 unreported (minus judicial review) decisions and are as described above. Accordingly, the total number of decisions in each appeal type in the stratified sample of 102 randomly selected decisions for second annotation were: Asylum: 13, Deport(ation): 5, Deprivation of citizenship: 1, EEA Freedom of Movement: 5, Entry clearance: 7, Family visit visa: 2, Human rights: 17, Managed migration: 29, Protection: 22, Revocation of protection: 1. Where according to percentages less than one decision should have been included, we randomly selected 1 decision to have at least one decision per appeal type in the double-annotated sample (hence numbers exceed 100).

The 102 decisions were double-annotated for decision outcomes in a first step, and 10 fully overturned decisions were double-annotated for error type information in a second step. To account for capacity and availability of the second annotator, the second annotation step of labelling error type information was not performed on all fully overturned decisions of the 102 annotated for outcomes, but on one overturned decision per appeal type only. For each appeal type, therefore, one decision was randomly sampled from the 292 decisions annotated for error information in the first round. To be able to compare annotations, the second annotator also compiled a spreadsheet for each annotation task, one detailing decision outcome labels and one capturing error type labels for every annotated decision. The spreadsheets for annotators 1 and 2 were linked for comparison in Python via the decision file name.

## 4 Results

We draw on the commonly used Cohen's kappa statistic $\kappa$ to assess inter-annotator agreement. Introduced by Jacob Cohen in 1960, the statistic corrects the percentage agreement between annotators by accounting for the possibility of chance agreement [7]. Cohen's $\kappa$ is calculated (see ibid. for details) as actual agreement (Pr(a)) minus chance agreement (Pr(e)) divided by 1 minus chance agreement, or $\kappa = (\Pr(a) - \Pr(e))/(1 - \Pr(e))$. In the first task – outcome annotation – inter-annotator agreement is high, with $\kappa = 0.96$ at the document level for labels of whether the FtTIAC decision was upheld or overturned. This can be interpreted as 'almost perfect' agreement (see Table 2). Agreement on the second task – error type annotation – is a lot lower, however, with $\kappa = 0.13$ for the exact same error type labels at document level and reaching $\kappa = 0.51$ for agreeing on at least one error type per decision at the document level. These values indicate 'no' to 'weak' levels of agreement (Table 2). Note that the interpretation of $\kappa$-values has been under discussion and is being regularly revisited; for further discussion, see [6, 7]. Comparison to $\kappa$-values in related work must also be heavily caveated as tasks and annotation bases were different. As mentioned above, [10] do not report double-annotation or $\kappa$-values; [4, p. 313] report 'good reliability' with $\kappa = 0.83$ at the sentence level.

Note that $\kappa$-values for the second task are based on a comparison of 10 labelled decisions only and therefore low numbers might explain some of the uncertainty in annotations as expressed in the low kappas. That said, the values do suggest that the second annotation task is trickier than the first and it might be more difficult to achieve agreement between humans on labelling the error type(s) a UTIAC judge finds in a FtTIAC decision. Indeed, inspection shows that divergence of labelling documents as containing a particular error of law occured between 'neighbouring' codes, e.g., one annotator assigned 'law' while the other assigned 'legal approach'. Similar disagreement was due to assigning 'conclusion' vs 'reasons', or 'fairness' vs 'procedure' labels (see 'full codes' column in Table 1).

This observation led to a revision of granularity of the coding scheme: the original 12 error type labels were condensed into five in a second annotation version (done post-annotation as categories are combined rather than newly created, see above). Repeating the inter-annotator agreement assessment for the so-condensed error type categories results in an improved Kappa of $\kappa = 0.42$ for the exact same error type labels at document level but remains similar for agreement on a minimum of one error type per document ($\kappa = 0.52$). This highlights the particular complexity of the error type annotation task, which might in future work benefit from more detailed annotator training, additional domain expert input, and a more collaborative/consensus-finding annotation approach to resolve ambiguities and further iterate the annotation scheme (see Discussion section below).

**Table 2.** Interpretation of Cohen's *kappa* values

| $\kappa$ value | Level of inter-annotator agreement |
|---|---|
| 0.00–0.20 | None |
| 0.21–0.39 | Minimal |
| 0.40–0.59 | Weak |
| 0.60–0.79 | Moderate |
| 0.80–0.90 | Strong |
| Above 0.90 | Almost perfect |

*Source:* = Own compilation, based on Table 3 in [7].

As we are, to the best of our knowledge, the first to label this type of corpus for the purposes of appeals analysis in terms of outcomes and errors of law, we are not aware of any other existing ground truth against which to further evaluate our annotation approach and validate our labels. One way to approximate an additional ground truth, however, for the outcome annotation only, are the publicly available and regularly published Tribunal Statistics (available at https://www.gov.uk/government/collections/tribunals-statistics, last accessed 2025/07/20). These provide receipt and disposal (determined/ remitted/ withdrawn) numbers as well as overall decision outcomes (allowed/ dismissed). For the years 2013 to Q1 2021, the time frame for the analysis presented here, we calculated rates of overturn based on "Allowed" and "Remitted" appeals, both for UTIAC decisions overall, and differentiated along appeal types.

**Table 3.** Correlation matrix of overturn rates

| | Annotations | Tribunal Stats | Pred_LinSVM | Pred_KW II | Year |
|---|---|---|---|---|---|
| Annotations | 1 | 0.52 (0.15) | 0.09 (0.81) | 0.27 (0.48) | 0.27 (0.49) |
| Tribunal Stats | 0.52 (0.15) | 1 | 0.63* (0.07) | 0.85*** (0.00) | 0.68** (0.04) |
| Pred_LinSVM | 0.09 (0.81) | 0.63* (0.07) | 1 | 0.86*** (0.00) | 0.75** (0.02) |
| Pred_Keywords II | 0.27 (0.48) | 0.85*** (0.00) | 0.86*** (0.00) | 1 | 0.80** (0.01) |
| Year | 0.27 (0.49) | 0.68** (0.04) | 0.75** (0.02) | 0.80** (0.01) | 1 |

*Notes:* Cells contain Pearson's correlation coefficient $r$ with $p$ values in parentheses. In the diagonal values are $r = 1$ because they represent the correlation of a curve with itself. Asterisks indicate significance levels as follows: * indicates $p < 0.10$, ** indicates $p < 0.05$, *** indicates $p < 0.01$.

*Source:* Own compilation.

We used these Tribunal Statistics figures as additional ground truth against which to evaluate the performance of the outcome classifiers that were trained on our labelled dataset. This comparison showed that all predicted overturn rates obtained from our classifier and keyword-based prediction models significantly correlate with Tribunal Statistics overturn rates (see Table 3): Linear SVM and Tribunal Statistics overturn rates have a medium positive correlation of $r = 0.63$, which is significant at the 0.10 level ($p = 0.07$); the best performing keyword-based prediction and Tribunal Statistics overturn rates have a strong positive correlation of $r = 0.85$, significant at the 0.00 level ($p = 0.00$). While none of the prediction curves significantly correlate with the annotations curve, the fact that all predicted overturn rates significantly correlate with Tribunal Statistics overturn rates adds confidence to the outcomes annotation part of our initial ground truth produced with the annotation process as that was the training input for our classifier models.

## 5 Discussion and Recommendations

Comparing the human annotations also needs to take account of annotator background. Ideally, manual annotations would be conducted by domain experts to generate sufficient trust in the accuracy of the ground truth. Recruiting annotators with specific expertise in UTIAC decisions to do annotations was not possible in this instance as available time and resources for this task were restricted due to it being but one (albeit important) aspect of a wider PhD project. Recruiting relevant domain expert annotators and/ or validating annotations undertaken by us with such experts in future work might further improve annotation quality and potentially increase inter-annotator agreement. This additional domain expert input and more detailed annotator training, possibly coupled with a consensus-finding, collaborative approach to annotation might in particular improve inter-annotator agreement for the error type annotation task. That said, against the background of time and resource constraints of the overall PhD project, we still achieved to recruit two annotators with relevant expertise: the first author had familiarised themselves with the UK immigration and asylum appeals system through the PhD research process and acquainted themselves with the language and peculiarities of UTIAC judicial decisions through detailed reading. The second annotator is a legally trained professional with relevant experience, albeit from outside the UK.

We clarified annotation tasks in a number of calls. Concretely, we first shared the annotation guidance and some example annotations with the second annotator. We then held a couple of Zoom calls: 1) to understand the appeals system and actors within it, to discuss the usual structure of a decision and to confirm the annotation tasks (~1 h); 2) to revisit the error type annotation task, explaining and jointly disentangling paragraphs referencing submissions and those actually containing the error assessment of the UTIAC judge (~20 min), at the end of which we decided to focus on the outcome annotation task first; 3) to re-revisit the error type annotation task, re-explaining and going through annotated examples together (~1 h), after which we decided to go ahead with a feasible number of 10 decisions for error annotation as described above.

At the same time, it has to be noted that both annotators are non-native speakers of English. The varied structure of decision documents, stylistic idiosyncrasies, and unfamiliar formulations made annotation a challenging and time-consuming task with room for our own errors. To give an indication of time, annotating decisions for outcomes (task 1) took about 20 min per decision, which reduced to about 5 min per document as we gained more familiarity and confidence with the task. Error type annotation (task 2) took around 1 h per document, which eventually reduced to between 20–30 minutes per decision. Taking the lowest times only, this equates to a minimum of 42h for annotator 1 (500 decisions à 5 min each) and a minimum of 8.5 h (102 decisions à 5 min each) for annotator 2 on the outcomes annotation task; on the error type annotation task, minimum times were 97h for annotator 1 (292 decisions à 20 min each) and just over 3 h for annotator 2 (10 decisions à 20 min each).

As two individuals who could potentially also become appellants in immigration appeals, this observation incidentally underscores the importance of simple, clear, and consistent formulation and structural placement of outcomes (and error types) in judicial decisions. This supports recommendations for courts and tribunals to consider more standardised decision formats, for example, for information on appeal parties, decision date, etc., and standardised outcome and, where a decision gets overturned, error information sentences. We appreciate that standardisation of outcome and error information sentences might be seen as undue interference with individual judicial styles. This concern could be alleviated by offering standardisation of a few clearly delimited pieces of information only which could build on existing formatting templates that already make use of phrases such as "Appeal allowed/dismissed". The existence of form-based dropdowns and pre-defined text fields was discovered during plain-text extraction of annotated text passages. Apart from posing a plain text extraction challenge, they also suggest that there is an existing practice of template use within judicial decision-writing. Sentences for standardisation could be, e.g., "The FtTIAC decision is upheld/set aside/remitted", "The judge made an error of law – law error/legal approach error/evidence error/etc.".

Standardised error information sentences could also alleviate the challenge of temporal stability of contents of our annotation labels. While overarching upheld/overturned outcomes are likely to remain the same, it is reasonable to assume that what exactly would be classified within the scope of each of the different types of errors of law could well change over time, for example, due to concept drift (change in the data) or semantic drift (change in how we think about the data; cf. [16]). In part, such drift could also be driven by changes in the law. Because statements about errors of law are less formulaic than outcome formulations, the annotated subset of decisions might have provided time-bound training input for classifiers. This means that formulations marking the same error type in different decision years might be more difficult to recognise during classification. Furthermore, domain knowledge, e.g., via input from judges or other relevant legal experts, could indicate whether assuming static error type labels is appropriate or whether different approaches, such as working with knowledge bases, would be needed to better support temporal transferability of labels as training input for corpus-based ML analysis of appeal decisions.

Beyond alleviating challenges to manual annotation of decisions, increased standardisation of outcome and error information could assist appeal parties, and indeed senior judges reviewing overturned decisions, in quickly locating key decision information. This could add both to increased understanding and transparency of decisions – key aspects of quality of justice in terms of access to justice – as well as to more effective recognition of training needs. Indeed, this recommendation might support on-going 'changes to ways of working' in the FtTIAC which have been introduced by the current FtTIAC President's "Programme for Change" [15, p. 38]: amongst a number of other changes, this programme sets out to offer 'more comprehensive and up to date jurisdictional support for judges through the maintenance of *online checklists, templates and sample judgments* for each cohort of work' (ibid., our emphasis).

## 6 Conclusion

This paper describes our annotation approach used to label a corpus of UTIAC decisions for decision outcomes and error types attested to overturned FtTIAC decisions in support of judicial training evaluation in the immigration and asylum appeals system. To the best of our knowledge, we are the first to develop a taxonomy for this purpose. Annotations were implemented via a low-cost, high-accessibility tool and validated calculating inter-annotator agreement. We discuss the pros and cons of our annotation tool and also critically reflect on annotator background. Our approach produces a suitable ground truth for our subsequent simple binary supervised classification tasks taking account of time and resource constraints provided by the wider PhD project of which the annotation task was part.

We successfully used the produced ground truth to train and evaluate supervised ML classifiers to identify overturned decisions (see [13]) and error types attested to those decisions. Significant correlation of predicted overturn rates with overturn rates calculated based on official published Tribunal Statistics adds further confidence to the suitability of our annotations for said tasks. We are considering options for releasing the corpus and annotations in ways that comply with ethics and data protection considerations for this sensitive data so that future work can safely apply further experiments based on our annotated and validated corpus.

**Acknowledgment.** This work was supported by the UK Economic and Social Research Council (ESRC; grant number ES/P000630/1). It received further support from the TORUS Project, which has been funded by the UK Engineering and Physical Sciences Research Council (EPSRC; grant number EP/X036146/1). We thank Gregory Tourte for his valuable technical contributions.

**Disclosure of Interests.** Author 1 is an associate at Exeter University, having completed their PhD there, and now works at the Judicial Office. This post was taken up after completion of the research presented in this article and is separate to the research. Any recommendations and statements made in this article are the author's own, based on their independent PhD research undertaken at Exeter University. Author 2 has no competing interests to declare that are relevant to the content of this article.

## References

1. Aletras, N., Tsarapatsanis, D., Preotiuc-Pietro, D., Lampos, V.: Predicting judicial decisions of the European Court of Human Rights: a natural language processing perspective. PeerJ Comput. Sci. **2**(e93), 1–19 (2016). https://doi.org/10.7717/peerj-cs.93
2. Armytage, L.: Educating Judges: Towards Improving Justice. A Survey of Global Practice. Brill Nijhoff, Leiden (2006)
3. Chalkidis, I., Androutsopoulos, I., Aletras, N.: Neural legal judgment prediction in English. arXiv preprint arXiv:1906.02059 (2019)
4. Hachey, B., Grover, C.: Extractive summarisation of legal texts. Artif. Intell. Law **14**, 305–345 (2006)
5. Howlin, N., Coen, M., Barry, C., Lynch, J.: Robinson Crusoe on a desert island? Judicial education in Ireland, 1995–2019. Legal Stud. **42**, 525–545 (2022)

6. Landis, J.R., Koch, G.G.: The measurement of observer agreement for categorical data. Biometrics **33**(1), 159–174 (1977)
7. McHugh, M.L.: Interrater reliability: the kappa statistic. Biochem Med (Zagreb) **22**(3), 276–282 (2012)
8. Medvedeva, M., Vols, M., Wieling, M.: Using machine learning to predict decisions of the European Court of Human Rights. Artif. Intell. Law **28**, 237–266 (2020)
9. Neves, M., Ševa, J.: An extensive review of tools for manual annotation of documents. Briefings Bioinf. **22**(1), 146–163 (2021)
10. Petrova, A., Armour, J., Lukasiewicz, T.: Extracting outcomes from appellate decisions in US state courts. In: Villata, S., Harašta, J., Křemen, P. (eds.) Legal knowledge and information systems – JURIX 2020: 33rd Annual Conference. Frontiers in Artificial Intelligence and Applications, pp. 133–142 (2020). https://doi.org/10.3233/FAIA200857
11. Richards, D.: Current models of judicial training: an updated review of initial and continuous training models across western democratic jurisdictions. Judicial Educ. Training. J. IOJT **5**, 41–52 (2016)
12. L. Scheinert: The 'bullet-proof vest' : remits and limits of judicial training and its evaluation. An exploration of the United Kingdom's First-tier Tribunal Immigration and Asylum Chamber. University of Exeter [unpublished PhD thesis], Exeter, UK (2024)
13. L. Scheinert and E.L. Tonkin: To err or not to err? Towards extracting error of law findings from the UK's Upper Tribunal Immigration and Asylum Chamber decisions. In: Presented at the PhD Forum of ECML PKDD 2021 – European Conference on Machine Learning and Principles and Practice of Knowledge Discovery in Databases (2021)
14. L. Scheinert and E.L. Tonkin: Towards ethical judicial analytics: assessing readability of immigration and asylum decisions in the United Kingdom. In: G. Marreiros, F. Melo, N. Lau, H. Lopes Cardoso, and L.P. Reis. EPIA2021 – 20$^{th}$ EPIA Conference on Artificial Intelligence (2021)
15. SPT: Senior President of Tribunals' annual report. Courts and Tribunal Judiciary (2023)
16. T.G. Stavropoulos, S. Andreadis, M. Riga, E. Kontopoulos, P. Mitzias, and I. Kompatsiaris: A framework for measuring semantic drift in ontologies. In: SEMANTiCS (Posters, Demos, SuCCESS) (2016)
17. O.-M. Şulea, M. Zampieri, M. Vela, and J. van Genabith: Predicting the law area and decisions of French Supreme Court cases. arXiv preprint arXiv:1708.01681v1 (2017)
18. R. Thomas: Immigration judicial reviews in the Upper Tribunal (Immigration and Asylum Chamber): an analysis of statistical data. https://ssrn.com/abstract=2766979 (2016)
19. R. Thomas: Mapping immigration judicial review litigation: an empirical legal analysis. Public Law 652, 1–27 (2015)
20. L. Toomey: Measuring the impact of judicial training. INPROL Consolidated Response (07-005) (2007)

# Span-Level Domain-Specific Annotated Student Feedback Pilot Dataset

Zhengyuan Feng, Mengyuan Cui, Meenu Bala, Henry Agaba, and Abe Kazemzadeh(✉)

University of St. Thomas, Saint Paul, MN 55105, USA
{feng2052,cui06590,bala5797,agab4826,abe.kazemzadeh}@stthomas.edu
https://software.stthomas.edu/

**Abstract.** This paper presents an annotated dataset of student feedback for end-of-semester reviews of teaching in a software engineering master's program. The annotation was performed at the word span level in order to capture inputs with mixed annotations. The annotation was performed by a combination of students and faculty using labels that capture not only sentiment categories (POSITIVE, NEGATIVE), but also domain-specific labels that are relevant to better understand and process the content of student feedback, namely a SUGGESTION label for feedback that can distinguish a purely negative response from constructive criticism, a COMPARISON label for capturing comparisons that are not clearly an absolute positive or negative sentiment, and a REDACT label for identifying personal information of instructors or students that should be removed prior to wider data collection and dissemination. This paper is a pilot in that it only covers one instructor's feedback from a variety of courses over several years. However, we supplement these data with non-official student feedback from online sources. Our primary contributions are the annotated dataset and preliminary machine learning results, including BERT, DistilBERT, and SpaCy span categorization models.

**Keywords:** teaching reviews · student feedback · annotation · natural language processing · text analysis

## 1 Introduction

This paper presents a small annotated dataset of student feedback from end-of-semester course reviews in a software engineering master's program. The student feedback was text-based sentence-to-paragraph length comments. Each comment was annotated by selecting text spans, i.e. at the word-, phrase-, or sentence-level, to capture parts with different meanings. We used not only sentiment labels like POSITIVE and NEGATIVE, but also more specific ones like SUGGESTION (to show helpful advice), COMPARISON (for comparing people or courses), and REDACT (to hide names or private details). The main data comes from one instructor's reviews over several years, but we also include examples from online student comments.


E. L. Tonkin et al. (Eds.): ARDUOUS 2025, CCIS 2706, pp. 147–156, 2026.
https://doi.org/10.1007/978-3-032-09117-8_9

### 1.1 Motivation and Challenges

Feedback from students is an important way to continually improve teaching, course materials, program curriculum, and class dynamics, especially in graduate programs where students may have clear goals and past educational experiences. Open-ended comments are ways to get feedback to inform such improvements, but quantifying and presenting these comments are not as convenient as Likert-valued surveys. Sentiment analysis and opinion mining are possible solutions, but these are domain-agnostic so having a dataset specifically for teaching evaluation will be a benefit both as a benchmark and a source of training data. Some of the challenges we address toward these goals are: dealing with subjectivity, dealing with label imbalance and limited data, and adapting an annotation system to machine learning (ML) model creation.

### 1.2 Contributions and Prior Work

Our primary contribution is the dataset which we make available to the community[1]. We also contribute preliminary results in ML model training. Our work builds on prior research that aims to use natural language processing (NLP) to automatically analyze student's feedback to instructors. A recent review paper [9] presents 28 papers in this area, which are divided into several different approaches: general sentiment analysis, categorical prediction complemented sentiment analysis, emotion prediction, opinion mining, lexicon creation, statistical and mathematical analysis. Sentiment analysis in this domain aims to classify student feedback into the typical sentiment categories, such as positive, negative, and neutral. Category prediction complemented with sentiment analysis aims to identify specific categories of educational design and assign sentiment or ratings to these. Emotion prediction is like sentiment analysis but with a categorical emotion vocabulary instead of binary or scalar sentiment values. Opinion mining aims to extract content that reflect opinions, suggestions, and advice. Lexicon creation aims to identify specific words in categories associated with aspects of teaching and education. Statistical analysis in this context refers to building regression and correlation models from additional sources of data, like rating scales.

Our work aims to identify both sentiment-related spans of text in teaching reviews as well as suggestions and comparisons, so it can be seen as a combination of sentiment analysis and opinion mining approaches. Of the 28 papers identified in [9], several took a similar approach to ours. In particular, [2,5,6] similarly used sentiment-related categories of *positive* and *negative* together with a more feedback focused *suggestion* category. These works used a rule-based ML analysis and linguistic features like part-of-speech tags to predict these categories, while ours uses BERT [1], DistilBERT [7], and SpaCy [3]. Although our data is from

[1] https://github.com/abecode/teaching_reviews.

master's level students, there are still typos and grammatical issues, so rule-based and lexical systems may struggle with this type of input, while modern language models like BERT have more robust tokenization.

## 2 Methodology

### 2.1 Data Collection and Preprocessing

The dataset used in this study consists of 192 textual feedback entries related to a single professor at the University of St. Thomas. These inputs were collected from two primary sources. **IDEA Surveys**[2] consist of 169 end-of-semester course evaluations officially administered by the university. **RateMyProfessors**[3] consist of 23 comments from an online platform where students post informal, public reviews of the same instructor.

All feedback instances are in free-text form and span multiple years and courses taught by the same instructor. The goal of this focused sampling was to create a pilot dataset that balances natural variability with a controlled scope. Each subset of the data provides a different distribution of labels. Although both subsets are fully anonymous, the officially administered IDEA was biased toward positive labels and suggestions, while the RateMyProfessors subset was characterized by a higher proportion of negative labels, as seen in Fig. 1.

### 2.2 Data Annotation

To enable fine-grained text analysis, we annotated the reviews at the word-span level using Prodigy [4], an annotation tool for NLP and other ML tasks. Annotators were allowed to label any contiguous sequence of words within each feedback input using the following six labels: **POSITIVE**, spans describing what the writer likes about the instructor or course materials; **NEGATIVE**, spans describing what the writer dislikes about the instructor or course materials; **SUGGESTION**, spans describing recommendations or ideas for improvement, **COMPARISON**, spans that compare two aspects of the teaching or course. These reflect relative preferences or contrasts rather than absolute sentiment (e.g., "the final was better than the midterm"); **UNSURE**, spans where the annotator is uncertain about which label to apply; and **REDACT**, personally identifiable information, such as names or gendered pronouns, which should be removed for privacy and fairness in future analyses. Because the annotations focused on span-level annotations, there was no explicit neutral category, since neutral is indicated by the lack of a span annotation, which is similar to named-entity recognition and other chunking NLP tasks (Fig. 2).

Spans could be a single label, multi-label, or no label at all, which represented an implied neutral category. They ranged in length from single words to full sentences. A total of seven annotators, including both students and faculty,

[2] https://www.ideaedu.org/.
[3] https://www.ratemyprofessors.com/.

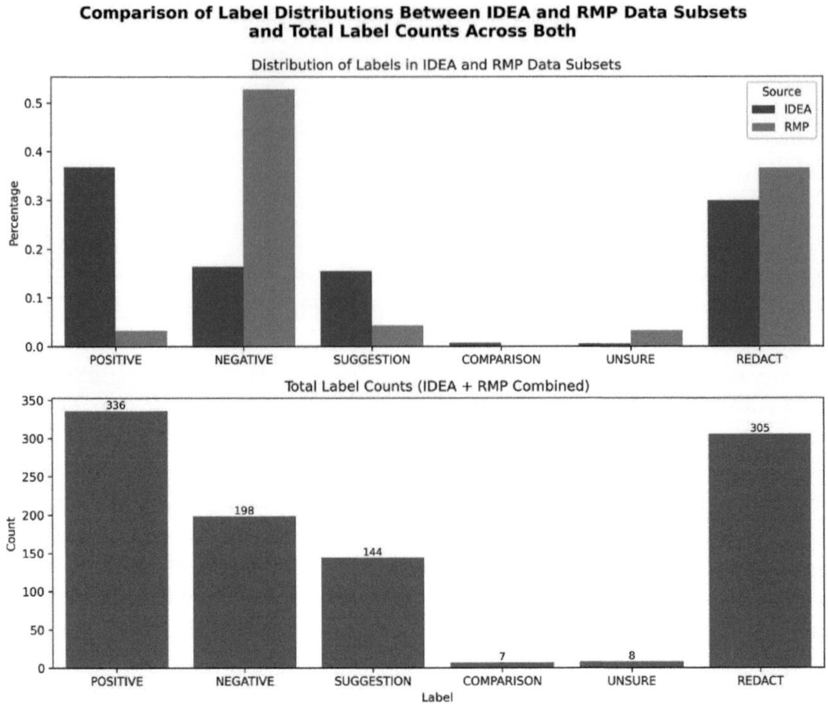


**Fig. 1.** The RateMyProfessor data contained more NEGATIVE annotation labels, which helped balance the overall bias toward positive reviews from the larger IDEA teaching reviews subset. COMPARISON and UNSURE labels showed up too infrequently to train models.

participated in the process. Each annotator followed written guidelines and was encouraged to consult with others in ambiguous cases. After the first annotation, we performed an annotation review task, also using Prodigy, where the annotators could revise their annotations while seeing other's annotations.

The output format of the annotation resulted in an `SQLite` database as the primary operational database and a `JSONL` document as serialized data extract to enable flexible downstream processing and integration with machine learning pipelines. The `JSONL` document consisted of lines of `JSON` records with the following attributes: `text`, an attribute for the input represented as a character string; `input_hash`, an attribute to uniquely represent the input as a hash function output; `annotator`, an attribute to store the annotator's username; `task_hash`, an attribute to uniquely represent the combination of input and annotator; and finally a list of span records, which consisted of `start`, `end`, `span`, and `label` attributes, which represent the start and end indices of the input text string, the span text, and the span label. In addition to these attributes which were the output of the Prodigy annotation tool, we also added a `filename` and `linenum` attribute to identify the origin of the original data in the files that were stored

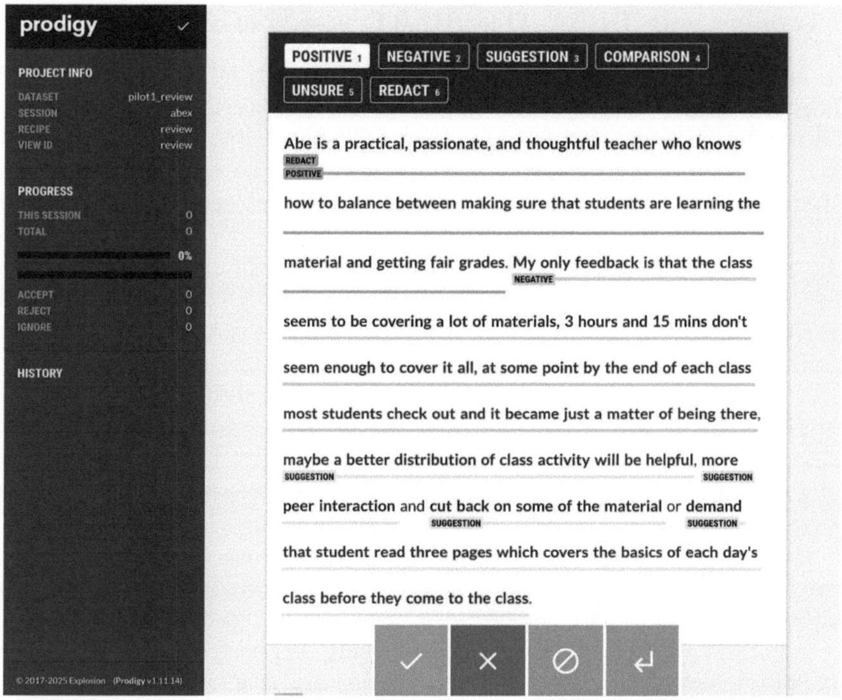


**Fig. 2.** Example of annotated feedback using the Prodigy tool. In this case, the REDACT label, which aims to anonymize the data, and POSITIVE are overlapping.

per class section for each of the two data subsets, IDEA surveys and RateMyProfessors comments.

The complete annotated dataset is available for public use and research replication at https://github.com/abecode/teaching_reviews.

# 3 Results

## 3.1 Annotation

Seven annotators contributed to the dataset. Each annotator annotated all teaching reviews, although the total number of spans labeled by annotators varied between 813 and 1,039 spans.

The annotator agreement was determined by Kripendorff's $\alpha$ to be 0.48 which represents low-to-moderate agreement. Having multiple overlapping annotators allowed us to tune our threshold for accepting annotated spans. Through experiments with training ML models, we determined that 3 or more agreeing annotators was the optimal amount of agreement for our ML model results.

### 3.2 Training with BERT, DistilBERT, and SpaCy

BERT and DistilBERT do not natively support multi-label classification, but our dataset includes the REDACT label, which often overlaps with other labels. To address this, we trained three models with differing approaches to overlapping labels. The first model simply classifies the input on the word level, the second model classifies on the chunk level similarly to named entity recognition, and the third model allows for overlapping spans.

The first, word-level model is based on DistilBERT and was trained in 4 epochs. The second, chunk-level model is based on BERT and was trained in 10 epochs. The third, span-level model uses SpaCy's span categorization and it has default settings except that the suggester n-gram length was increased to 30 to accommodate long spans. We used a train-validation-test split based on the `input_hash` field, i.e. a hash function of the teaching review's raw text. The first and second models used the same parameters: batch size of 8, and a learning rate of $5 \times 10^{-5}$. In all the experiments we disregarded COMPARISON and UNSURE labels due to lack of training examples.

In the first modeling experiment, we also removed the REDACT labels because this word-level classification model does not support multi-label classification (e.g. both POSITIVE and REDACT). However, to classify the REDACT labels in parallel, we also trained a model solely on the REDACT label. These two models achieved low loss, fast predictions, and high precision, recall, and F1-scores on the test set. The performance for the main model is displayed in Table 1. The REDACT-only model also achieved high performance: precision 0.9956, recall 0.9960, and F1-score 0.9954.

In the first model experiments, DistilBERT and BERT performed comparably but DistilBERT trained faster, so we report its results in Table 1. BERT's performance on the REDACT-only model was slightly lower (F1, precision, and recall around 0.97), with a longer training time. This suggests that BERT's added complexity yields minimal performance gains for this task. In Table 4 are some examples from the DistilBert model classification. Note that despite the higher classification performance, the word-level classification task results in spans being split up irregularly. Also, notice the presence of typos in the input data.

**Table 1.** Word-level DistilBert classification report without REDACT. Here "O" represents outside labeled span, i.e. neutral.

| Label | Precision | Recall | F1-Score | Support |
|---|---|---|---|---|
| NEGATIVE | 0.8305 | 0.8189 | 0.8247 | 359 |
| O | 0.9965 | 0.9911 | 0.9938 | 13778 |
| POSITIVE | 0.6302 | 0.8909 | 0.7382 | 440 |
| SUGGESTION | 0.6627 | 0.4133 | 0.5091 | 271 |
| **Macro Avg** | 0.7800 | 0.7786 | 0.7664 | 14848 |
| **Weighted Avg** | 0.9755 | 0.9734 | 0.9733 | 14848 |

**Table 2.** Chunk-level BERT `seqval` (IOB format) classification report without REDACT.

| Label | Precision | Recall | F1-Score | Support |
|---|---|---|---|---|
| NEGATIVE | 0.3243 | 0.4800 | 0.3871 | 25 |
| POSITIVE | 0.2361 | 0.5152 | 0.3238 | 33 |
| SUGGESTION | 0.1667 | 0.2667 | 0.2051 | 15 |
| **Macro Avg** | 0.2424 | 0.4206 | 0.3053 | 73 |
| **Weighted Avg** | 0.2521 | 0.4521 | 0.3211 | 73 |

**Table 3.** SpaCy span-level classification report. SpaCy span classification supports overlapping labels so REDACT labels did not have to be classified in a separate step.

| Label | Precision | Recall | F1-Score | Support |
|---|---|---|---|---|
| NEGATIVE | 0.5454 | 0.2000 | 0.2927 | 25 |
| POSITIVE | 0.4186 | 0.3673 | 0.3913 | 33 |
| SUGGESTION | 0.3076 | 0.2105 | 0.2500 | 15 |
| REDACT | 0.8780 | 0.6000 | 0.7129 | 43 |
| **Macro Avg** | 0.5374 | 0.3445 | 0.4117 | 116 |
| **Weighted Avg** | 0.6018 | 0.3972 | 0.3972 | 116 |

**Table 4.** Examples of word-level DistilBERT model classification output.

**Example 1:**

```
SUGGESTION [ 0: 111] → apply book chapter skills to the class project on a
weekly basis like the quizzes quizd us on the book knowleage
SUGGESTION [ 113: 181] → it would be more helpful to abosrb and retain the
learning matrials.
```

**Example 2:**

```
SUGGESTION [ 0: 12] → Maybe find a
NEGATIVE [ 13: 68] → textbook that only includes the language that is taught
NEGATIVE [ 70: 147] → - sometimes it was confusing when the information did
not apply to oracle SQL
```

**Example 3:**

```
POSITIVE [ 0: 105] → Good teacher, appreciated the lectures greatly and
appreciated his seeking feedback on course improvement
```

In Table 2, we show the results for the chunk-based model, which uses an IOB (inside, outside, beginning) sequence labeling task. This model is a fine-tuned based on BERT base uncased. In this case our performance was less than the word-level classification labeling task in Table 1, but it more closely matches the annotation task of labeling discrete, contiguous spans of input content. In Table 3, the results of training SpaCy's span-level model include the REDACT label because it allows for overlapping span labels.

# 4 Discussion

## 4.1 Annotation Challenges

Our presented study is the result of several iterations of annotation experiments. We first annotated at the whole input level (i.e. sentence- or paragraph-length text). At this resolution we observed much mixed positive and negative sentiment so we had a MIXED annotation label. Next, we tried annotating at the sentence level, using SpaCy's sentence splitting functionality. This did not entirely eliminate the MIXED annotation label because sentences could still have clauses of both positive and negative content. Also, the SpaCy sentence splitting functionality was not robust given the informal spelling and grammar of our input text. In particular, R (as in the programming language) at the end of the sentence (i.e. followed by a period) was sometimes treated as an abreviation rather than the end of a sentence. Bulleted lists were another source of sentence splitting errors.

As seen from Kripendorff's $\alpha$ agreement figure, .48, the annotation task was difficult and involved subjective judgments. One source of disagreement is that the annotators were a combination of faculty and students, so this offered different perspectives. Also, some of the annotators were non-native English speakers. Ambiguity is another factor, but the UNSURE label allowed annotators to indicate confusion and in practice this led to fewer cases of other overlapping labels, with the exception of REDACT, which frequently overlapped with other labels.

Choosing a set of labels was an iterative process that was informed primarily by looking at the data. This is a source of bias that a wider source of data or a more top-down approach may have solved. For example, after our paper was reviewed, we considered applying our annotation scheme to the paper reviews instead of teaching reviews. The labels fit to some extent, but the paper submission reviews contained questions, a phenomenon we did not observe in the teaching reviews.

Structured analysis and structured design are traditional methodologies used to model and develop information systems. They focus on defining system functions, processes, and data flow using tools like data flow diagrams [8]. These methods offer one type of top-down approach that may help guide the choice of labels by situating the choice in the context of building systems based on an understanding of how information moves through the system and how different components interact functionally. The goal is to create a well-organized framework for software systems based on input, processes, and outputs. Our paper does not involve designing or modeling a complete information system. Instead, it focuses on descriptively annotating student feedback data and applying NLP techniques using machine learning models like BERT and SpaCy. The work focuses on text classification, span-level annotation, and sentiment labeling, rather than defining system behavior or structure. However, we hope that this pilot project can inform future work in developing software functionality or system architecture.

The span labeling aspect of annotation also was a factor in the difficulty of the task. Determining when to start and end a span was part of the instructions but still led to some disagreements, especially with respect to punctuation and determining what was the end of one span and the beginning of another. Our instructions told annotators to exclude punctuation from the ends of spans except when the punctuation was important to the span class, like exclamation points. The segmentation issue is one of the reasons why the word-level classification (Table 1) results were better than the chunk- and span-level classification results (Tables 2 and 3), where identifying discrete, contiguous spans is critical.

### 4.2 Model Training

Ideally, annotation and model training would be in close correspondence. However, in practice, there are often mismatches between this ideal. In our case, the annotation labels corresponded to phenomena we wished to study in the data and post-processing, such as redacting names and pronouns that could inhibit anonymity. The Prodigy tool conveniently let us annotate data with these overlapping spans. However, machine learning models for overlapping spans are not as well-supported as chunking models like named entity recognition, where the spans cannot overlap. However, SpaCy's span categorization performed better than the chunking IOB method, so this showed that although the raw performance was not as high as the first, word-level model, the annotation-model fit may explain why the third, Spacy span-based model outperformed the second, IOB chunk-based BERT model.

## 5 Conclusion

Our preliminary results with model training indicate that, while the span categorization is a good model for convenient annotation, it is not the best fit in terms of model performance. Our best model results came from BERT and DistilBERT using a word-level classification task, which does not allow overlapping spans but rather requires separate pipeline that accounts for spans that overlap, like REDACT in our case. Our future research will aim to augment these data with other sources, including more official student feedback and synthetic data. Large language models (LLMs) could be used to generate these synthetic data. In addition, LLMs could be used in the future to compare the performance of zero-shot and few-shot models with the models we have described in this paper. Finally, another next step is to integrate the ML models into operational use in applications that can be useful for teachers and schools.

**Acknowledgments.** Thanks to Sakthi Srikanthan, Yue Fu, Rohith Ambarish, and Manoj Ravi Kumar for discussion and help with annotation.

**Disclosure of Interests.** We have no conflicts of interest to declare.

## References

1. Devlin, J., Chang, M.W., Lee, K., Toutanova, K.: BERT: Pre-training of deep bidirectional transformers for language understanding. In: Burstein, J., Doran, C., Solorio, T. (eds.) Proceedings of the 2019 Conference of the North American Chapter of the Association for Computational Linguistics: Human Language Technologies, Volume 1 (Long and Short Papers), pp. 4171–4186. ACL, Minneapolis, Minnesota, June 2019. https://doi.org/10.18653/v1/N19-1423, https://aclanthology.org/N19-1423/
2. Gottipati, S., Shankararaman, V., Lin, J.R.: Text analytics approach to extract course improvement suggestions from students' feedback. Res. Pract. Technol. Enhanc. Learn. **13**(1), 6 (2018). https://doi.org/10.1186/S41039-018-0073-0
3. Honnibal, M., Montani, I.: spaCy 2: natural language understanding with Bloom embeddings, convolutional neural networks and incremental parsing (2017), to appear
4. Montani, I., Honnibal, M.: Prodigy: a modern and scriptable annotation tool for creating training data for machine learning models, https://prodi.gy/
5. Pyasi, S., Gottipati, S., Shankararaman, V.: SUFAT - an analytics tool for gaining insights from student feedback comments. In: IEEE Frontiers in Education Conference, FIE 2018, San Jose, CA, USA, 3–6 October 2018, pp. 1–9. IEEE (2018). https://doi.org/10.1109/FIE.2018.8658457
6. Rashid, A., Asif, S., Butt, N.A., Ashraf, I.: Feature level opinion mining of educational student feedback data using sequential pattern mining and association rule mining. Int. J. Comput. Appl. **81**, 32 (2013) https://doi.org/10.5120/14050-2215
7. Sanh, V., Debut, L., Chaumond, J., Wolf, T.: Distilbert, a distilled version of bert: smaller, faster, cheaper and lighter. ArXiv arXiv:1910.01108 (2019), https://api.semanticscholar.org/CorpusID:203626972
8. Stevens, W.P., Myers, G.J., Constantine, L.L.: Structured design. IBM Syst. J. **13**(2), 115–139 (1974). https://doi.org/10.1147/sj.132.0115
9. Sunar, A.S., Khalid, M.S.: Natural language processing of student's feedback to instructors: a systematic review. IEEE Trans. Learn. Technol. **17**, 741–753 (2024). https://doi.org/10.1109/TLT.2023.3330531

# Relation Extraction from Real-World Unstructured Text in the Domain of Dementia

# Assessing Privacy-Friendly Local Open-Source Voice Annotation for Participants with Parkinson's Disease

Emma L. Tonkin[1](✉) and Gregory J. L. Tourte[2]

[1] Digital Health, University of Bristol, Bristol, UK
e.l.tonkin@bristol.ac.uk
[2] Advanced Research Computing, University of Oxford, Oxford, UK
gregory.tourte@it.ox.ac.uk

**Abstract.** There is significant potential clinical benefit to be gained in capturing symptom data from individuals with Parkinson's Disease (PD). For this purpose, sensor data is often collected. However, labels (ground truth) data is also beneficial, both to train (supervised learning) and to validate outcomes from automated monitoring systems. With the increasing use of voice assistants, this modality has been proposed for labelling. In this study, we examine some design patterns for voice-agent-supported labelling, identify failure modes, and make use of the MDVR-KCL dataset to benchmark a widely used key component, a speech-to-text pipeline. We identify that this component shows rapid increase in several error metrics (WER, CER, WIL) when employed on data from mildly symptomatic participants. We identify some potential mitigating steps and discuss potential future work.

**Keywords:** Parkinson's Disease · Privacy-first engineering · Voice assistants

## 1 Introduction

The increasing use of in-home technology for assistance, support and monitoring, such as for the aged and for those living with conditions such as Parkinson's or Alzheimer's, has led to an ongoing need for training and validation data to ensure that these systems are functioning as planned. For this purpose, a broad swathe of technologies may be used, ranging from paper diaries, tablet, phone or wearable based questionnaires or voice assistants, through to post-hoc annotation of identifiable data such as video or audio. It has also led to ongoing concern about the potential costs and risks surrounding the externalisation of this data and its processing from the home, since a great deal of the data collected is likely to be identifying or contain re-linkable features. In recent years, the problem of privacy-preserving and decentralised approaches to data processing with machine learning (ML) has received a great deal of attention. For example, federated learning is often proposed, in which models are trained in-home and in


E. L. Tonkin et al. (Eds.): ARDUOUS 2025, CCIS 2706, pp. 159–176, 2026.
https://doi.org/10.1007/978-3-032-09117-8_10

principle may be tuned by comparison to other models by centralising operations on model weights, rather than raw data and labels. Since the raw data and features do not leave the home, the residual risk of this data sharing is solely that attached to the model weights, and is consequentially lower.

In this paper, we examine a subset of the design challenges of building an affordable, auditable voice assistant suitable for supporting clinical trials within the home, with a particular focus on participants with Parkinson's Disease (PD). Our aim is to assess the current technology readiness of a key component widely used for open source voice assistants. Ultimately, we restrict our focus to privacy-friendly, decentralised approach: for the present study, our interest is in voice assistant implementations in which data does not leave the home (that is, in which audio is processed via on-device processing entirely within the home).

The paper is structured as follows: we begin by characterising PD, discuss a number of potential uses of data annotation/labelling, and review potential effects of the symptoms of PD on the individual's voice and hence on the technologies. We then discuss scenarios of use for a voice assistant suitable for data annotation purposes, drawn from individual and collaborative ideation and refined using a design-fiction approach to develop scenarios. Our methodology is to make use of an existing dataset created by King's College London (KCL) to characterise the performance of standard components of a voice assistant speech-to-text pipeline of changes in speech or voice due to PD. This enables us to establish the effects of performance limitations on the system requirements. In our discussion, we discuss the methodological limitations of this study and explore further work, discuss key findings, and briefly review potential mitigations of these issues.

## 2 Characterising PD

PD is a neurodegenerative disorder. Motor function is impaired, resulting in symptoms such as slowness of motion or decrease in amplitude of motion (bradykinesia), tremor, and disturbance to gait and balance [40]. The patient is likely to experience nonmotor symptoms such as pain [38], and individual patients report finding a range of symptoms particularly troublesome. Nonmotor symptoms such as abnormalities of sensation, behavioural changes and sleep disturbance are also important components of PD [37].

People with Parkinson disease are very likely to have identified, or had others notice, changes in their speech or voice [16]. In particular, Holmes *et al.* [22] identified that people with PD are likely to speak with lower intensity (quieter), have a breathier voice, and display reduced variation in pitch and loudness compared to a control group. People with longer disease duration are more likely to experience higher magnitude of frequency tremor [20]. However, it is important to be aware that the experiences of people with PD vary widely [12]. There is also evidence that voice self-assessment is complex for people with PD compared to individuals with general voice disorders [8]. Hence, in this study, we have chosen to work with a dataset that is labelled via expert assessment.

PD symptoms are likely to fluctuate [39]. This occurs in the short term, as in the case of motor fluctuations such as freezing – a sudden and temporary inability to move – and paradoxic kinesis [15], in which fluid motion is briefly exhibited, potentially as a consequence of external cueing [28]. Within the day, there is fluctuation – for example, in gait – potentially due to factors such as depletion of medication [35]. Additionally, the Hawthorne effect, change in performance due to the awareness that an activity is observed, is likely to be a factor in short-term observation of people with PD [33].

The variance described in the previous paragraph adds complexity to 'snapshot-based' evaluation of PD, meaning that ratings such as the Unified Parkinson's Disease Rating Scale (UPDRS) have difficulty capturing the full picture [21]. As a consequence of this complex picture, there is considerable interest in making use of mobile, pervasive and wearable sensors to characterise the ongoing activities of people with PD, and in particular, of the symptoms that they experience. This is perceived as likely to enable a fuller picture of the ebb and flow of symptoms throughout the day and over time, facilitating evaluation of interventions such as medication or other therapies.

### 2.1 Data Labelling in PD

In this section, we briefly discuss the challenge of data labelling in PD.

Existing literature shows a wide range of potential approaches to data annotation in PD. One popular approach is app-based scripted data collection. For example, the mPower dataset [5] made use of a smartphone-based app strategy to implement and record a series of scripted activities, including participants with and without PD, with the intention of quantifying the fluctuation in PD symptoms. The activities included were well-chosen for an app-based delivery mechanism and for the available sensors, and included a memory task, a 'tapping' task to assess dexterity, a voice-based task to assess sustained phonation, and a walking activity involving walking 20 steps in a straight line, turning, standing still and walking back. However, the IMU data did not receive ground truth labelling within this task, possibly because there was no convenient mechanism to achieve this without disrupting the task itself. Similarly, Borzì *et al.* [4] describe the use of mobile phone sensors to record a scripted activity, with data recording started and stopped after each case. As Little [26] summarises the problem: labelling often requires expert decisions, and hence requires care, potentially training for the assessor, assessment of inter-rater variability, and a high degree of ongoing adherence, which may become a significant burden for the labeller. In-situ labelling also has the potential to disrupt activities, adding a further burden to the participant: on a very basic level, the need to carry a device with one and interact with it periodically is itself a burden.

By contrast, Morgan *et al.* [32] present a taxonomy consisting of a series of features in PD that may be of interest for annotation, including: activity level and intensity (walking, sitting, lying down), activities of daily living (e.g. watching television, food prep, cleaning, chatting,...), global spontaneity of movement (slowness), gait (from unproblematic independent walking to requiring assistance or unable to walk), and level of impairment in the activity of sit-to-stand, going from a seated position to standing up. These are then labelled using RGB video data taken from within the home, by a medically trained specialist with support from other annotators. Such an approach has challenges, notably those related to the limited field of view of a camera: the body will tend to occlude some features, especially if the individual is not well placed in front of the camera, and especially when the activity takes place in a small space.

## 2.2 The Challenge of Voice Annotation in PD

Partially in response to the challenges of other methodologies, it has been proposed that voice agents provide a potential solution for data labelling in the wild in the general case, whether via automated assessment of audio cues [18], via semi-automated means through interaction with a voice agent [10] or via straightforward voice-based logging [42]. Audio recording, however, is a privacy-intrusive approach, and hence there is the potential that at least some demographics of participant will react negatively to this as a consequence of privacy concerns, requiring appropriate mitigations to be put in place to safeguard privacy [17].

From a privacy perspective, voice annotation poses challenges. As Germanos *et al.* [19] indicate, typical voice assistants coexist with a wider ecosystem, in which a large quantity of data, some of which is classifiable as personal data, is either temporarily or permanently stored outside the user's immediate physical context. In particular, commercial voice assistants are increasingly moving toward LLM-based approaches and cloud architectures rather than on-device processing, a trend encapsulated by the recent decision by Amazon to discontinue the 'Do not send voice recording' option, meaning that recordings that may previously have been retained locally are now sent to remote processing venues. Where medical information is annotated and logged, this may be a greater concern than for other applications of this technology. Hence, in this paper, we focus on the challenge of voice annotation using technology situated within the home.

The use of voice assistants for data labelling in contexts such as human activity recognition is not widely explored, compared to the use of data labelling on voice commands (in order to improve performance), which is common place, or, in the case of PD, the analysis of voice recordings to directly assess the progression of PD symptoms. However, the designer is led to consider the possibility by observing, firstly, that voice assistants or agents are currently widespread and widely used, including amongst older adults [2], for purposes such as setting up reminders, weather information and search; secondly, that the technology is reasonably mature; thirdly, that voice agents are well-placed for use where the hands and eyes are busy [23]; and finally, that there is also some anecdotal evidence that the practice of making use of a voice agent may lead to improvements in the speech of people with PD [16]. A key question for our purposes is therefore whether the technology as implemented in the home is adequately mature to support this use case, and to what extent.

In the following section, we discuss generic interaction scenarios that are envisaged to be relevant to supporting voice annotation. These are included as a

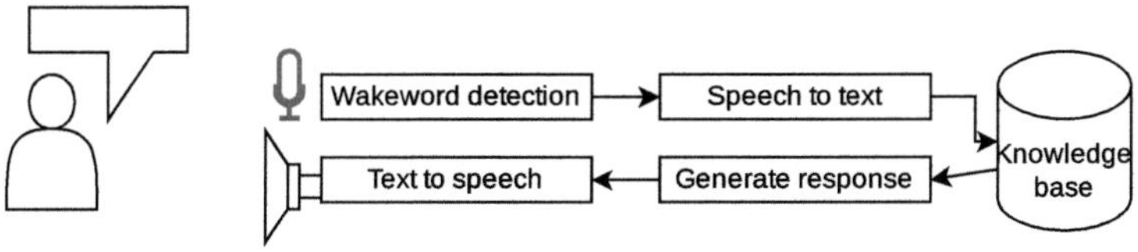


**Fig. 1.** Simplified architecture for a voice agent.

lens through which to consider the required quality of voice transcription (speech-to-text). In this paper, we primarily consider participant-initiated information logging. We acknowledge that more complex patterns may mitigate many quality concerns. Additionally, patterns that primarily involve information presented by the voice assistant are likely to be useful in many annotation scenarios, such as prompting the participant to engage in scripted activities.

## 3 Samples of Design Patterns for Voice Annotation

The methodology used for collecting scenarios was as follows: scenarios of use for voice annotation in PD are elicited from several sources, including: literature review; individual and group ideation; symptom-led discussion; clinical requirements for study data; and a design-fiction approach, using design stories to elicit and explore potential uses and accompanying concerns and risks. This last approach may be used informally in technical teams to communicate functionality and illustrate perceptions and expectations regarding factors such as user acceptance, functional constraints and practical risks. While these scenarios will not be reported in full in this workshop paper, as they are beyond the scope of this work, we provide a summary of the underlying design patterns here alongside an illustrative example for each case. By design patterns, we refer to generic, reusable patterns of dyadic [27] interaction [14] that can take place between the participant and the voice agent. These generic capabilities define the base functional requirements for a voice assistant framework in this context.

### 3.1 Pattern 1: Participant-Initiated Information Logging

Example: Recording events and activities without system prompting.

> *Human speaker:* Assistant name/Wakeword, I'm taking my medication.
> *Voice assistant (VA):* Noted, you took your medication at nine fifty three AM. I'll add an entry to the log.

This type of speech act is described by Mahmood *et al.* [27] as a statement. The VA's response indicates that the relevant action is taken and that the interaction is at an end.

### 3.2 Pattern 2: Device-Initiated Query-Response

Example: Activity recognition validation.

*Voice assistant [triggered by ML device prediction]:* Hey, [participant name], are you cooking something?
*Human speaker:* Yes, I'm making lunch. It's sardines on toast.

This is also potentially useful for many other types of validation task, such as re-identification, quality of motion and so forth. An **informational device-initiated announcement** is also possible that does not expect any kind of response: for example, a voice assistant announcing that there is a person at the door, that post has been received or that a device is low on battery and needs recharging. However, in the context of data annotation it is likely that dyadic interactions with confirmation will be preferred where possible, principally because the purpose is usually to elicit information from the participant, and secondly because this is likely to lead to more robust communication, in that it is more likely for communication failures to be identified and potentially repaired.

### 3.3 Pattern 3: Participant-Led Longer Unscripted Interaction or Continued Conversations

Example: participant chats to device

### 3.4 Pattern 4: Lengthier Scripted Interactions, Such as Completion of Standard Movement Scripted Activities

Example: Device leads participant through several tasks that provide adequate proxy data for estimating standardised results such as UPDRS score, or device talks participant through standardised instruments such as the Pittsburgh Sleep Quality Index (PSQI) test.

### 3.5 Failure Pattern in Participant-Initiated Interaction: System Does Not Recognise that Interaction Is Occurring

In some cases the system wake word is not recognised, resulting in the voice assistant failing to process the following statement at all.

It is also possible in device-initiated interactions that the participant will not recognise that the sound they are hearing is the voice assistant starting an interaction. Mitigating patterns that are often suggested for this are visual and audible indicators preceding the utterance to clearly link the utterance with the source.

### 3.6 Failure Patterns: System Misunderstands the Participant, or Vice Versa

This is a key problem in voice assistant design. Appropriate recovery strategies are an issue.

### 3.7 Key Concerns in Voice Assistant Design

While the present study essentially examines feasibility and practicality by evaluating the performance of a key component, there are further major areas of concern for us as implementers. The first is usability and user acceptance. For example, according to Mahmood *et al.* [27], lag time in response is a significant concern. Voice assistants frequently implement a 'wait pattern' in the event that queries will take more than a couple of seconds. Similarly, a voice assistant with a high error rate is likely to frustrate the user, either because it does not detect that an error has occurred or, to a lesser extent, if it overcorrects [11]. Implementing repair in a domestic voice assistant is beyond the scope of this study, which aims only to explore the likelihood that such errors occur: however, we will touch on this topic again in the discussion of this paper. In general, voice assistants may be viewed as intrusive [36] in privacy terms, and this may affect user acceptance. Some of the design patterns mentioned above are potentially disruptive in nature, which, Jamshed, Nurain and Brewer [25] observes, may be beneficial depending on the precise purpose of use. For example, as Zargham *et al.* [43] find, proactivity in voice assistants is preferable during opportune moments, which implies a certain level of context-awareness in system design. Perceived appropriateness is of importance: however, in that study, participant opinions of proactive interventions vary between participants, and there is a negative correlation between perceptions of usefulness and invasiveness. A further system feature not examined within this study is identification of the speaker: speaker identification is a requested feature for home-deployable systems. Again, a detailed discussion of these concerns is beyond the scope of this study: however, it is useful to recognise that reduced-quality voice detection, keyword detection and transcription may have a significant effect on the ability of a system to achieve the desired design and user acceptance.

The second key subject area for implementers is security and privacy. Although the technical and organisational concerns of voice assistants are within the scope of our broader study, detailed discussion is beyond the scope of this paper. Perhaps the most commonly discussed issue with voice assistant implementations is the potential to retain data for system improvement purposes [7], for example, finetuning [30]: there is genuine potential benefit for system users in doing so, yet the retention of the data, even if appropriate technical and organisational measures are taken to protect it, raises significant risks for participant privacy. Cheng and Roedig [6] highlights many concerns with potential uses of participant data and the need to ensure transparency, such as participant awareness of recording, the destinations of recordings, and the potential for one's voice (and data) being picked up by others' devices, as well as the possibility for detection of activities (e.g. laughter, crying, or eating, or indeed medical state, such as a cold [1]), room characteristics, or even of active audio sensing of room features, occupancy and so on. Technologies such as speaker recognition offer the potential of access control on data input and system control, yet these are subject to attacks such as speech synthesis based on existing samples of data, known as replay attacks [13]. Furthermore, some uses of voice-based annotation for digital health purposes, for participants in multi-occupancy homes, for example living with other family members or friends, have the effect of exposing others in the home to healthcare data: this may not be desired by participants, for example because there may be tensions around these topics, or participants may, as Binda *et al.* [3] describes, be concerned about causing other family members to worry. Voice assistant use in these contexts may limit participant control over disclosure, and hence it may be beneficial to provide parallel solutions, such as an app, according to participant preference. Crotty *et al.* [9] find that information sharing practices for older people are often fluid, designed to maximise autonomy, and that preferences vary significantly. To summarise, data from voice recordings has the potential for considerable abuse and information leakage, and the appropriateness of spoken interaction varies significantly between participants, so practical implementations of this kind require effective technical and organisational measures to be taken throughout the design, implementation and deployment processes, as well as involvement of stakeholder groups (for example, through co-design) to assess and address concerns.

## 4 Methodology: Assessing Performance of Voice Assistant Software

The key research question on which we focus in evaluating the performance of voice assistant software for this purpose is: to what extent can we expect voice assistant software performance to be affected by PD symptoms? For this purpose, we focus on the performance of the key speech-to-text component (depicted in Fig. 1) – that is, the component that takes arbitrary speech input and attempts to convert it to text in order to extract commands, store information, or take other action as described above.

The other key component that may be affected is the problem of *wakeword detection* – that is, the system's ability to recognise when it is being addressed. This is also an important problem, particularly since wakeword detection often takes place on the edge – which is to say, on small machines such as ESP32 microprocessors, which have severe technical limitations. Wakeword failure means that the system will fail to recognise that it is being addressed, or alternatively that the system will wake inappropriately (false positive). We acknowledge that wakeword detection is also an important area, but it is out of scope for the present study.

For the purpose of evaluating the performance of speech-to-text in this context, we make use of the KCL MDVR-KCL dataset [24], Mobile Device Voice Recordings at King's College London (MDVR-KCL) from both early and advanced Parkinson's disease patients and healthy controls. This dataset was chosen on several grounds, including accessibility for reuse, appropriate licensing, compatibility with the broad aims of the original dataset, and clear and relevant data annotation, in that the dataset was annotated by subject matter experts for participant UPDRS scores related to speech characteristics (see discussion of voice self-assessment in Sect. 2). The MDVR-KCL dataset is recorded

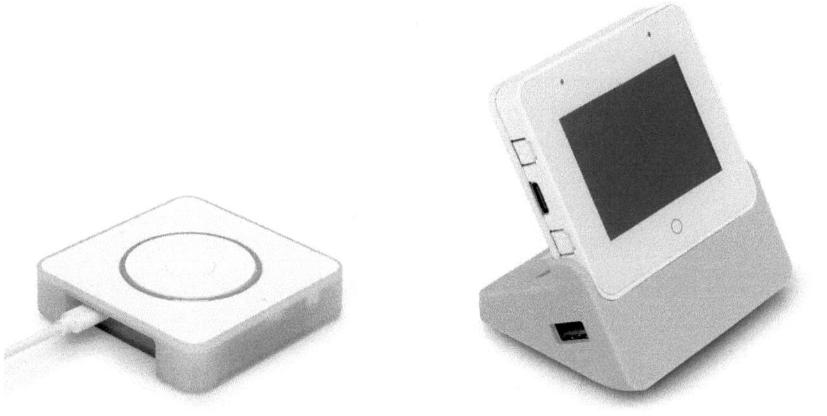

(a) (b)

**Fig. 2.** Example of home deployable voice assistant hardware compatible with Home Assistant (a) Nabu-Casa Home Assistant Voice Preview Edition and (b) Espressif ESP-32 S3 Box-3.

using a mobile phone rather than high-quality microphones, which is somewhat analogous to the likely conditions for use of home-deployed voice assistant hardware (see Fig. 2).

This dataset contains voice recordings from sixteen participants with PD, and 21 healthy control (HC) participants. The dataset contains both scripted speech and unscripted spontaneous dialogue: for ease of comparison within this initial study, we focus on the scripted data. Each participant is asked to read at least one of two readings, 'The North Wind and the Sun' and 'Tech. Engin. Computer applications in geography snippet'. Each file is annotated with a pseudonym, a health status label (PD or control), a Hoehn and Yahr (H&Y) scale rating, a UPDRS II-5 (expert peer-reviewed) score and a UPDRS III-18 (expert assessed score). To interpret the latter two [41], the UPDRS II-5 assesses speech within 'activities of daily living', and rates speech between 0 (Normal), 1 (Mildly affected, no difficulty being understood), 2 (Moderately affected. Sometimes asked to repeat statements), 3 (Severely affected. Frequently asked to repeat statements) and 4 (Unintelligible most of the time). The UPDRS III-18 score assesses speech within the motor examination, and assesses speech on the following scale: 0 (Normal), 1 (Slight loss of expression, diction and/ or volume), 2 (Monotone, slurred but understandable; moderately impaired), 3 (Marked impairment, difficult to understand) and 4 (Unintelligible). The H&Y scale is a system for grading severity of PD symptoms, as follows: [31]: 1) minimal or no functional disability, 2) bilateral involvement, without impairment of balance, 3) mild to moderate bilateral disease, with some postural instability, 4) severely disabling, still able to walk or stand unassisted, 5) wheelchair bound or bedridden unless aided.

In this section, we test the performance of speech-to-text transcription on these files, as this is a key component of voice assistants in general. We develop a ground truth for these audio files. We calculate word error rate and processing time based on a standard setup. We compare several models chosen from OpenAI's Whisper. In this manner we aim to assess the technology readiness of this component to this use case.

### 4.1 Developing a Ground Truth

Since the audio files contain extraneous audio before and after the participants' readings of the texts, the first author made note of the times in which individuals other than the participant were speaking and stored these for automated cropping. Following this process, the audio files were manually transcribed by the first author. Attention was paid to accurate transcription of the participants' speech. The second author then reviewed each of these transcriptions for accuracy, resulting in a consensus ground truth. These timings and transcriptions are intended for eventual publication, as we feel that they form a useful resource alongside the existing dataset.

### 4.2 Scoring Speech-to-Text Output with Word, Character and Match Error Rates

Word error rate (WER) and character error rate (CER) are standard metrics by which to measure the performance of speech recognition systems. Similarly to the Levenshtein edit distance algorithm, the goal of WER and CER are to establish the minimum edit distance between the ground truth string and the hypothesis (e.g. the speech to text system's 'guess' at the correct answer). This can be understood by the following equation:

$$\text{error\_rate} = \frac{I + D + S}{N_{ER}} \tag{1}$$

where $I$ is the number of insertions, $D$ the number of deletions, and $S$ the number of substitutions required to generate the hypothesis from the ground truth string, $H$ is the number of correct matches and $N$ is the overall number of terms: in the case that word error rate is calculated, $N$ is the number of words in the string, while where character error rate is calculated $N_{ER}$ is the number of characters $(H + S + D)$. In other words, word error rate is the ratio of the number of errors to the number of words provided [34].

As an intuitive explanation, comparing a ground truth string of 'This is a fact' to a version, 'This is fact', we note that one word has been omitted. One word must be deleted from the ground truth in order to achieve the hypothesis text. If our hypothesis text has an additional word, e.g. 'This is indeed a fact', one word must be added to generate the hypothesis text. Hence, two identical strings have an edit distance of zero. The larger the *WER* or *CER*, less accurate the system.

$$WIL = 1 - \frac{H}{N} \times \frac{H}{P} \tag{2}$$

The Word Information Lost (WIL) metric attempts to approximate which proportion of word information is unsuccessfully transmitted, quantifying the proportion of information lost. This differs from *WER* in that *WER* calculates the cost of reconstructing the input. In the above equation, $P$ is the number of words in the automated transcript.

There are known shortcomings to the use of these metrics for evaluating voice systems, principally that they do not accurately reflect human perception of the accuracy of such systems [29]. That is to say, technical error and perception of error are likely to differ, according to the area of application in which the technology is used.

### 4.3 Processing Time

When running these models, we have collected processing time as a loose indicator of relative requirements in terms of processing power and time. We stress that this does not signify that these models are necessarily slow or that their deployment will involve lag. It is clear that, in practice, deployment of a larger model with more parameters will involve making and evaluating suitable hardware choices prior. Rather, we wish to highlight that deployment cost of the larger models is accordingly higher, and potentially that there is less pragmatic likelihood of running these models in a low-power home environment context, such as that indicated in a private federated learning context. We collect this information alongside system performance scoring data in order to establish whether there is clear benefit in deploying the larger models, in this specific user context.

## 5 Results

### 5.1 Error in Voice Annotation by UPDRS Score

Unsurprisingly, direct comparison of error metrics between the PD and HC groupings demonstrates that average performance of models is notably worse in the former group ($\overline{WER_{PD}} = 0.16$, $\overline{WER_{HC}} = 0.1$; $\overline{CER_{PD}} = 0.11$, $\overline{CER_{HC}} = 0.07$; $\overline{WIL_{PD}} = 0.2$, and $\overline{WIL_{HC}} = 0.12$).

A more nuanced picture can be seen by examining the performance of the system relative to participant UPDRS scores (see Fig. 3). As the figure shows, the speech-to-text system has difficulties dealing with 'moderately affected' (level 2) speech in UPDRS II 5, and significant difficulties with severely affected speech. It also displays increased error on speech scored as 'mildly affected' under UPDRS-II 5. Concretely, WER increases from 0.09 for those with a UPDRS-II 5 score of 0 to 0.17 for those with a score of 1, while WIL almost doubles (0.12 and 0.21 respectively). This is interesting, in comparison with the experience of the annotators participating in this project, who found that as human listeners, speech scored in this way was as comprehensible as that of control participants. This suggests that the speech-to-text system may be somewhat susceptible to errors as a result of features of mildly affected speech. A UPDRS-III 18 score of

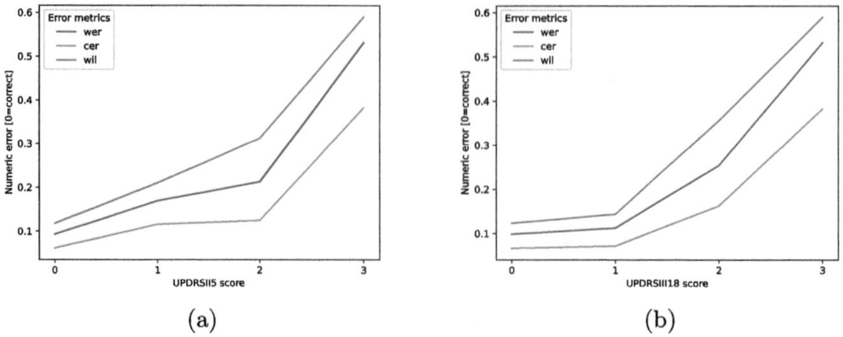


**Fig. 3.** Performance of text-to-speech segmented by Unified Parkinson's Disease Rating Scale (a) UPDRS-II 5 score and (b) UPDRS-III 18 score.

1 has relatively little effect: the WER increases only very slightly, as does CER and WIL. However, a UPDRS-III 18 score of 2 has a significant effect (WER increases from the range of 0.1 to 0.2 in the case of a score of 0 or 1 to 0.25, whilst WIL increases from 0.12 to 0.14 [UPDRS-III 18 score of 0 or 1 respectively] to 0.36. A score of 3 has a similar effect, with WER and WIL exceeding 0.5. Hence, moderate impairment of speech on the motor examination aspect of UPDRS may be expected to significantly impair performance of speech-to-text systems of this kind.

It is worth noting that H&Y scores of 0 and 1 are very similar in performance: indeed, we find that the performance improves very slightly between the two, an effect that we attribute to variation in demographic and selection strategies between the groups. However, samples with a H&Y score of 3 experience approximately double the error rate to the baseline, with samples with H&Y of 4 seeing error rates of around 4 to 5 times the baseline on average depending on metric.

Perhaps the most significant point to take from this analysis is that performance of speech-to-text systems appears to degrade faster than we might expect, given the comprehensibility of voice to the human listener. Informally, it is worth noting that many of the participants in this study, especially in the HC (control) group, have accents that the annotators viewed as regional or international, and while this has not been systematically encoded in the study, it is notable that these accents do not seem to have had similar impact on system performance, potentially implying that the speech-to-text systems used are more resilient to accent variation than to PD symptoms.

### 5.2 Model Performance in Each Group

Model performance in each group is summarised in Table 1. The best-performing by each metric in the healthy control group (HC) and the PD group are highlighted in bold. See the following subsection for further discussion.

**Table 1.** Performance of Whisper models in control (HC) and PD groups

| Model | Parameter Count | Overall Aggregate WIL | Performance by Group | | | | | |
|---|---|---|---|---|---|---|---|---|
| | | | PD WER | HC WER | PD CER | HC CER | PD WIL | HC WIL |
| tiny | 39 000 000 | 0.206 | 0.197 | 0.093 | 0.107 | 0.042 | 0.283 | 0.147 |
| base | 74 000 000 | 0.156 | 0.142 | 0.078 | 0.080 | 0.038 | 0.203 | 0.120 |
| small | 244 000 000 | **0.104** | **0.105** | **0.048** | **0.065** | 0.030 | **0.149** | **0.069** |
| medium | 769 000 000 | 0.108 | 0.110 | 0.051 | 0.073 | **0.029** | 0.151 | 0.075 |
| turbo | 809 000 000 | 0.183 | 0.256 | 0.151 | 0.203 | 0.123 | 0.234 | 0.145 |
| large | 1 550 000 000 | 0.194 | 0.154 | 0.172 | 0.111 | 0.138 | 0.196 | 0.193 |

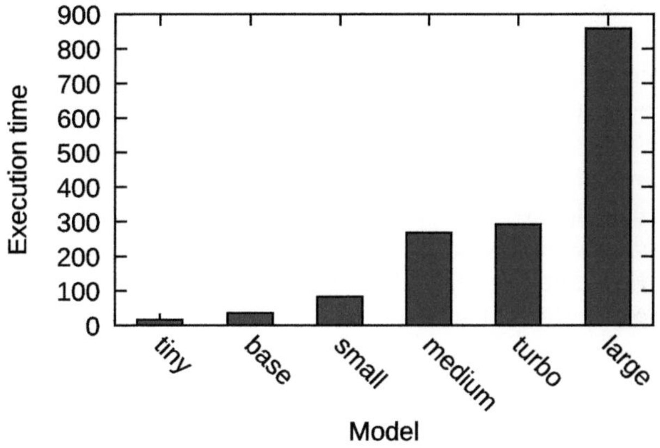


**Fig. 4.** Model average processing time across all segments (mean).

## 5.3 Processing Time

As can be seen in Fig. 4, the processing time of the larger models is very significant (e.g. efficient use of these models would require specialised hardware, which likely involves cloud processing). Fortunately from a privacy perspective, there is little apparent benefit of using the larger models in this specific context of use. There is anecdotal evidence that in general voice assistant implementers find the Whisper Base model to be an adequate compromise between execution speed/hardware requirements and accuracy. However, given the increased error rate and information loss identified in this study for participants with PD, it is likely that the 'small' model would be the better compromise in this population, as this would provide, for example, a WER only slightly higher than the base model would produce for input from the control group. In effect, the average WIL experienced for individuals with PD where a 'small' model is used is equivalent to that experienced by individuals in the control group using the 'tiny' model. However, there are several important caveats to this, which are discussed in the following section.

## 6 Discussion

There are some methodological limitations to this study. Principally, the KCL dataset does not provide demographic data, and therefore it is not possible to comment on other factors that may confound the findings. For example, the age range of participants in each cohort is not provided, nor is information provided about screening regarding other diagnoses or confounding factors, other than UPDRS/H&Y scoring of the HC participants. Secondly, we have excluded from the scope of the present paper any detailed examination of the features of the participants' voices other than UPDRS scores, and therefore we are not able to comment within this study on the impact of different features that may be present in individuals – for example, features detectable via software analysis, such as variance in amplitude or pitch [22]. We view this as a potentially fruitful topic for further work. Thirdly, we note that the dataset also has the confounding feature that the participants are engaging in scripted reads of standard texts. It is possible that, depending on the selection criteria of the participants, the control group may be more familiar with this activity, and hence more practised at reading aloud. As one participant [ID29] states, 'I'm not used to reading aloud to people'. There is potential to examine other types of speech – indeed, the KCL dataset itself includes spontaneous speech. However, this is beyond the scope of the present study, and may be explored in future work.

Our first finding is that speech-to-text systems display a higher error rate when processing speech from individuals diagnosed with PD, versus a control group. While this is to be expected with individuals with relatively severe PD, the results suggest that mild to moderate PD has a noticeable effect on transcription error. Our second finding is that, using stock models provided alongside Whisper, the optimal choice of model in terms of accuracy in this particular dataset is the so-called 'small' model. For users with PD, the error rate on smaller models is otherwise quite high. However, since this model has over two hundred million parameters, a device with 2 GB of video RAM is a reasonable minimum requirement for deployment within the home.

Having established that it is reasonable in general, from the evidence available, to expect a loss of accuracy when a speech-to-text system is used by a person with even mild PD versus an individual from a control group, we then question what, other than larger models and better hardware, may help to mitigate this concern. One such approach is that proposed by [44], who demonstrated that fine-tuning may be a beneficial strategy when working with dysarthria. As discussed in Sect. 3.7, this is facilitated by the logging and retention of diagnostic data, including user utterances captured by the system: however, this significantly impacts participant privacy. Beyond this, an analysis that takes into account the features of individual speech would be helpful in indicating in greater detail how features of speech in PD affect the performance of the speech-to-text system: once their relative significance is understood, it may be possible to use this information to guide efforts to design systems that better mitigate these limitations. For example, an improved microphone system may be an effective mitigation of quiet speech. A further mechanism that may be beneficial is the development of systems that support and actively engage in repair: for example, query of indistinct input and correction of erroneously recorded data or false positives [11].

## 7 Conclusion

In this study we have discussed design patterns for use of a voice agent designed to support an individual in annotating their actions, responding to system-triggered validation requests, interacting and participating in scripted activities. We have also discussed failure patterns that may occur between the individual and the device. Using an open dataset of spoken passages including participants with PD and control participants, we have benchmarked the performance of a key component of voice agent software, the speech-to-text application Whisper, in several configurations. In so doing, we have shown that according to standard error metrics, even mild PD symptoms affecting speech, which do not appear significant to comprehensibility of the audio to human annotators, appear to have a significant effect on the performance of this tool. We note that this can be partially countered by making use of the 'base' model, although this increases the hardware requirements of home installations of this software.

The question of the suitability of this approach for collecting speech annotation data in the wild still remains to be answered. We would argue that there are several facets to this question: there is the engineering challenge, of building a system that performs as optimally as possible in the intended context of use on both the hardware and software levels. There is the human-interaction challenge of building a system that supports the participant in repairing interactions when error occurs and minimises the frustration of systems that are prone to error. Finally, there is the broader question of the suitability of speech and interaction as a medium for annotating the types of information that are commonly labelled in PD, and the extent to which these actions or activities are susceptible to self-annotation by participants: the use of augmentative and alternative communication methods (AAC) is often recommended, and it is likely that exploring these approaches may be a useful direction for future research.

**Acknowledgments.** This work was supported by the TORUS Project, which has been funded by the UK Engineering and Physical Sciences Research Council (EPSRC), grant number EP/X036146/1.

## References

1. Ai, H., Wang, Y., Yang, Y., Zhang, Q.: An improvement of the degradation of speaker recognition in continuous cold speech for home assistant. In: International Symposium on Cyberspace Safety and Security, pp. 363–373 (2019)
2. Arnold, A., Kolody, S., Comeau, A., Cruz, A.M.: What does the literature say about the use of personal voice assistants in older adults? a scoping review. Disability Rehabilitation: Assistive Technol. **19**(1), 100–111 (2024). https://doi.org/10.1080/17483107.2022.2065369

3. Binda, J., Park, H., Carroll, J.M., Cope, N., Yuan, C.W., Choe, E.K.: Intergenerational sharing of health data among family members. In: Proceedings of the 11th EAI International Conference on Pervasive Computing Technologies for Healthcare, PervasiveHealth 2017, pp. 468–471. Association for Computing Machinery, Barcelona, Spain (2017). https://doi.org/10.1145/3154862.3154895
4. Borzì, L., et al.: Smartphone-based estimation of item 3.8 of the MDS-UPDRS-III for assessing leg agility in people with parkinson's disease. IEEE Open J. Eng. Med. Biol. **1**, 140–147 (2020). https://doi.org/10.1109/OJEMB.2020.2993463
5. Bot, B.M., et al.: The mPower study, Parkinson disease mobile data collected using ResearchKit. Sci. Data **3**(1), 1–9 (2016)
6. Cheng, P., Roedig, U.: Personal voice assistant security and privacy–a survey. Proc. IEEE **110**(4), 476–507 (2022)
7. Cho, E., Sundar, S.S., Abdullah, S., Motalebi, N.: Will deleting history make alexa more trustworthy? effects of privacy and content customization on user experience of smart speakers. In: Proceedings of the 2020 CHI Conference on Human Factors in Computing Systems, pp. 1–13 (2020)
8. Contreras-Ruston, F., et al.: Voice self-assessment in individuals with Parkinson's Disease as compared to general voice disorders. Parkinsonism & Related Disorders **123**, 106944 (2024). https://doi.org/10.1016/j.parkreldis.2024.106944
9. Crotty, B.H., et al.: Information sharing preferences of older patients and their families. JAMA Intern. Med. **175**(9), 1492–1497 (2015)
10. Cruz-Sandoval, D., et al.: Semi-automated data labeling for activity recognition in pervasive healthcare. Sensors **19**(14) (2019). https://doi.org/10.3390/s19143035
11. Cuadra, A., Li, S., Lee, H., Cho, J., Ju, W.: My bad! repairing intelligent voice assistant errors improves interaction. Proc. ACM Hum.-Comput. Interact. **5**(CSCW1), 1–24 (2021). https://doi.org/10.1145/3449101
12. Davis, J.T., Ehrhart, A., Trzcinski, B.H., Kille, S., Mount, J.: Variability of experiences for individuals living with Parkinson disease. J. Neurol. Phys. Ther. **27**(2), 38–45 (2003)
13. Dhiya'Mardhiyyah, A., Latif, J.J.K., Tho, C.: Privacy and security in the use of voice assistant: an evaluation of user awareness and preferences. In: 2023 International Conference on Information Management and Technology (ICIMTech), pp. 481–486 (2023). https://doi.org/10.1109/ICIMTech59029.2023.10277724
14. Díaz-Oreiro, I., López, G., Quesada, L., Guerrero, L.A.: Conversational design patterns for a UX evaluation instrument implemented by voice. In: Rocha, Á., Ferrás, C., Méndez Porras, A., Jimenez Delgado, E. (eds.) ICITS 2022. LNNS, vol. 414, pp. 530–540. Springer, Cham (2022). https://doi.org/10.1007/978-3-030-96293-7_44
15. Distler, M., Schlachetzki, J.C.M., Kohl, Z., Winkler, J., Schenk, T.: Paradoxical kinesia in Parkinson's disease revisited: anticipation of temporal constraints is critical. Neuropsychologia **86**, 38–44 (2016). https://doi.org/10.1016/j.neuropsychologia.2016.04.012
16. Duffy, O., Synnott, J., McNaney, R., Brito Zambrano, P., Kernohan, W.G: Attitudes toward the use of voice-assisted technologies among people with parkinson disease: findings from aweb-based survey. JMIR Rehabil Assist Technol. **8**(1), e23006 (2021). https://doi.org/10.2196/23006
17. Dunbar, J.C., Bascom, E., Boone, A., Hiniker, A.: Is someone listening? audio-related privacy perceptions and design recommendations from guardians, pragmatists, and cynics. Proc. ACM Interact. Mobile, Wearable Ubiquitous Technol. **5**(3), 1–23 (2021)

18. Garcia-Constantino, M.., et al.: Semi-automated annotation of audible home activities. In: 2019 IEEE International Conference on Pervasive Computing and Communications Workshops (PerCom Workshops), pp. 40–45 (2019). https://doi.org/10.1109/PERCOMW.2019.8730729
19. Germanos, G., Kavallieros, D., Kolokotronis, N., Georgiou, N.: Privacy issues in voice assistant ecosystems. In: 2020 IEEE World Congress on Services (SERVICES), pp. 205–212 (2020). https://doi.org/10.1109/SERVICES48979.2020.00050
20. Gillivan-Murphy, P., Miller, N., Carding, P.: Voice tremor in parkinson's disease: an acoustic study. J. Voice **33**(4), 526–535 (2019). https://doi.org/10.1016/j.jvoice.2017.12.010
21. Goetz, C.G., et al.: Movement disorder society sponsored revision of the unified parkinson's disease rating scale (MDS-UPDRS): scale presentation and clinimetric testing results. Movement Disorders: Offi. Movement Disorder Soc. **23**(15), 2129–2170 (2008)
22. Holmes, R.J., Oates, J.M., Phyland, D.J., Hughes, A.J.: Voice characteristics in the progression of Parkinson's disease. Inter. J. Lang. Commun. Disorders **35**(3), 407–418 (2000). https://doi.org/10.1080/136828200410654
23. Jaber, R., et al.: Cooking with agents: designing context-aware voice interaction. In: Proceedings of the 2024 CHI Conference on Human Factors in Computing Systems, pp. 1–13 (2024)
24. Jaeger, H., Trivedi, D., Stadtschnitzer, M.: Mobile Device Voice Recordings at King's College London (MDVR-KCL) from both early and advanced Parkinson's disease patients and healthy controls. Zenodo (2019). https://doi.org/10.5281/zenodo.2867216
25. Jamshed, H., Nurain, N., Brewer, R.N.: Designing accessible audio nudges for voice interfaces. In: Proceedings of the 2025 CHI Conference on Human Factors in Computing Systems. CHI 2025. Association for Computing Machinery, New York (2025). https://doi.org/10.1145/3706598.3713563
26. Little, M.A.: Smartphones for remote symptom monitoring of Parkinson's disease. J. Parkinsons Dis. **11**(s1), S49–S53 (2021)
27. Mahmood, A., Wang, J., Yao, B., Wang, D., Huang, C.-M.: User interaction patterns and breakdowns in conversing with LLM-powered voice assistants. Int. J. Hum Comput Stud. **195**, 103406 (2025)
28. McDonald, L.M., Griffin, H.J., Angeli, A., Torkamani, M., Georgiev, D., Jahanshahi, M.: Motivational modulation of self-initiated and externally triggered movement speed induced by threat of shock: experimental evidence for paradoxical kinesis in Parkinson's disease. PLoS ONE **10**(8), e0135149 (2015)
29. Mishra, T., Ljolje, A., Gilbert, M.: Predicting human perceived accuracy of ASR systems. In: INTERSPEECH, pp. 1945–1948 (2011)
30. Mitra, V., et al.: Analysis and tuning of a voice assistant system for dysfluent speech. arXiv preprint arXiv:2106.11759 (2021)
31. Modestino, E.J., Reinhofer, A., Blum, K., Amenechi, C., O'Toole, P.: Hoehn and Yahr staging of Parkinson's disease in relation to neuropsychological measures. Front Biosci (Landmark Ed) **23**(7), 1370–1379 (2018)
32. Morgan, C., et al.: Data labelling in the wild: annotating free-living activities and Parkinson's disease symptoms. In: 2021 IEEE International Conference on Pervasive Computing and Communications Workshops and other Affiliated Events (PerCom Workshops), pp. 471–474 (2021). https://doi.org/10.1109/PerComWorkshops51409.2021.9431017

33. Morgan, C., et al.: Understanding how people with Parkinson's disease turn in gait from a real-world in-home dataset. Parkinsonism & Related Disorders **105**, 114–122 (2022)
34. Morris, A.C., Maier, V., Green, P.D.: From WER and RIL to MER and WIL: improved evaluation measures for connected speech recognition. In: Interspeech, pp. 2765–2768 (2004)
35. Morris, M.E., Matyas, T.A., Iansek, R., Summers, J.J.: Temporal stability of gait in parkinson's disease. Phys. Therapy **76**(7), 763–777 (1996). https://doi.org/10.1093/ptj/76.7.763
36. Pal, D., Babakerkhell, M.D., Roy, P.: How perceptions of trust and intrusiveness affect the adoption of voice activated personal assistants. IEEE Access **10**, 123094–123113 (2022). https://doi.org/10.1109/ACCESS.2022.3224236
37. Pfeiffer, R.F.: Non-motor symptoms in Parkinson's disease. Parkinsonism & Related Disord. **22**, S119–S122 (2016). https://doi.org/10.1016/j.parkreldis.2015.09.004
38. Politis, M., Wu, K., Molloy, S., Bain, P.G., Chaudhuri, K.R., Piccini, P.: Parkinson's disease symptoms: the patient's perspective. Mov. Disord. **25**(11), 1646–1651 (2010). https://doi.org/10.1002/mds.23135
39. Quinn, N.P.: Classification of fluctuations in patients with Parkinson's disease. Neurology **51**(2_suppl_2), S25–S29 (1998). https://doi.org/10.1212/WNL.51.2_Suppl_2.S25
40. Sveinbjornsdottir, S.: The clinical symptoms of Parkinson's disease. J. Neurochem. **139**(S1), 318–324 (2016). https://doi.org/10.1111/jnc.13691
41. MISC
42. Woznowski, P., Tonkin, E., Laskowski. P., Twomey, N., Yordanova, K., Burrows, A.: Talk, text or tag? In: 2017 IEEE International Conference on Pervasive Computing and Communications Workshops (PerCom Workshops), pp. 123–128 (2017)
43. Zargham, N., et al.: Understanding circumstances for desirable proactive behaviour of voice assistants: the proactivity dilemma. In: Proceedings of the 4th Conference on Conversational User Interfaces. CUI 2022. Association for Computing Machinery, Glasgow, United Kingdom (2022). https://doi.org/10.1145/3543829.3543834
44. Zheng, X., Phukon, B., Hasegawa-Johnson, M.: Fine-Tuning Automatic Speech Recognition for People with Parkinson's: An Effective Strategy for Enhancing Speech Technology Accessibility. arXiv preprint arXiv:2409.19818 (2024)

# Relation Extraction from Real-World Unstructured Text in the Domain of Dementia

Sumaiya Suravee(✉), Dipendra Yadav, and Kristina Yordanova

Institute of Data Science, Universität Greifswald, 17489 Greifswald, Germany
{sumaiya.suravee,dipendra.yadav,kristina.yordanova}@uni-greifswald.de

**Abstract.** Relation extraction (RE) identifies semantic relations between named entities and is crucial for tasks such as knowledge graph construction and question answering. RE can be leveraged for automatic relationship annotation by employing trained RE models to identify and annotate semantic relationships between ontology-driven entities in unstructured, conversational texts. This paper examines RE in real-world conversational texts collected from an online dementia forum comprising 45,216 sentences, where language is often ambiguous and departs from standard medical terminology. We present a unified RE pipeline based on the domain-specific annotations and conduct a comparative evaluation of two model types: (i) a neural network-based architecture combining a bidirectional long-short-term memory (Bi-LSTM) model with static GloVe: Global Vectors for Word Representation (GloVe) and a conditional random field (CRF) classifier, and (ii) a transformer-based language model, BERT-Large, followed by a CRF layer. The results show that the use of GloVe embedding in the Bi-LSTM model achieves a significantly higher F1 score of 0.81, compared to 0.64 with the BERT-Large model. Despite lacking contextualised embeddings, the GloVe embedding captures relation patterns more effectively in this low-resource, domain-specific setting. These results demonstrate that lightweight models can outperform large pre-trained transformers in challenging real-world scenarios. The output of the RE task is a set of structured annotations, which can be integrated into downstream knowledge bases. Therefore, the investigated RE models have the potential to be applied as automatic annotators of informal texts from the domain of dementia, transforming the text into richly annotated resources by systematically annotating entity relationships without human intervention.

**Keywords:** Relation extraction · Data annotation · Recurrent neural network · Transformer architecture · Dementia

## 1 Introduction

Dementia has become a global health concern, currently affecting over 55 million individuals worldwide. While memory loss is one of its most prominent symptoms, people with dementia (PwD) often experience additional impairments,


E. L. Tonkin et al. (Eds.): ARDUOUS 2025, CCIS 2706, pp. 177–188, 2026.
https://doi.org/10.1007/978-3-032-09117-8_11

including language and communication difficulties, impaired judgment, mood and behavioural changes [1]. PwD may exhibit agitation, screaming, crying, wandering, biting, and other aggressive and non-aggressive behaviours that can be distressing for both PwD and their caregivers [2]. These behaviours are often recorded in informal and unstructured language in clinical notes, online forums, caregiver logs, and qualitative interviews. Extracting relevant information from these dementia texts is necessary to improve behavioural understanding and care strategies. RE, the task of identifying semantic relationships between named entities (NEs) in text, allows a deeper understanding of behavioural dynamics by transforming unstructured information into structured relational data. In the domain of dementia, RE can link challenging behaviour, such as agitation in PwD, to causal factors that trigger agitation in PwD. This structured information has the potential to influence clinicians and researchers in the development of personalised care strategies and assist caregivers in the planning of interventions.

This study develops an experimental pipeline for the use of RE in unstructured texts collected from dementia-related forums, where the goal is to extract relationships between the ontology-driven entities, which can later be used for generating rapid relational annotation of informal texts from the domain of dementia. Therefore, RE reduces the demand for manual annotation, accelerates the generation of high-quality relationship-annotated corpus, and allows large-scale analysis of relationships within massive corpora. We conducted a comparison study on the RE task using a traditionally trained Bi-LSTM with a CRF classifier and masked-based language models such as Bidirectional Encoder Representations from Transformers (BERT) with the CRF classifier. The contributions of the paper are as follows: 1) We propose an approach for extracting the relationship between ontology-driven entities in dementia texts where entities, derived from the eDEM-Connect: Ontology of Dementia-related Agitation and Relationship between Informal Caregivers and Persons with Dementia (EDEM-CONNECTONTO); 2) We introduce a relationship dataset for the domain of agitation of PwD; 3) We present results from experiments that use traditional neural networks and transformer architecture. The remainder of the paper is structured as follows. Section 2 discusses related work on the RE task, while Sect. 3 presents our proposed approach and outlines the evaluation strategy. Section 4 details the experimental setup while Sect. 5 reports and critically analyzes the evaluation results. Finally, Sect. 6 outlines directions for future work.

## 2 Related Works

The automatic extraction of NE and the relationship between NE have become a prominent area of research in the biomedical field. RE transforms unstructured text into structured knowledge by identifying semantic relationships between entities. For instance, if the sentence is "Maria was born in Madrid," we can produce a relational tuple like (Maria, birth_place, Madrid), where "Maria" and "Madrid" are NE, and "birth_place" denotes the relationship between these

NEs. Generally, RE specifies the relationship between the extracted NE in texts using either heuristic rules, machine learning or deep learning techniques. For instance, Ben Abacha and Zweigenbaum [13] focused on extracting semantic relations from medical texts, especially the relationship between diseases and treatments. Their approach combined defining relation patterns by experts with a machine learning method using support vector machines, achieving a high F1-score of 94.07%. Deep learning-based approaches such as convolutional neural networks (CNNs) and Bi-LSTM networks have gained substantial attention in biomedical RE. For example, Liu et al. [21] introduced a CNN architecture that learns hierarchical features from sentence representations to extract drug-drug interactions on the DDIExtraction-2013 dataset without explicit feature design, achieving an F-score of 69.75%. Similarly, Sahu and Anand [20] employed a joint attention-based LSTM to capture long-range contextual relations between biomedical entities, achieving an F1-score of 69.39%.

Recently, pre-trained transformer-based language models (LM) such as BERT [10] and RoBERTa [14], which are trained on a large corpus, have demonstrated impressive performance in addressing RE tasks by capturing and leveraging deep semantic representations. In [15], the authors introduced BioRED, a biomedical RE dataset that includes diverse entity types—such as gene/protein, disease and multiple relation pairs, compiled from 600 PubMed abstracts. To evaluate its effectiveness, they benchmarked several state-of-the-art models, including BERT-based architectures, on named entity recognition (NER) and RE tasks. Their findings indicated that the PubMedBERT model achieved significant performance, attaining F1 scores of 93.5% for NER and 58.9% for RE. Their results demonstrated that a well-annotated dataset, such as BioRED [15], can significantly improve the performance of RE models in the biomedical domain. In [16], the authors introduced an attention model for the joint NER and RE task. They used the BERT model [10] to learn together using a dynamic range attention mechanism in coronary angiography texts accumulated from Shuguang Hospital. Their results demonstrated F1-scores of 96.89% for NER and 88.51% for RE, respectively. In [17], the authors incorporated large langauge model (LLM) on the DDIExtraction-2013 dataset for the RE task, which focuses on identifying drug-drug interactions from biomedical literature. They employed a few-shot learning-based prompting technique with Gemini-Pro [18]. Additionally, they also fine-tuned PubMedBERT [19] using entity descriptions automatically generated by the LLM. Their study reveals that incorporating contextual few-shot learning with LLMs underperforms in biomedical RE tasks while incorporating LLM-generated entity explanations with fine-tuned PubMedBERT can significantly enhance classification-based RE performance, achieving an F1-score of 85.61% on the DDIExtraction-2013 dataset. Unfortunately, there is no research on the RE in real-world informal texts in the dementia domain where meaningful relationships have been extracted between the PwD and the challenging behaviours of people experiencing dementia. Hence, we focus on extracting such kinds of relationships from the online dementia forum using traditional recurrent-based neural networks and transformer architecture-based LM.

# 3 Method and Materials

This study uses ontology: EDEM-CONNECTONTO to describe our target domain. The EDEM-CONNECTONTO is developed on the agitation-related behaviours exhibited by PwD. Based on this ontology, we design an annotation codebook that guides the annotation process. The annotated dataset comprises unstructured texts collected from online dementia forums, capturing real-world caregiver narratives. For the RE task, we evaluate two different architectures: a classical recurrent neural network architecture (Bi-LSTM with CRF) and a transformer-based masked LM (BERT-Large with CRF). The overall experimental pipeline, is illustrated in Fig. 1.

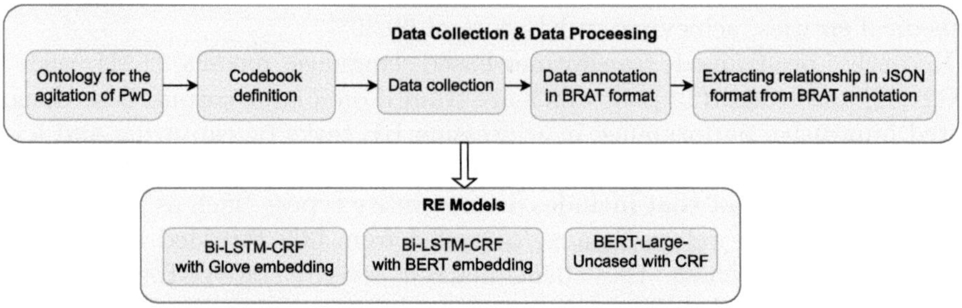


**Fig. 1.** Proposed pipeline for the relationship extraction task in the domain of dementia.

## 3.1 Dementia Dataset

We collected a total of 45,216 informal and unstructured conversational sentences from an online dementia forum[1], comprising 775 questions and 5,571 answers. These dementia forum texts contain information about the personal experiences and the challenges of the caregivers of the PwD. To process dementia texts, we applied preprocessing steps using the Clean-Text, TextBlob, and StanfordNLP Python libraries to correct punctuation, remove extraneous whitespace, and address typos, misspellings, and grammatical inconsistencies. Each document was segmented so that one sentence appeared per line. The dataset was structured into three components:"T" for the topic title, "Q" for dementia-related questions, and "A" for user-provided answers corresponding to each question. Given that many responses contained sensitive PwD's information, we anonymised such content using placeholder tags: <name>, <location>, <age>, <time_period>, <distance>, <date>, <professional_practitioner>, <medicine>.

[1] https://www.healingwell.com/.

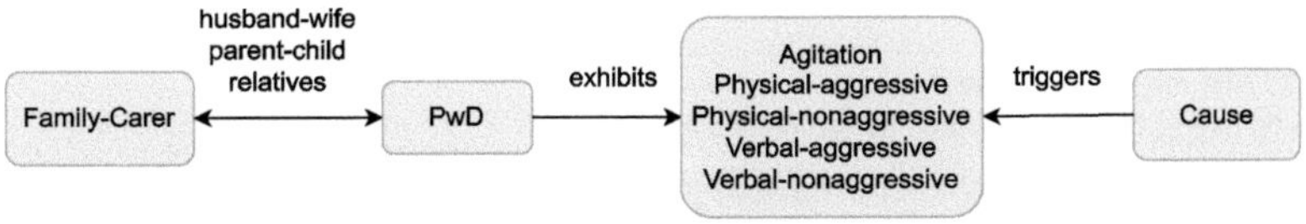


**Fig. 2.** Ontology-driven entities and the relationship between them.

### 3.2 Relationship Annotation Scheme

We define a set of domain-specific relationships to capture meaningful associations between the ontology-driven entities in the dementia-related texts. These relations are derived from the EDEM-CONNECTONTO[2], which we have manually developed, consisting of 241 concepts, 240 individuals and 10 relationships, which describe the types of agitation in PwD, causal factors that trigger exhibiting agitated behaviour, along with non-pharmacological interventions. Based on the ontology, we introduced an annotation scheme in [4] that contains the eight most hierarchical concepts and seven relations. The annotation scheme consists of the following entities: **PwD, Family-Carer, Cause, Agitation, Physical-aggressive, Physical-nonaggressive, Verbal-aggressive, Verbal-nonaggressive** and relationship entities: **exhibits, triggers, co-reference, husband-wife, parent-child, relatives**. Each relation connects with two annotated entities such as **exhibits** defines relationship between "PwD" and "Agitation, Physical-aggressive, Physical-nonaggressive, Verbal-aggressive, Verbal-nonaggressive" (see Fig. 2). Similarly, "triggers" defines relationship between "Cause" and "Agitation, Physical-aggressive, Physical-nonaggressive, Verbal-aggressive, Verbal-nonaggressive". We also define relationship **Co-reference** between noun phrase and pronoun phrase if the pronoun phrase refers to the same noun phrase. For example, if the sentence is: **"My bother is taking care of my mother and he is very stressed"** where we annotated **"brother"** and **"he"** as "Family-Carer" and defined a relationship **"Co-reference"** between **"brother"** and **"he"** as both referred to the same person. Our annotation scheme [4] also defined the following relationship: **husband-wife, parent-child, relatives** between the entities: **PwD** and **Family-Carer** (see Fig. 2).

### 3.3 Relationship Annotation

The publicly available BRAT annotation tool [5] is being used to annotate the ontology-driven entities and the relationship entities in the dementia forum texts. In Fig. 3, the word ***"She"*** is annotated as **"PwD"** and the phrase ***"repeats herself"*** is annotated as "**Verbal-nonaggressive**" where we annotated the relationship **"exhibits"** between **"PwD"** and **"Verbal-nonaggressive"**. Three annoators were asked to participate in the annotation process where the first annotator was considered the *expert annotator* who developed the annotation

[2] https://bioportal.bioontology.org/ontologies/EDEM-CONNECTONTO.

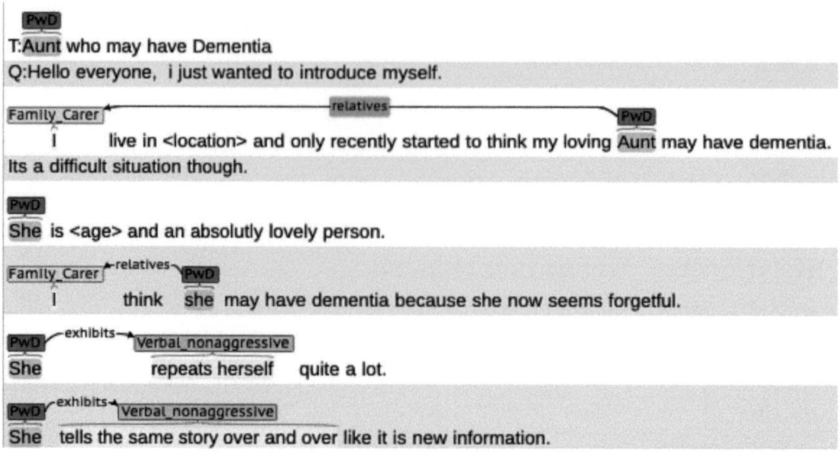


**Fig. 3.** Relationship annotation (e.g., exhibits, relatives) between the entities using the BRAT annotation.

scheme, dementia ontology, and had advanced expertise in the domain of PwD; the *expert annotator* trained the other annotators, and their annotation were reviewed and manually evaluated by the expert annotator and the domain experts. Because the dementia-related text is often vague and context dependent, it was challenging to distinguish whether a given passage referred to the PwD or to a family caregiver, making it difficult to define the relationship between these concepts. To ensure consistency and accuracy, we conducted annotations in three iterative phases, each followed by an expert review and domain expert consultation, resulting in three consecutive annual revisions of the corpus.

In this experiment, 84 files were selected to annotate the entities and the relationship entities simultaneously by considering the files with the most entity labels and relationships (see [11]). Table 1 presents the annotated dementia corpus, comprising a total of 9,757 relationship annotations. The relationship entity annotation reveals a notable class imbalance, with a large number of 4174 "Co-reference" relationships, whereas there are only 160 "Husband-wife" relationships and 168 "Triggers" relationships (see Table 1).

### 3.4 Model Development

We adopt a classical neural network architecture based on Bi-LSTM, a model that combines static GloVe embeddings [9] and a CRF classifier, which is considered a baseline model. Each sentence is first tokenised and represented as a sequence of pre-trained GloVe embeddings, which encode semantic relationships among the words based on global co-occurrence vectors. These embedded vectors are then passed to a Bi-LSTM, which was introduced by Huang et al. [6]. The Bi-LSTM can analyse each sequence in both directions, grasping the context from both past and future tokens in a sentence, enabling the model to capture contextual dependencies that are crucial for identifying relations in unstructured text. The resulting token-level hidden states are mapped to label scores via a

**Table 1.** Number of relationship annotations in the dementia corpus for each relationship type.

| Relationship Type | No. of Annotations |
|---|---|
| Exhibits | 717 |
| Triggers | 168 |
| Co-reference | 4174 |
| Parent-child | 1656 |
| Husband-wife | 160 |
| Relatives | 782 |
| **Total Annotations** | 7657 |
| **Total Sentences** | 9737 |

linear layer. Finally, a CRF layer introduced in [7] and implemented by the PyTorch framework[3], is applied to enforce global consistency in the predicted label sequence, leveraging the relationship between adjacent tags.

To conduct a comparison study with the baseline model, we employed a hybrid sequence-labelling architecture that leverages a domain-adapted transformer-based BERT embedding with the Bi-LSTM and CRF classifier. Initially, each document is divided into sentences. Then, each input sentence is tokenised into sub-tokens by a BERT tokeniser, incorporated from Hugging Face[4]. Each sentence token is mapped to a vector representation sequence, where we use pre-trained BERT [8] that provides context-sensitive embeddings for every sub-token. BERT is pre-trained on a large amount of English Wikipedia. These embeddings are fed as contextual vectors into a Bi-LSTM layer (256 hidden units per direction) and then learned by a forward and backwards LSTM layer. Finally, it is passed into the CRF layer, which delivers the most likely sequence of the expected labels based on the sequence of probability vectors from the previous layer.

Lastly, we adopt a fully pre-trained LM which has been widely used in the biomedical and clinical domains recently. In this experiment, pre-trained LM like transformer-based BERT [10] model with a CRF classifier is also employed to perform RE. BERT is a pre-trained masked LM that generates deep, context-aware embeddings for each token by jointly attending to both left and right contexts using self-attention mechanisms. In our setup, each input sentence containing two target entities is first tokenised using BERT's tokeniser and fed into the BERT-Large encoder. BERT outputs a sequence of contextualised embeddings for each token, capturing complex semantic and syntactic relationships in the input text. These embeddings are then passed through a linear classification layer that projects them to a label space corresponding to the possible relation types. Finally, a CRF layer is applied on top of the output logits to capture the relationships between the entities.

[3] https://pypi.org/project/TorchCRF/.

[4] https://huggingface.co/docs/transformers/en/model_doc/bert.

**Table 2.** Hyper-parameters for all experiments.

| Hyper-parameter | Value |
|---|---|
| LSTM hidden state | 256 |
| Dropout | 0.1 |
| Learning rate | 0.00001 → 0.00005 |
| Batch size | 8 |
| Optimizer | Adam |
| Decay rate | 0.01 |
| Token length | 512 |

## 4 Experimental Setup

Our study assesses the performance of the baseline model: Bi-LSTM-CRF using 300-dimensional GloVe embeddings for the RE task. We further compare this with a Bi-LSTM-CRF model utilizing BERT embeddings and a transformer-based architecture, specifically BERT-Large-Uncased. All models were implemented using the PyTorch framework. To accommodate input length limitations (maximum 512 tokens), longer sentences were segmented into multiple parts, ensuring each segment remained within the token constraint. The Bi-LSTM model was trained with a batch size of 8 and an LSTM hidden size of 256. The training was conducted up to 100 epochs. The experiments were carried out on a corpus related to dementia comprising 9,737 sentences, divided into sets of training (60%), development (20%) and test (20%). RE models were trained on the training set, with hyperparameter tuning on the development set. The test set was used to evaluate the performance of RE models.

We calculated the macro F1 score to evaluate the performance of RE models for each relationship entity. F1-score is a performance metric that combines precision and recall by calculating their harmonic mean [12]. This metric provides a balanced measure, making it especially reasonable when assessing classification models on unbalanced datasets. To ensure robust performance estimation, each experiment on the dementia corpus was repeated three times with different random initialisations. The final results were calculated as the macro average F1-score of these three runs. Detailed parameter settings are provided in Table 2.

## 5 Results and Discussions

The performance of the baseline model: Bi-LSTM-CRF model using GloVe embeddings is evaluated and then compared with two enhanced approaches: a hybrid model that combines the recurrent Bi-LSTM-CRF architecture with transformer-based BERT embeddings, and a fully transformer-based BERT-Large-Uncased model paired with a CRF classifier. All models were evaluated in the dementia corpus. Table 3 shows the macro average (avg.) F1-score using the baseline Bi-LSTM-CRF model with the GloVe embedding, the Bi-LSTM-CRF model with the BERT embedding and the BERT-Large uncased model, where each experiment is conducted 3 times, following the same parameter setup. In terms of macro avg. F1-score considering all relationship entity type, our baseline model: Bi-LSTM-CRF with GloVe embeddings outperformed the transformer-based BERT-Large-Uncased model, achieving a significantly higher F1-score of 0.81 compared to 0.64. Surprisingly, our hybrid model, which combines the recurrent Bi-LSTM-CRF architecture with transformer-based BERT embeddings, performs slightly better in identifying relationship entities: "Exhibits", "Triggers", "Co-reference", "Parent-child", and "Relatives" (see Table 3). In contrast, the baseline model significantly outperformed the hybrid and fully transformer-based models in identifying the "Husband-wife" relationship, achieving an F1-score of 0.47. Neither the hybrid model nor the BERT-Large model was able to correctly identify any instances of "Husband-wife" relationship in the dementia texts. One possible reason for the poor classification of the "Husband-wife" relationship is the limited number of instances of this relationship entity type in the dataset. Besides, the BERT-Large model performed moderately in identifying relationship entities in texts with a F1-score of 0.64.

Although transformer-based models such as BERT have demonstrated significant improvement in a wide range of NLP tasks, our results indicate that the BERT-Large model with a CRF classifier underperforms for RE task compared to the simpler Bi-LSTM-CRF architecture using static GloVe embeddings. One key explanation for this is the domain mismatch, as BERT is pre-trained on large English raw texts collected from Wikipedia and BooksCorpus, which may not grasp the informal, context-specific language and caregiving nuances found in dementia-related texts. This mismatch limits BERT's ability to generalise to domain-specific relation patterns effectively. Furthermore, with the sequential nature of LSTM, GloVe embeddings provide stable lexical representations that perform robustly in low-resource scenarios. The CRF layer further contributes by modelling label dependencies more effectively in structured prediction tasks. These characteristics enable the Bi-LSTM-CRF architecture to capture the relationship between the entities more effectively in loosely structured conversational text, ultimately yielding outstanding performance for the RE task in the dementia domain.

**Table 3.** F1 scores for each relationship tag: Exhibits, Triggers, Co-reference, Parent-child, Husband-wife, Relatives using relationship extraction models.

| Relationship Tag | Bi-LSTM-CRF with GloVe emb. | Bi-LSTM-CRF with BERT emb. | BERT-Large-uncased-CRF |
|---|---|---|---|
| Exhibits | 0.98 | **1.00** | 0.93 |
| Triggers | 0.98 | **0.99** | 0.69 |
| Co-reference | 0.96 | **0.98** | 0.93 |
| Parent-child | 0.86 | **0.89** | 0.85 |
| Husband-wife | **0.47** | 0.00 | 0.00 |
| Relatives | 0.63 | **0.67** | 0.46 |
| **Macro avg. F1-Score** | **0.81** | 0.75 | 0.64 |

## 6 Conclusion and Future Work

This study proposes an approach for the relation extraction task by employing a traditional recurrent neural network as a baseline model and comparing its performance with transformer-based architectures on real-world texts collected from an online dementia forum. We created an annotation scheme, which was used as an annotation codebook, and then manually annotated the ontology-driven entities and the relationships between them where entities and relationship derived from the eDEM-Connect: Ontology of Dementia-related Agitation and Relationship between Informal Caregivers and Persons with Dementia, creating a valuable corpus for the domain of challenging behaviour of PwD. Our developed dementia corpus comprising 7,657 relationship annotations was subsequently utilised for the relation extraction task using three models: (1) a baseline Bi-LSTM-CRF model with GloVe embeddings, (2) a hybrid model combining the Bi-LSTM-CRF architecture with transformer-based BERT embeddings, and (3) a fully transformer-based BERT-Large-Uncased model. Our findings indicate that the Bi-LSTM-CRF architecture with GloVe embeddings achieved a significantly higher F1-score of 0.81, compared to the transformer-based BERT language model, which attained an F1-score of 0.64. The higher F1-score achieved by the Bi-LSTM-CRF model implies that simpler architectures, when integrated with well-suited embeddings, may outperform more complex models like BERT in a domain-specific, unstructured scenario such as syntactic ambiguity, informal language, and limited in-domain training data. In addition, these trained relation extraction models can be used to automatically annotate relationships, generating rapid and structured relationships in dementia-related texts without requiring human intervention.

In the future, to address the issue of an imbalanced dataset, we plan to generate synthetic dementia texts and annotate these synthetic texts for under-represented relationship types. Furthermore, we intend to utilise the state-of-the-art large language model, LLaMA 3, for the relation extraction task by adopting a few-shot prompting approach, which has shown significant improvements in downstream applications. We also plan to develop an end-to-end sequential experimental pipeline for the joint domain-specific entity recognition and relation extraction task.

## References

1. Dementia. https://www.who.int/news-room/fact-sheets/detail/dementia, Accessed 5 June 2025
2. Vithanage, D., Zhu, Y., Zhang, Z., Deng, C., Yin, M., Yu, P.: Extracting symptoms of agitation in dementia from free-text nursing notes using advanced natural language processing. In: MEDINFO 2023—The Future Is Accessible, pp. 700–704. IOS Press (2024)
3. Blinded: Blinded for double blind reviewing (2025)

4. Suravee, S., et al.: Annotation scheme for named entity recognition and relation extraction tasks in the domain of people with dementia. In: 2022 IEEE International Conference on Pervasive Computing and Communications Workshops and other Affiliated Events (PerCom Workshops), pp. 236–241. IEEE (2022)
5. Stenetorp, P., Pyysalo, S., Topić, G., Ohta, T., Ananiadou, S., Tsujii, J.: BRAT: a web-based tool for NLP-assisted text annotation. In: Proceedings of the Demonstrations at the 13th Conference of the European Chapter of the Association for Computational Linguistics, pp. 102–107 (2012)
6. Huang, Z., Xu, W., Yu, K.: Bidirectional LSTM-CRF models for sequence tagging. arXiv preprint arXiv:1508.01991 (2015)
7. Lafferty, J., McCallum, A., Pereira, F.: Conditional random fields: probabilistic models for segmenting and labeling sequence data. In: ICML, Williamstown, MA, vol. 1, no. 2, pp. 3 (2001)
8. Alsentzer, E., et al.: Publicly available clinical BERT embeddings. arXiv preprint arXiv:1904.03323 (2019)
9. Pennington, J., Socher, R., Manning, C.D.: Glove: global vectors for word representation. In: Proceedings of the 2014 Conference on Empirical Methods in Natural Language Processing (EMNLP), pp. 1532–1543 (2014)
10. Devlin, J., Chang, M.-W., Lee, K., Toutanova, K.: BERT: pre-training of deep bidirectional transformers for language understanding. In: Proceedings of the 2019 Conference of the North American Chapter of the Association for Computational Linguistics: Human Language Technologies, vol. 1 (Long and Short Papers), pp. 4171–4186 (2019)
11. Suravee, S., Stoev, T., Konow, S., Yordanova, K.: Assessing large language models for annotating data in Dementia-Related texts: a comparative study with human annotators. In: INFORMATIK 2024, pp. 487–498. Gesellschaft für Informatik e.V. (2024)
12. Sokolova, M., Lapalme, G.: A systematic analysis of performance measures for classification tasks. Inform. Process. Manag. **45**(4), 427–437 (2009)
13. Ben Abacha, A., Zweigenbaum, P.: A hybrid approach for the extraction of semantic relations from MEDLINE abstracts. In: Gelbukh, A. (ed.) CICLing 2011. LNCS, vol. 6609, pp. 139–150. Springer, Heidelberg (2011). https://doi.org/10.1007/978-3-642-19437-5_11
14. Liu, Y., et al.: Roberta: a robustly optimized bert pretraining approach. arXiv preprint arXiv:1907.11692 (2019). https://arxiv.org/abs/1907.11692
15. Luo, L., Lai, P.-T., Wei, C.-H., Arighi, C.N., Lu, Z.: BioRED: a rich biomedical relation extraction dataset. Briefings Bioinform. **23**(5), bbac282 (2022)
16. Xue, K., Zhou, Y., Ma, Z., Ruan, T., Zhang, H., He, P.: Fine-tuning BERT for joint entity and relation extraction in chinese medical text. In: 2019 IEEE International Conference on Bioinformatics and Biomedicine (BIBM), pp. 892–897 (2019). https://doi.org/10.1109/BIBM47256.2019.8983370
17. Asada, M., Fukuda, K.: Enhancing relation extraction from biomedical texts by large language models. In: International Conference on Human-Computer Interaction, pp. 3–14. Springer (2024). https://doi.org/10.1007/978-3-031-60615-1_1
18. Team, Gemini, Anil, R., et al.: Gemini: a family of highly capable multimodal models. arXiv preprint arXiv:2312.11805 (2023)
19. Gu, Y., et al.: Domain-specific language model pretraining for biomedical natural language processing. ACM Trans. Comput. Healthcare (HEALTH) **3**(1), 1–23 (2021)

20. Sahu, S.K., Anand, A.: Drug-drug interaction extraction from biomedical texts using long short-term memory network. J. Biomed. Inform. **86**, 15–24 (2018). https://doi.org/10.1016/j.jbi.2018.08.005
21. Liu, S., Tang, B., Chen, Q., Wang, X.: Drug-drug interaction extraction via convolutional neural networks. Comput. Math. Methods Med. **2016**, 6918381 (2016). https://doi.org/10.1155/2016/6918381

# Correction to: Towards Standardized Dataset Creation for Human Activity Recognition: Framework, Taxonomy, Checklist, and Best Practices

Friedrich Niemann, Fernando Moya Rueda, Moh'd Khier Al Kfari, Nilah Ravi Nair, Stefan Lüdtke, and Alice Kirchheim

## Correction to:
## Chapter 5 in: E. L. Tonkin et al. (Eds.): *Annotation of Real-World Data for Artificial Intelligence Systems*, CCIS 2706, https://doi.org/10.1007/978-3-032-09117-8_5

The original version of chapter 5 has been republished, with Updating the image in page 84.

The updated version of this chapter can be found at
https://doi.org/10.1007/978-3-032-09117-8_5


E. L. Tonkin et al. (Eds.): ARDUOUS 2025, CCIS 2706, p. C1, 2026.
https://doi.org/10.1007/978-3-032-09117-8_12

# Supplementary Material

# Annotation for Multi-Channel Time Series Data of Human Activities

Fernando Moya Rueda[1(✉)], Nilah Ravi Nair[2], Raphael Spiekermann[3], Erik Altermann[3], Philipp Oberdiek[4], Christopher Reining[2], and Gernot. A. Fink[3]

[1] Motion Miners, Dortmund, Germany
fernando.moya@motionminers.com
[2] Chair of Materials Handling and Warehousing, TU Dortmund University, Joseph-von-Fraunhofer-Str. 2-4, 44227 Dortmund, Germany
[3] Pattern Recognition in Embedded Systems Groups, TU Dortmund University, Otto-Hahn-Str. 16, 44227Dortmund, Germany
[4] ControlExpert GmbH, Marie-Curie-Strae 3, 40764 Langenfeld, Germany

## 1 Results

### 1.1 Retrieval Evaluation on LARa

We conducted two experiments to evaluate the retrieval-based annotations for HAR. First, we evaluated human activity retrieval on the Logistic Activity Recognition Challenge (LARa) dataset, measuring its global performance in terms of $mAP$. Second, we used this retrieval approach as part of a semi-automated annotation procedure, measuring the annotation effort in terms of annotation time and consistency, following the same procedure from [1] for comparison.

**Table 1.** mAP metric for QbAR and QbC using the tCNN-IMU on different window sizes $W$, and similarities on the $\text{LARa}^{\text{Test}}$ dataset.

| Network | QbAR | | QbC | |
|---|---|---|---|---|
| | COS | PRM | COS | PRM |
| tCNN-IMU W050 | 0.350 | 0.360 | 0.609 | 0.619 |
| tCNN-IMU W100 | 0.382 | 0.396 | 0.629 | 0.635 |
| tCNN-IMU W150 | 0.414 | 0.426 | 0.647 | 0.658 |
| tCNN-IMU W200 | 0.433 | **0.445** | **0.651** | **0.661** |
| tCNN-IMU W400 | **0.439** | 0.441 | 0.616 | 0.622 |


W. Senn et al. (Eds.): ICANN 2025, LNCS 16071, pp. 191–201, 2026.
https://doi.org/10.1007/978-3-032-04555-3

1. **QbAR and QbC:**
   We evaluated retrieval for different sequence lengths $W$. Multiple tCNN-IMU networks have been trained on $\text{LARa}_{MoCap}$ for different $W$, following [5]. The sequence segments are extracted following a sliding-window approach with a window size of $W$ and a step size of $s = \frac{W}{4}$ (75.0% overlapping). For comparison, the average class length in the LARa dataset is $4.12s$ ($\approx 800$ frames). The networks are trained by minimising the binary-cross entropy loss using stochastic gradient descent with the RMSProp update rule [2, 6]. The layers are initialized with orthogonal initialization. Moreover, dropout with a probability of 50% is used in the fully connected layers. Gaussian noise with $\mu = 0$ and $\sigma = 0.01$ is added to the sequence input. Following [3, 4], every channel is normalized to a range of $[0, 1]$. Table 1 shows $mAP$ vs. different $W$. For QbC, *tCNN-IMU W200* outperformed every other network. For QbA, the *tCNN-IMU W400* outperforms the *tCNN-IMU W200* when using the cosine similarity. For the PRM similarity, the *tCNN-IMU W200* outperforms the *tCNN-IMU W400*. As the LARa annotation tool uses QbC, all further experiments will be done using the *tCNN-IMU W200*.
2. **QbA:**
   Table 4 shows the $mAP$, column in colour , for each attribute. The attributes in the first three groups have high $mAP$ values, meaning that retrieval is viable for Human Activity Recognition (HAR). Since the $mAP$ values for Attributes in group IV are all rather low, the annotator should pay special attention to these attributes to ensure that everything is correctly annotated.

**Revision Performance (time and Consistency)** We perform a set of annotations for the $\text{LARa}_{15,16}^{\text{Test}}$, evaluating the feasibility of retrieval on an existing semi-automated annotation framework. Four annotators, two experts, and two beginners annotate eight recordings from $\text{LARa}_{15,16}$ using the LARa annotation tool. The tool uses the *tCNN-IMU W200.* This annotation follows the same annotation procedure in [1]. We aim to compare the semi-automated approach using retrieval against the manual+revision annotation, and the automatic-classifier+revision annotation from [1] in terms of time and consistency.

1. **Annotation Time** Figure 1 shows the annotation times of the retrieval-based annotation using the cosine and PRM similarities. Besides, it compares with the manual annotations of [1]. Annotations were faster using the retrieval-based annotations for both similarities vs. the manual annotations. A learning process by the annotators is seen as the variation in the annotation time decreases with more recording units or files. Different from semi-automated annotations from [1], a revision is integrated into the retrieval process, as annotators get suggestions based on the ranked segments, which have to be accepted or rejected. The annotation tool also brings the option to change the attribute representation before accepting manually. Following a ranked order based on QbC, accepting the annotations and directly correcting the attribute representation was reported by the expert annotators as less

mentally demanding. Beginner annotators experienced a comfortable annotation process for *Walking*, *Standing*, and *Handling* without the attribute *Utility/Auxiliary*.

2. **Class-wise Consistency**
We compare the semi-automated approach using retrieval against the manual-revised annotation procedure from [1]. The latter ones will be considered the ground truth. Table 2 presents the comparison of the annotations from the four annotators vs. the $\text{LARa}^{\text{Test}}_{15,16}$ annotations. It shows different metrics, classification metrics (Acc, $wF1$ and $mF1$), and consistency ones $\kappa$– here, manual annotations are not considered ground truth. In general, the $\kappa$ values lie within a small interval and hint towards a substantial agreement, i.e., $0.61 < \kappa \leq 0.8$. Table 3 compares the between-annotator consistency in terms of $\kappa$ among the four annotators and the two similarities using the retrieval approach for annotating the $\text{LARa}^{\text{Test}}_{15,16}$ recordings. In general, the annotators agree substantially. Interestingly, the agreement is superior with respect to the average agreement shown in [7] for the LARa dataset and similar to the semi-automated annotations in [1] for the $\text{LARa}^{\text{Test}}_{15,16}$.
3. **Attribute-wise consistency** Table 4 presents the between-annotator consistency in terms of $\kappa$ among the four annotators and the two similarities for each attribute. After the semi-automated annotation, the between-annotator consistency for the attributes remains substantial. Even though the tCNN-IMU network performs poorly for attributes in the IV group, annotators correct the predictions—except on the *Handy Unit*. The attributes *Torso Rotation*, *None*, and *Error* were not selected by the annotators.

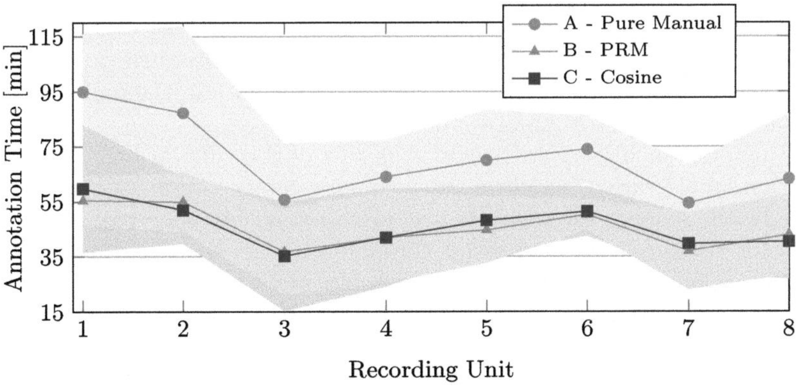


**Fig. 1.** Annotation-time of retrieval-based and manual annotation [1] procedures on the $LARa^{\text{test}}_{15,16}$. Retrieval-based approaches use cosine and PRM similarities. Here, recording unit refers to the each of the recording files of 2 mins each.

**Table 2.** Consistency metrics: Acc.[%], $wF1$ [%], $mF1$ [%], and between-annotator consistency $\kappa$ of activity class annotation of $\text{LARa}_{15,16}^{\text{Test}}$ by 4 annotators.

| Metric | Cosine | | | | PRM | | | |
|---|---|---|---|---|---|---|---|---|
| | A1 | A2 | A3 | A4 | A1 | A2 | A3 | A4 |
| Acc | 0.8675 | 0.8487 | 0.8542 | 0.8345 | 0.8514 | 0.8208 | 0.8332 | 0.8312 |
| F1w | 0.8751 | 0.8664 | 0.8752 | 0.8543 | 0.8645 | 0.8535 | 0.8569 | 0.8186 |
| F1m | 0.6188 | 0.5833 | 0.5687 | 0.5678 | 0.5990 | 0.5332 | 0.5565 | 0.5788 |
| kappa | 0.7961 | 0.7647 | 0.7801 | 0.7444 | 0.7711 | 0.7178 | 0.7502 | 0.7441 |

**Table 3.** Between-annotator consistency $\kappa$ of activity class annotation of 8 recordings (960$s$) from two subjects by 4 annotators. ▒: consistency among annotators using the cosine similarity. ▓: consistency among annotators using the PRM similarity.

| **Procedure** | | **Annotator** A1 | A2 | A3 | A4 |
|---|---|---|---|---|---|
| **Annotator** | A1 | - | 0.7955 | 0.7704 | 0.7658 |
| | A2 | 0.7652 | - | 0.7859 | 0.7960 |
| | A3 | 0.7926 | 0.7414 | - | 0.7867 |
| | A4 | 0.7623 | 0.7548 | 0.7725 | - |

### 1.2 Retrieval Evaluation on Kitchen Dataset

In order to take part in the Arduous Challenge 2022, the creators of the LARa annotation tool modified the existing tool for Optical marker-based Motion Capture (MoCap) data to accommodate the RGB-video data from the CMU-MMAC kitchen dataset to facilitate manual annotation. Though the dataset consisted of MoCap data, the challenge was to either use the multi-view camera data or the OBD data available, and thus, for ease of visualization, the multi-view RGB camera data was used for annotation.

The annotation labels were provided as part of the annotation challenge. The annotation labels varied based on three cooking recipes, namely, brownie, eggs, and sandwich. A large set of labels was provided within each recipe, making it difficult for the annotators to scroll through the list to select the appropriate annotation. Consequently, to help the annotators, the annotation labels were simplified to a sentence structure format; the annotation labels were restructured into a verb followed by four attribute groups referring to the first object, the second object, the place/placement of the object/subject, and a temporal instance. For example, the given annotation label, *fill-brownie mix-brownie bag-bowl-partially* activity, was separated into a class fill and four attributes – brownie mix, brownie bag, bowl, partially – following the attribute structure discussed.

Here, we present the result of the manual annotation of the challenge. One experienced annotator performed the manual annotation of the Kitchen dataset. The annotator was familiar with the annotation tool as they had previously par-

**Table 4.** Semantic Attributes in LARa Dataset. In Gray: $mAP$ for QbA using the *tCNN-IMU W200* on the $LARa^{Test}$ dataset. Each attribute's mAP was calculated independently. In White: and average between-annotator consistency $\kappa$ of the four annotators following the retrieval-based approach on the $LARa^{Test}_{15,16}$. Manual annotations * are taken from [1].

| Attributes | $mAP$ | Manual* | Cohen's $\kappa$ COS | Cohen's $\kappa$ PRM |
|---|---|---|---|---|
| I-A Gait Cycle | 0.833 | 0.91 | 0.67 | 0.66 |
| I-B Step | 0.744 | 0.85 | 0.36 | 0.30 |
| I-C Standing Still | 0.887 | 0.87 | 0.69 | 0.64 |
| II-A Upwards | 0.888 | 0.98 | 0.83 | 0.81 |
| II-B Centred | 0.828 | 0.91 | 0.82 | 0.80 |
| II-C Downwards | 0.561 | 0.99 | 0.83 | 0.84 |
| II-D No Int. Motion | 0.838 | 0.92 | 0.81 | 0.80 |
| II-E Torso Rotation | 0.080 | - | - | - |
| III-A Right Hand | 0.941 | 0.92 | 0.67 | 0.74 |
| III-B Left Hand | 0.838 | 0.93 | 0.73 | 0.75 |
| III-C No Hands | 0.647 | 0.98 | 0.84 | 0.87 |
| IV-A Bulky Unit | 0.441 | 0.95 | 0.79 | 0.75 |
| IV-B Handy Unit | 0.560 | 0.87 | 0.55 | 0.63 |
| IV-C Utility/Auxiliary | 0.310 | 0.92 | 0.58 | 0.59 |
| IV-D Cart | 0.568 | 1.00 | 1.00 | - |
| IV-E Computer | 0.287 | 1.00 | 1.00 | 1.00 |
| IV-F No Item | 0.784 | 0.98 | 0.87 | 0.89 |
| V-A None | 0.072 | - | - | - |
| VI-A Error | 0.000 | - | - | - |
| All Attributes | 0.743 | - | - | - |

ticipated in the annotation process of the LARa dataset. The authors proposed attribute-based annotations for the different tools, articles, and places in the three tasks. Thus, the learning here was focused on understanding the classes and the structure of class-attribute annotation based on the kitchen dataset annotation rules.

To understand the class-attribute rules, the annotator analyzed the annotated files provided for semi-automatic annotation. One file per recipe was viewed. This step helped in understanding the label-to-activity relations. Next, a trial run of annotation was performed by the annotator under the supervision of the label designer. One pre-annotated video for all three recipes was selected for this trial. The annotation duration of the trial runs was not captured. Table 5 shows the details of the annotation time of the recordings of the challenge as was given by the organizers.

Due to the long list of first, second, and third attributes, the annotator found it difficult to navigate the list to identify the correct labels. As a result, further modifications were performed on the annotation tool and annotation labels. A dependency table was derived based on the class-to-attribute relationships that were given by the annotation label designers of the Arduous Challenge. To elaborate, if the annotator selects the class *close*, only attributes pertaining to the class will be made available on the first level of attribute selection. This selection of the attribute would then further affect the attributes presented in the following levels based on the dependency table. This reduces the list of attributes presented on the annotation tool pop-up, thus facilitating the annotator to perform faster annotations.

Table 5 shows the time taken to perform the annotation task. The annotation duration is mentioned as *Ann.*. The annotator was required to mark any breaks they may have taken during the annotation period. This is mentioned as duration. The Revision was performed if it was deemed necessary by the annotator and was accounted as duration. The total annotation period is calculated as $annotation - breaks + revision$.

The annotator noted that in a few cases, the activities were not within the viewing range of the camera placed on the head of the actors. In such cases, a second video was viewed, separate from the annotation tool, using a video player. The second video was selected based on the view required to access the blind spot to support annotation.

The annotator performed a revision based on their annotation experience. Few files do not have a revision process. The process was performed in the 'Label Correction' mode of the LARa annotation tool.

As discussed previously, we manually annotated recordings of the Kitchen dataset provided as part of the Arduous Challenge 2022. Building on this work, the SARA annotation tool now includes retrieval for the videos in the Kitchen Dataset, specifically for the recipes: Brownie, Eggs, and Sandwich. The CMU MMAC dataset has numerous recordings that are not annotated yet. This contribution aims to facilitate researchers in this field by providing a seamless method for annotating recordings, leveraging SARA's retrieval support.

We have used a pre-trained ResNet-18 on ImageNet and three parallel MLPs, one per recipe, for retrieval. The output of each MLP consists of a concatenation of a softmax layer for activity classification and a sigmoid layer for attribute predictions. These three MLPs are trained individually for each recipe video input; the Resnet18 is shared across all recipes. The network is trained using the training data proposed in the ARDUOUS Challenge 2022 with the following hyperparameters: window length of 30 frames of $[256 \times 256]$, batch of 30, with a loss combing the cross-entropy and binary-cross entropy, learning rate of $10^{-3}$, and epochs of 90. This network is available at the Sequence Attribute Retrieval Annotator (SARA)-Zenodo [8].

To test the efficiency of this retrieval method, the annotator who performed the manual annotations of the Arduous Challenge annotated the same recordings using the retrieval method. Firstly, in Table 6, we present the total annotation time for each recording. Second, in Table 7, we present the annotation time comparison between manual and retrieval annotation of the recordings from Arduous Challenge. Finally, Table 8 presents Cohen's Kappa of the annotations

**Table 5.** Manual Annotation Time for the Kitchen dataset as part of the Arduous Challenge

| Recipe | Rec. | Dur. mm:ss | Ann. h:mm | Break h:mm | Rev. h:mm | Total h:mm |
|---|---|---|---|---|---|---|
| **Brownies** | S54 | 6:51 | 2:01 | 1:15 | 0:11 | 0:57 |
| | S32 | 4:59 | 0:36 | 0:00 | 0:08 | 0:44 |
| | S31 | 8:11 | 0:41 | 0:00 | 0:08 | 0:49 |
| | S09 | 7:47 | 2:23 | 1:12 | 0:08 | 1:10 |
| **Sandwich** | S16 | 3:25 | 0:23 | 0:00 | 0:00 | 0:23 |
| | S25 | 2:38 | 0:21 | 0:00 | 0:00 | 0:21 |
| | S34 | 2:06 | 0:14 | 0:00 | 0:00 | 0:14 |
| | S15 | 1:39 | 0:14 | 0:00 | 0:00 | 0:14 |
| **Eggs** | S08 | 3:08 | 0:31 | 0:00 | 0:00 | 0:31 |
| | S20 | 5:13 | 0:33 | 0:00 | 0:00 | 0:33 |
| | S16 | 4:06 | 0:37 | 0:00 | 0:00 | 0:37 |
| | S50 | 4:45 | 0:29 | 0:00 | 0:00 | 0:29 |

**Table 6.** Retrieval Annotation Time for the Kitchen dataset of recordings from the Arduous Challenge

| Recipe | Rec. | Dur. mm:ss | Retrieval h:mm | Ann. h:mm | Break h:mm | Revision h:mm | Total h:mm |
|---|---|---|---|---|---|---|---|
| **Brownies** | S54 | 6:51 | 0:09 | 0:04 | 0:29 | 0:00 | 0:42 |
| | S32 | 4:59 | 0:07 | 0:04 | 0:23 | 0:00 | 0:34 |
| | S31 | 8:11 | 0:10 | 0:08 | 0:33 | 0:00 | 0:51 |
| | S09 | 7:47 | 0:06 | 0:12 | 2:31 | 1:19 | 1:30 |
| **Sandwich** | S16 | 3:25 | 0:02 | 0:06 | 0:18 | 0:00 | 0:26 |
| | S25 | 2:38 | 0:02 | 0:06 | 0:16 | 0:00 | 0:24 |
| | S34 | 2:06 | 0:02 | 0:06 | 0:11 | 0:00 | 0:19 |
| | S15 | 1:39 | 0:01 | 0:08 | 0:15 | 0:00 | 0:24 |
| **Eggs** | S08 | 3:08 | 0:04 | 0:05 | 0:20 | 0:00 | 0:29 |
| | S20 | 5:13 | 0:06 | 0:05 | 0:19 | 0:00 | 0:30 |
| | S16 | 4:06 | 0:06 | 0:08 | 0:20 | 0:00 | 0:34 |
| | S50 | 4:45 | 0:06 | 0:06 | 0:22 | 0:00 | 0:34 |

of each recording between the manual and retrieval annotation for the same annotator.

Table 6 presents the total annotation time of each recording. Here, the total time is calculated to be a sum of the annotation time, the retrieval interval loading duration, annotation using the retrieval method, and the overall revision of the annotation. Any breaks that were taken during this period are noted by the annotator and reduced from the total annotation time. Thus, the total annotation time can be presented as $retrieval + annotation - breaks + revision$. It is to be noted from the table that depending on the recording length, the retrieval network took longer to load the predictions per interval. For instance, the recipe Brownies were longer in comparison to the recipe Sandwich. The average retrieval interval loading time difference between the two is $6,25min$. Often, the time spent by the annotator on the annotation using the retrieval method depends on the quality of the queried predictions. On the one hand, where the query was apt, the annotator spent time modifying the attributes to suit the annotation of the window. On the other hand, when the predictions were poor, the annotator pressed reject and quickly completed the retrieval-based annotation. Overall, the annotator recommended improving the network as the retrieval query was not up to the mark as the retrieval-based annotation of LARa dataset. The annotator further noted that the recipe Eggs and Sandwich predictions had more correct predictions in comparison to the recipe Brownies. This could be because of the numerous frames pertaining to a single activity, such as 'filling-jam-jam glass-bread' in the Sandwich recipe or 'stir-bowl-whisk' in the Eggs recipe, whereas in the case of Brownies, there are frequent changes in activities being performed.

**Table 7.** Comparison between time taken for manual and retrieval-based annotation for the Arduous Challenge Kitchen Dataset

| Recipe | Rec. | Dur. mm:ss | Manual h:mm | Retrieval h:mm |
|---|---|---|---|---|
| **Brownies** | S54 | 6:51 | 0:57 | **0:42** |
| | S32 | 4:59 | 0:44 | **0:34** |
| | S31 | 8:11 | **0:49** | 0:51 |
| | S09 | 7:47 | **1:10** | 1:30 |
| **Sandwich** | S16 | 3:25 | **0:23** | 0:26 |
| | S25 | 2:38 | **0:21** | 0:24 |
| | S34 | 2:06 | **0:14** | 0:19 |
| | S15 | 1:39 | **0:14** | 0:24 |
| **Eggs** | S08 | 3:08 | 0:31 | **0:29** |
| | S20 | 5:13 | 0:33 | **0:30** |
| | S16 | 4:06 | 0:37 | **0:34** |
| | S50 | 4:45 | **0:29** | 0:34 |

On comparing the total annotation time between manual and retrieval annotation Table 7, it can be noticed that retrieval has supported the annotator in a few of the recordings to reduce annotation duration. When evaluating the average difference in total annotation time, both manual and retrieval annotation methods here are close; however, manual shows an overall shorter annotation duration than retrieval. We strongly believe that with improvements in the retrieval network for video-based Kitchen dataset annotation, the total annotation time for retrieval can be considerably improved.

**Table 8.** Comparison Annotations: Manual with LARa vs. Retrieval with SARA on the Kitchen Dataset. Average between-annotator consistency $\kappa$ of the two annotators following the retrieval-based approach.

| Recipe | Rec. | Cohen's $\kappa$ |
|---|---|---|
| **Brownies** | S54 | 0.6149 |
| | S32 | 0.6133 |
| | S31 | 0.8112 |
| | S09 | 0.8832 |
| **Sandwich** | S16 | 0.8691 |
| | S25 | 0.7661 |
| | S34 | 0.7288 |
| | S15 | 0.8329 |
| **Eggs** | S08 | 0.7174 |
| | S20 | 0.5174 |
| | S16 | 0.6369 |
| | S50 | 0.7111 |

On comparing the manual vs. the retrieval annotations of the Kitchen dataset, we found that the annotation achieved substantial and, in some cases, high consistency for the annotations. Only one annotation fell into the category of moderate consistency. We noted a subtle trend where the retrieval annotation took more time than manual annotation, where Cohen's $\kappa$ was greater than 0.81. Given that the network requires improvement, we believe that training the network to detect and track the object in use for the kitchen could considerably improve the predictions and, thus, the annotation time.

## References

1. Avsar, H., Altermann, E., Reining, C., Moya Rueda, F., Fink, G.A.: Benchmarking annotation procedures for multi-channel time series HAR dataset. In: 2021 IEEE International Conference on Pervasive Computing and Communications Workshops and other Affiliated Events (PerCom Workshops), pp. 453–458. Kassel, Germany (2021). https://doi.org/10.1109/PerComWorkshops51409.2021.9431062

2. Moya Rueda, F., Fink, G.A.: Learning attribute representation for human activity recognition. In: 2018 24th International Conference on Pattern Recognition (ICPR), pp. 523–528. IEEE (2018). https://doi.org/10.1109/ICPR.2018.8545146
3. Moya Rueda, F., Grzeszick, R., Fink, G., Feldhorst, S., ten Hompel, M.: Convolutional neural networks for human activity recognition using body-worn sensors. MDPI Inform. (2018). https://doi.org/10.3390/informatics5020026
4. Münzner, S., Schmidt, P., Reiss, A., Hanselmann, M., Stiefelhagen, R., Dürichen, R.: CNN-based sensor fusion techniques for multimodal human activity recognition. In: Proceedings of the 2017 ACM International Symposium on Wearable Computers (2017)
5. Niemann, F., et al.: LARa: creating a dataset for human activity recognition in logistics using semantic attributes. Sensors **20**(15) (2020)
6. Ordóñez, F., Roggen, D.: Deep convolutional and LSTM recurrent neural networks for multimodal wearable activity recognition. MDPI Sensors 1 (2016). https://doi.org/10.3390/s16010115
7. Reining, C., Rueda, F.M., Niemann, F., Fink, G.A., t. Hompel, M.: Annotation Performance for multi-channel time series HAR Dataset in Logistics. In: 2020 IEEE International Conference on Pervasive Computing and Communications Workshops (PerCom Workshops), pp. 1–6. PERCOM Workshops, March 2020. https://doi.org/10.1109/PerComWorkshops48775.2020.9156170
8. Niemann, F., et al.: Logistic Activity Recognition Challenge (LARa Version 03) – A Motion Capture and Inertial Measurement Dataset. Zenodo (2023). https://doi.org/10.5281/zenodo.8189341

# Author Index





E. L. Tonkin et al. (Eds.): ARDUOUS 2025, CCIS 2706, p. 203, 2026.
https://doi.org/10.1007/978-3-032-09117-8

MIX
Papier aus verantwortungsvollen Quellen
Paper from responsible sources
FSC® C105338

If you have any concerns about our products,
you can contact us on
**ProductSafety@springernature.com**

In case Publisher is established outside the EU,
the EU authorized representative is:
**Springer Nature Customer Service Center GmbH**
**Europaplatz 3, 69115 Heidelberg, Germany**

Printed by Libri Plureos GmbH
in Hamburg, Germany